Public-Private Partnerships in Africa

Public-Private Partnerships in Africa

Exploring Africa's Growth Potential

Edited by
Thekiso Molokwane,
Muhiya Tshombe Lukamba, Alex Nduhura,
and Innocent Nuwagaba

LEXINGTON BOOKS
Lanham • Boulder • New York • London

Published by Lexington Books
An imprint of The Rowman & Littlefield Publishing Group, Inc.
4501 Forbes Boulevard, Suite 200, Lanham, Maryland 20706
www.rowman.com

86-90 Paul Street, London EC2A 4NE

British Library Cataloguing in Publication Information Available

Library of Congress Cataloging-in-Publication Data Available

ISBN: 978-1-66693-128-0 (cloth)
ISBN: 978-1-66693-129-7 (ebook)

The book is dedicated to scholars and practitioners in the fields of public administration and public management.

Contents

List of Figures

List of Tables

Foreword

The public sector is facing fundamental challenges. Climate change, demographic change, international competition for investors, customers and resources and the changing demands of citizens, as well as the considerable upheavals caused by international and regional conflicts, are exerting considerable pressure on public authorities to act. How the ability of public authorities to act can be secured through efficient and effective management is therefore a central topic of public management research and consultancy. However, the focus is too often on the Anglo-American, European and Asian expert debates about the best approaches and tools. This anthology is dedicated to shed more light on the specific conditions for public management reforms in Africa with a specific focus on public-private partnerships (PPPs).

Why should you as a reader be interested in this rather specific reform instrument and its application in an African context? Let me give you some arguments that I hope will convince you to take a closer look at this publication.

With the transition to the new millennium, almost all countries worldwide agreed on common goals, namely the Millennium Development Goals (MDGs) in development policy. The MDGs comprise eight main goals, the first of which is a drastic reduction in poverty. The essential task in development policy is therefore to set measures that support poverty reduction. A major focus is on the development of the infrastructure sector, which is considered to be an enabling factor. Infrastructure is thus an important component in achieving the MDGs. One of the biggest challenges in this context is the financing of the required infrastructure, which can basically come from three sources: the state, development aid, or the private sector. In addition, there is the hybrid form of public-private models, which have gained recognition in both development economics and business administration through the term 'public-private partnerships'.

PPP stands for a variety of forms of cooperation between government or public agencies on the one hand and actors from the private sector or the civil society non-profit sector on the other. Such forms of cooperation are characterised by the fact that the partners involved work together to fulfil public tasks through an interaction based on the division of labour.

Even though public task fulfilment is a key feature of PPPs, it should not be concealed that different interests and motives may be decisive for the parties involved in such partnerships. On the public side, the hope will be to relieve the burden on public budgets by tapping private financial resources, as well as access to the expertise of the private sector and certainly time and cost efficiencies in complex projects. On the private side, PPPs promise additional profit opportunities, the development of new business areas and participation in public capacities and resources. It is therefore not surprising that, against the backdrop of increasingly uncertain global economic development and new and old crises, PPP is being put forward by both sides as a promising alternative to the traditional fulfilment of public tasks.

Inadequate infrastructures, investment backlogs and tight budgets are the buzzwords currently dominating the public debate in many African countries. In the search for new approaches and solutions, PPP has frequently become the focus of public interest in recent years. Advocates in Africa, but also among international financial institutions and development aid agencies, have hailed PPP as a silver lining on the horizon, even as the ideal way out of the chronic financial crisis in the public sector. For some, PPP suggests progress, signals a willingness to cooperate, and at the same time exudes the charm of the legally non-binding. Critical voices, on the other hand, accuse PPP of lacking transparency, obscuring public debt through shadow budgets, as well as hidden additional costs and greater time expenditure. Others degrade PPP to a mere buzzword that has no sharp conceptual contours and is unsuitable for legal problem solving—two opposing positions on PPP that could not be more different.

What new forms of financing and safeguarding have emerged in the field of promoting private infrastructure investment, especially in Africa? What are the challenges in political control and governance of legal regulation and operational implementation of PPP? How can these challenges be addressed? What is the contribution of public-private-funded projects to the achievement of key policy objectives? How can the impact of PPPs be evaluated in the first place? Which specific African contextual conditions influence the success of these approaches and instruments? The editors of this anthology, as well as the authors of the individual contributions, have addressed precisely these and other relevant questions. The very knowledgeable case studies from different sectors and countries in Africa (chapters 6 to 11 of this book) provide a variety of exciting answers. The special value of this anthology, however, lies in the linking of this current picture of public-private partnerships in Africa with a conceptual and analytical perspective, which can be found in particular in chapters 1 to 5 as well as in the conclusion of this book.

I wish all readers of this inspiring book much pleasure in reading and many exciting and new insights!

Prof. Dr. Jörg Röber
University of Applied Sciences Kehl

Acknowledgements

The sub-field of public-private partnerships is a comparatively contemporary area of study that requires acute attention from both scholars and practitioners. This book project brought together scholars from Africa south of the Sahara. The development of the book and its successful completion are attributed to various stakeholders. Of primary significance are the book chapter contributors from various parts of the African content. The success of this book would have not been realised had it not been for their unwavering support and patience owing to the length of time taken to complete the project from the very first call issued. Acquisition of expert knowledge of public-private partnerships in the era is golden as going forward, this method of procurement is bound to take precedence over other methods of procurement in the developing world as majority of governments and public officials are still acclimatising themselves with the same. In this regard the adept knowledge and analysis shared by contributors of this book will go a long way in educating students, scholars, as well as the public and private sector practitioners in the affairs of public-private partnerships. The editors of this book thank their families for support rendered during its development. Gratitude also goes to the publisher for accepting our manuscript and according it an international platform. Access of this book by the global community will accord it the necessary latitude of reaching a wider audience and sharing African experiences on the subject matter of PPPs.

List of Abbreviations

ANC	African National Congress
BCHSL	Bi-Courtney Highway Services Limited
BOT	Build Operate Transfer
BOOT	Build Own Operate Transfer
BRT	Bus Rapid Transit
BTO	Build Transfer Operate
BVM	Best Value for Money
BVP	Best value procurement
CRBC	China Road and Bridge Construction Corporation
CPI	Consumer Price Index
DBFOM	Design-Build-Finance-Operate-Maintain
DCFOM	Design, Construct, Finance, Operate and Maintain
DFBOM	Design, Finance, Build, Operate and Maintain
DBOM	Design, Build Operate and Maintain
DFBOT	Design, Finance, Build, Operate and Transfer
DOT	Department of Transport
EAC	East African Community
ECOWAS	Economic Community of West African States
EDD	Economic Diversification Drive
EFF	Economic Freedom Fighters
GFIP	Gauteng Freeway Improvement Project
IFC	International Finance Corporation
IFMOT	Improve, Finance, Maintain, Operate and Transfer
IPPs	Independent Power Producers
KPLC	Kenya Power and Lighting Company
NHF	National Housing Fund

NDB	New Development Bank
NDP	National Development plan
N3TC	N3 Toll Concession (RF) Proprietary Limited
OECD	Organisation for Economic Co-operation and Development
OUTA	Organisation Undoing Tax Abuse
PIIP	Privately Initiated Investment Proposals
PFMA	Public Finance Management Act
PPPs	Public-Private Partnerships
RFA	Road Freight Association
ROT	Rehabilitate-Operate-and-Transfer
RSA	Republic of South Africa
SADC	Southern African Development Community
SAFTU	South African Federation of Trade Unions
SAPs	Structural Adjustment Programs
SANRAL	South African National Roads Agency
SOE	State-Owned Enterprise
SOT	Supply-Operate-and-Transfer
SPV	Special Purpose Vehicle
UEB	Uganda Electricity Board
UEDCL	Uganda Electricity Distribution Company Limited
UEGLC	Uganda Electricity Generation Company Limited
UETCL	Uganda Electricity Transmission Company Limited
UNRA	Uganda National Roads Authority
UK	United Kingdom
UN	United Nations
UNCITRAL	United Nations Commission on International Trade Law
VFM	Value for Money
ZERA	Zimbabwe Energy Regulatory Authority

Part I

PUBLIC-PRIVATE PARTNERSHIPS

THEORETICAL AND PRAGMATIC UNDERPINNINGS

Introduction

Muhiya Tshombe Lukamba and
Thekiso Molokwane

In the twenty-first century, governments around the world began to engage the private sector with the objective of achieving public service delivery targets. The essence of this collaboration was to address the inefficiencies of the public sector—chiefly, the red-tape. The need for collaboration was instigated by, among others, the constraint to raise funds for infrastructural developments and, the ever shrinking public purse. The African continent has as such been experiencing transformation particularly since the introduction of Public-Private Partnerships (PPP), as a measure of reform and method of procurement.

PPPs have become a tool for many governments in the sub-Saharan Africa region (SSA), convenient for achieving public policy goals. The aim of implementing PPPs is to improve the delivery of goods and services that would ordinarily be provided by the state (Tshombe and Molokwane, 2016a, p. 131). PPPs refer to a contractual obligation between the private sector and a government entity for the construction of specific project based on the terms agreed between the two parties. This is true to the service sector as well.

ORIGINS OF PUBLIC-PRIVATE PARTNERSHIPS

Literature attributes PPPs to different points in time. This reform involves the collaboration between the public and private sectors as such; some literature use this relationship to argue the genesis of PPPs. To illustrate, Grimsey and Lewis (2004) trace that the participation of the private sector in infrastructure sector development began well over two centuries ago in Europe and North America. In the United Kingdom, the utilisation of tollgates was authorised by law in 1364. The first turnpike model was established in

1664. The mechanism became popular in developed countries in the 1980s and 1990s particularly in the construction of government facilities. In SSA, PPPs became in vogue in the twenty-first century as governments explored alternative means of financing various sector projects. Amongst others, infrastructure in the water, energy and road sectors benefited from this arrangement. Greenfield projects such as dams, power plants, roads, supply and distribution of water, and generation of electricity are further cases in point. As of 2010, the World Bank espoused that there was a huge gap in SSA in terms of infrastructure development, with an infrastructure financing gap of almost US$34 billion (World Bank, 2010). A close view at the African context nonetheless reveals that much has to be done in order to attain considerable levels of success in the implementation of PPPs. The institutional and legal frameworks are amongst factors to be given priority. The lack of political will both in countries with little and full capacity to implement PPPs remains an issue of concern. A need to create an enabling environment remains paramount.

Governments throughout the African continent must, in light of this observation, improve the ease of doing business so as to make the economic ambience conducive for both internal and external investors. Countries in the continent still require significant amounts of funding to improve their infrastructure. The African Development Bank (2018) reported that the infrastructure need across the 54 countries is estimated to be around $130–170 billion a year. The estimated gap ranges around $67.6–$ 107.5 billion (AfDB, 2018). The report from the AfDB 2018 shows that the African infrastructure stock is very low when you want to compare with another continent. That kind of a gap is discernible in the energy sector. More than 640 million Africans do not have access to energy, giving an electricity access rate for African states at just over 40%, the lowest in the world. For the majority of the countries in the continent, filling these gaps in a very short period will certainly be impractical.

Due to the many challenges facing governments in the sub-Saharan Africa, the economic performance of the countries remains a continuous source of concern. To close the infrastructure disparity in the states, collaboration with the private sector is both imperative and compelling. The governments must put in place a mechanism to work with the private sector particularly under the PPP arrangements that will assist the closing of the aforementioned gaps. Emirullah and Azam (2014) raise a further suggestion arguing that because of scarce state resources, financing the development of infrastructure has forced governments to turn to the private sector and ask for their participation through the PPP arrangement. The logic behind this partnership is to: generate greater efficiency and synergies; increase financial revenues; and reduce deficits; quicker market development, faster foreign investments, and increased competition are also on the development agenda (Tshombe and Molokwane, 2016b, p.73).

In Europe and America, countries now understand that in order to fast track infrastructure projects, there is a need to work in partnerships with private sector as this will improve not only the quality of delivery and output, but value for money (VfM) as well. The implication of adopting PPP in the African continent as such is to bring about a positive impact across different sectors of the economy. The presence of PPP ushers in competition in the markets thus offering the ordinary citizen choice. This element of choice is propounded by the public choice theorists. Public choice is a theory which posits that people are egoistic, rational, and utility maximisers, a characterisation which affects the state in that this behaviour is exhibited not only by voters, who seek to maximise their individual utility, but also by legislators and bureaucrats, who seek the same end (Wright, 1993, p. 1; Schuster, 2017, p. 2251). Put simply, public choice theorists contend that public bureaucracies are inherently less efficient than private enterprises.

Simplified further, the theory postulates that government officials behave in a manner that maximises their personal gain, rather than furthering the public's interests. The theory also suggests that democratically elected legislators depend on re-election to make a living (2017, p. 2251). Such a setting is one that would create monopoly in the provision of public goods and services. In this regard, the decision many governments in sub-Saharan Africa took to work with the private sector can be seen as a good one predominantly for the development and expansion of industries, and the expansion of infrastructure in the continent. What the government officials need to do is to focus on the 'quality of investment' and avoid the 'volume of a project'. By this, it must be understood that there is a need to prioritise critical projects that ascertain attainment of VfM.

In order to attain quality infrastructure investment in government projects, project quality analysis is required prior to inviting a private partner. Through this, government officials must ascertain the potential of 'profit' or 'benefit' in engaging the private party. In other words, the government must evaluate the benefit for undertaking a project through a PPP arrangement. There is a need to determine the VfM before awarding the project to an entity outside government. The same applies to the private sector; the project should offer good VfM, as no private investor will otherwise want to invest. A project should also offer the local authorities an opportunity to carry out its functions in a cost-effective manner through generating revenue or achieving cost saving.

The proposal should demonstrate how VfM would be achieved, considering estimated costs, benefits and risks involved in undertaking the project (Lewis, 2004). When inviting the private sector to participate in government project, the two parties (private investor and government) must take the view raised above into consideration. It is crucial for the government institutions to consider the interest of private investor experiences in the field, and as a result, innovative ideas in the project will be implemented. When there is a PPP project the reality in the field is that all parties will benefit as the project is being built.

Government officials in different countries in SSA need to develop expertise in the field of PPPs that will help them to considerably level private sector knowledge during the negotiation. That expertise puts the government institution in a strong position during the infrastructure project negotiation. Public officials should have a good understanding of the PPP model that the government favours. This should assist the state to avoid hiring consultant to negotiate on their behalf. Scholars such as Niekerk, Ruiter, Mcwabeni, Kruger, and Grinker (1999, p.55) support the above view. 'It seems that the successful application of PPP demands a relatively high level of administrative capacity from the structure which assumes overall contractual control of the process.' Government officials' expertise or knowledge in the field of PPP is paramount during a negotiation with potential investors.

SELECTED GLOBAL EXPERIENCES OF PPPs: A SYNOPSIS

Asia

The demand for new infrastructure and improvement of existing one is still felt in Asian countries. At present, inadequate roads, ports and airports represent a drag on trade, tourism and employment, impeding the flow of people and goods within and between countries and imposing higher transaction costs. Power shortages often reduce output resulting in lower productivity. Proper management of water for goods (such as potable water and irrigation) and services (such as electricity generation) benefits agriculture, industry and households (Economist Intelligence Unit, 2014). The Asia-Pacific region continues to be a global leader in economic development.

The rapid industrialisation and accompanying urbanisation of many of the region's economies, as their growth models transitioned from being factor-led to being driven more by efficiency gains, are creating greater demand for vital infrastructure, particularly for energy, transportation, water supply and sanitation. Cases in point for PPP projects include the AsiaWorld–Expo, Hong Kong Theme Park and Eastern Harbour Crossing in Hong Kong (Osei-Kyei & Chan, 2017, pp. 1222–1245).

Australasia

Australian PPPs have been used for delivering projects such as major toll roads, hospitals, prisons, schools, utilities and support facilities. The first generation of PPP projects for the country principally involved Build-Own-and Operate (BOO)- and Build-Own-Operate- Transfer (BOOT)-style projects. The first of these projects was the Sydney Harbour Tunnel (commenced in 1988) and projects of this form were progressively undertaken until the Victorian government released its Partnerships Victoria policy in June 2000. The policy significantly changed the government's involvement in PPP projects as they sought to retain direct control of 'core services and to involve the private sector where such involvement could deliver improved services to the community through innovative solutions and the development of VFM outcomes' (Duffield, p. 1).

An observation made by English (2006, pp. 256–260) is that, for citizens, and presumably government, the service provision is not just about realising lowest process and associated efficiencies. In the Australian historical, socio-economic and political context, it is about adequacy, quality and accessibility of services provided, maximising overall VfM, ensuring proper accounting for the use of public resources and the achievement of agreed results that often involve significant non-monetary elements. A study by Infrastructure Partnerships Australia (nd. p. 27) illustrates that PPPs demonstrated superior cost efficiency over traditional procurement.

The study further shows that PPPs provided superior performance in both costs and time dimensions and that PPPs were more transparent compared to traditional procurement. For New Zealand, the PPP programme was established in 2009 with the creation of a PPP Centre of Expertise within the Treasury. PPP procurement in the country has been implemented for the primary purpose of improving the focus on, and delivery of, required service outcomes from major infrastructure assets (New Zealand Government, 2015, pp. 1–27). PPPs in various sectors have been recorded in China (Guo, Chen & Feng, 2022), India (Asian Development Bank, 2022, pp. xxiii–196) and Taiwan (Hsu, Shen & Chiu, 2017), as well.

Europe

European experiences with PPPs are diverse. The history of PPPs in Europe can be traced to different times. In the United Kingdom, the collaboration between public and private sectors can be traced to 1364 when the use of tollgates was authorised by law. The first turnpike model was established in 1664 (Grimsey & Lewis, 2004). Other scholars, however, trace the origins of PPPs in the UK to the early 1990s when the country experienced the 'off-balance-sheet' public accounting treatment (Vickier, 2004). The aim was to seek Value for Money (VfM). For France, literature demonstrates that the PPP concept is older than that of other European nations. The country's national experience has had influence in the implementation of PPPs in francophone countries particularly in West Africa (World Bank, 2017, pp. 1–76). Legislatively, PPPs were introduced in the Italian legislations in 1998 (Rossi & Civitillo, 2014, p. 146). Ireland is also considered a late adopter of PPPs as it adopted the same only in 1998. By mid-2009, Ireland had only six PPP projects in operation representing less than 0.5% of all PPP EU contracts signed from 1990–2009 (Sheppard & Beck, 2016).

A bigger picture of Europe shows that in the years 2004/05, there were more than 1,150 PPP deals worth USD 26 billion that closed in Europe (Kong, 2007). Between 1990 and 2019, the European market had 1,749 PPP projects worth a total of 336 billion that reached financial close in the EU PPP market (European Court of Auditors, 2018, p. 16). Whilst there has been tendency towards a more intensive leverage of public funds with private funds through PPPs, there have also been PPP projects that combine EU fund with private finance. They are referred to as blended PPPs (European Court of Auditors, 2018, pp. 35–40). The contemporary challenges for PPPs in Europe show that in cases, risk allocation was often inappropriate resulting in less incentive or excessive risk exposure for the private sector. The long-duration PPP contracts were also poorly sorted to the rapid pace of technological change and that for most audited projects, PPPs were often selected without any prior comparative analysis to demonstrate VfM (European Court of Auditors, 2018, pp. 35–40).

A RECAP OF THE THEMATIC AND COUNTRY CASES: ONTOLOGICAL AND EPISTEMOLOGICAL AND DEPARTURES

This book is a result of exertions of scholars resident in the SSA region. The chapters presented herein capture fresh and captivating insights on PPPs in Africa. A diverse book project typically makes it enigmatic to determine a specific research gap for the entire book. The reason is, every scholar has their own eccentric way of viewing the same object. Ordinarily each chapter has its own research gap; however, it is penitent to share the overarching gaps for this book namely the 'empirical' and 'practical knowledge gap'. Any issue located in the academic space stimulates a need for inquiry hence the continued research for evidence of research problems, causes and the consequential search for solutions. In the twenty-first century, what has come out clear in academia is the need to conducting *problem-solving research.*

This book serves not only to unearth new findings on specific subject matters on PPPs in Africa but also offers potential solutions beneficial to scholars, governments and industries.

In view of the aforementioned, this book ushers insights into the theoretical underpinning of various contemporary PPP issues. In addition to this, a forecast of various key PPP issues is provided. The first substantive chapter of this book, by Lukamba (chapter 1), lays down the theoretical underpinnings of PPPs. The philosophical foundations of public/private collaboration are elaborated in this chapter. The governance, agency, network, transaction cost economics, resource-based view theories provide a basis for arguments raised in subsequent chapters of the book. In chapter 2, Botlhale raises pertinent issues on public procurement in Africa. Notable are that exogenous factors such as the recessions and pandemics compel African counters to embrace PPPs. The author also reveals that monocultural economies disproportionately predominate the SSA region of the continent thus instigating a need to diversify. Empirical evidence of the demand for alternative needs of financing public goods (e.g., infrastructure) and services is unearthed. The general consensus is that PPPs are increasingly being used as a competitive alternative to traditional public procurement.

Ndhuhara and Twinomuhwezi (chapter 3) offer a systematic and integrated approach on how PPPs have been and continue to be adopted in the Africa's electricity market. Their chapter serves both as a structured introduction for those who are new to the subject of PPPs in electricity markets, whether in the academic, public, private or social sectors, investment, finance or contracting fields such as procurement and supply chain, and as an aide-mémoire for those developing PPP policies and negotiating PPPs in the electricity sector. A comparative analysis of Egypt, Ghana, Kenya, Morocco, Nigeria and South Africa strengthen the study's case namely Uganda. In chapter 4, the Lekgowe examines the PPP legal frameworks in selected African jurisdictions analysing the trends and future prospects of the same. The author observes that the lack of expertise in understanding PPPs constitutes some of the bottlenecks in unlocking the benefits of this reform and procurement method. The chapter unravels the core ingredients of PPP law.

Chapter 5 by Nuwagaba explores the politics behind managing public-private partnership (PPP) projects in Africa to ensure Value for Money (VFM) in the roads sector with the Uganda National Roads Authority as its case study. The chapter acknowledges that in African counties, PPP policies have been formulated. It also emphasises that a well-designed, detailed and clear legal framework is often noted as a prerequisite for all types of PPP activity. Revelations by the chapter illustrate that: politics highly influences the adoption of PPP projects in the roads sector in African Union member states; policy frameworks affect the PPP projects used in the roads sector and that

African countries should understand that failure to harmonise the technical and political expectations at design, implementation, monitoring and evaluation stages will restrain PPP project sustainability.

In chapter 6, Molokwane provides an account of PPPs in Botswana. It is observed in the chapter that whilst the policy and regulatory framework has been established, the PPP-focused legal framework is still requisite. The country relies on its procurement laws for PPP-related matters; however, this has its own inadequacies. Further to this, the demand for infrastructure in the country is detailed with PPP projects in the pipeline documented as of May 2023. The author proposes consideration for government to explore in more detail, the use of domestic capital and debt funding in financing PPPs. Obosi identifies and analyses the drivers and impediments of PPP in Kenya in chapter 7. The author demonstrates that the country has made substantial investment by implementing multiple projects through the PPP model. The conclusion is that the implementation of PPPs in Kenya is driven by the need for enhanced service delivery, value for money, public interest and the potential benefits. T the major impediment is the cost factor.

In chapter 8, Iroanya, Nguluwe and Ndapulamo assess socio-economic and national security impact and challenges in Nigeria. The chapter adopts a multisectoral approach with a contextual analysis of PPPs in the road, infrastructure, energy and national security sectors. The observation made is that PPPs have not achieved a high level of success in Nigeria in terms of stimulating economic growth and development as well as enhancement of the national security. One of the reasons for this underdevelopment is that challenges confronting PPP operations in Nigeria take various forms. The chapter concludes nonetheless among others that, if rightly implemented, PPPs are indeed a veritable alternative means of infrastructure development in Nigeria. Attesting to this is the noticeable improvement in service delivery in some privatised sectors of the economy.

Borole (chapter 9) reveals that the South African government has had some degree of relief in the financing, designing, constructing, operating and maintenance of the infrastructure on the toll road concessions. This has been experienced since the introduction of PPP in South Africa's toll road subsector in the late 1990s. Borole explains that there are alternative free roads in the country; however, the state of these roads is undesirable. The author proposes a suitable model for the toll roads in South Africa namely the Improve, Finance, Maintain, Operate and Transfer (IFMOT). In chapter 10, Settumba and Nduhura provide a detailed account of the PPPs in Uganda's health sector.

The authors ascertain that PPPs bridge the financial gaps through funding many health programmes and infrastructural development, medical supplies, and equipment. They further conclude that PPPs should be fully implemented as a significant option if the government of Uganda wishes to expand and improve its infrastructure and healthcare services delivery to the community. Malisase, Chewe and Nyirenda (chapter 11) analyse the PPPs and the quality of public service delivery in Zambia. The authors identify, despite the existence of legal and institutional framework, constraints associated with delivering services through PPPs in the country.

Their study reveals that project implemented thought PPPs in Zambia have mixed outcomes. The quality of services provided from PPPs has been mixed. Some projects have improved quality of service delivery while others failed leading to cancellation of contracts. In the conclusion, Basera, Zhou and Chilunjika make not of the significance of IPPs as models of the PPPs in increasing electricity supply in Zimbabwe given that country constrained fiscal capacity. The authors recommend seven specific measures to strengthen the effective governance of the PPPs in the electricity sector in Zimbabwe. These include among others: the need for a cost reflective and competitive tariff framework, enhanced servicing and maintenance of the grid network as well as increasing or upgrading transmission grid capacity to accommodate the IPP demands.

REFERENCES

Asian Development Bank. (2022). *Public Private Partnerships Monitor India.* Asian Development Bank, Philippines,

African Development Bank. (2018). *African Economic Outlook. Africa's Infrastructure.* African Development Bank, Abidjan. Cote D'Ivoire.

Duffield, C. F. (2001). PPPs in Australia, in Ng. T. S (Ed.) *Public Private Partnership Opportunities and Challenges*, Center for Infrastructure and Construction Industry Development, The University of Hong Kong, Pokfulam, pp. 5–14.

English, L. M. (2006). Public Private Partnerships in Australia: An Overview of their Nature, Purpose, Incidence and Oversight, *UNSW Law Journal*, Vol. 29(3), pp. 256–260.

European Court of Auditors. (2018). *Public-Private Partnership in the EU: Widespread Shortcomings and Limited Benefits*, European Court of Auditors Luxembourg, pp. 35–40.

Grimsey, D and Lewis, M. K. (2004). *Public-Private Partnership the Worldwide Revolution in Infrastructure Provision and Project Finance*, Edward Elgar Publishing Limited, Cheltenham.

Guo, X., Chen, B and Feng, Y. (2022). Public-Private Partnership Transportation Investment and Low-Carbon Economic Development: An Empirical Study Based on Spatial Spill over and Project Characteristics in China, *Sustainability*, Vol.14 (9574), pp. 1–22.

Hsu, F., Shen, M and Chiu, C. (2017). Examining Public-Public and Public-Private Partnership of Information Systems in Taiwan, Pan Asia Conference on Information Systems, 2017 Proceedings, Association for Information Systems.

Infrastructure Partnerships Australia (nd). Performance if PPPs and Traditional Procurement in Australia, Allen Consulting Group and the University of Melbourne, p. 1. Available from: https://infrastructure.org.au/wp-content/uploads/2016/12/IPA_PPP-FINAL.pdf. Date of access 20 January, 2023.

Kong, Y. H. (2007). European Experiences in PPP, Cross-Border Infrastructure, A Toolkit, PPIAF, ADB, Available from: https://ppiaf.org/sites/ppiaf.org/files/documents/toolkits/Cross-Border-Infrastructure-Toolkit/Cross-Border%20Compilation%20ver%2029%20Jan%2007/Session%204%20-%20Private%20Sector%20Participation/Private%20Sector_03%20Regional%20Experiences%20in%20PPP%20-%2029%20Jan%2007.pdf. Date of Access: 24, February 2023.

Lewis, E. (2004). *Public Private Partnership Fund for Local Authorities Startup Funding for Projects*. Department of Environment and Local Government. United Kingdom.

Niekerk, S.Van, Ruiter. G, Mcwabeni. L, Kruger.V, and Grinker.R. 1999. *Public Private Partnerships Lesson and Case Studies from the Eastern Cape*. South Africa.

Molokwane, T. (2016a). An Analysis of Public Private Partnership in Emerging Economies, *Risk Governance & Control: Financial Markets & Institutions*, Virtus, Enterprises, Vol. 6(4), Fall, 2016, pp. 306–316.

New Zealand Government. (2015). *Public Private Partnership Programme—The New Zealand PPP Model and Policy: Setting the Scene*, A guide for Public Sector Entities, pp. 1–27.

Osei-Kyei, R and Chan, A. P. C. (2017). Emperical Comparison of Critical Success Factors for Public Private Partnerships in Developing and Developed Countries: A Case of Ghana and Hong Kong, *Engineering and Construction Management,* Vol. 24(6), Emerald, pp. 1222–1245.

Rossi, M and Civitillo, R. (2013). Public Private Partnerships: a general overview of Italy, 2nd World Conference on Business, Economics and Management—WCBEM 2013, *Procedia—Social and Behavioural Science*, Vol. 109(2014), pp. 140–149.

Tshombe, L. M & Molokwane, T. (2016b). An Analysis of Public Private Partnership in Sub-Saharan Africa, *African Journal of Public Affairs* (AJPA), African Consortium of Public Administration, Vol. 9(2), June 2016, pp. 72–86.

Schuster, W. M. (2017). Public Choice Theory, the Constitution, and Public Understanding of the Copyright System, *51 UC Davis Law Review,* 2247 (2018), Available at SSRN: https://ssrn.com/abstract=3026394. Date of Access 15 April, 2023.

Sheppard, G & Beck, M. (2016). The Evolution of Public Private Partnerships in Ireland: a sustainable pathway? *International Review of Administrative Sciences,* Queens University Belfast.

Wright, M. D. (1993). A Critique Of The Public Choice Theory Case For Privatization: Rhetoric And Reality, *Ottawa Law Review/Revue de droit d'Ottawa*, Vol. 25(1), p. 1

World Bank. (2010). Public Private Partnership Reference Guide, Version 3, International Bank for Reconstruction and Development, PPP Knowledge Lab. Available from: https://ppp.worldbank.org/public-private-partnerships/sites/ppp.worldbank.org/files/documents/PPP%20Reference%Guide%20Version%203.pdf. Date of Access: 23 April, 2023.

World Bank. (2010). Moving forward with Public Private Partnerships in Francophone Africa. The World Bank, Washington, DC. Available from: https://www.worldbank.org/en/news/feature/2010/03/17/moving-forward-public-private-partnerships-francophone-africa. Date of Access 25 April, 2023.

Chapter 1

Theoretical Framework for Public-Private Partnerships

Muhiya Tshombe Lukamba

Africa is experiencing a significant transformation as many countries in the region are making progress in infrastructure development. This has been made possible through the implementation of public-private partnerships (PPPs) by various African governments. Developed countries began using PPPs extensively in the 1990s (Davies & Eustice, 2005), as they enable governments to achieve value for money (VFM) and benefit the community. Such collaborations have allowed governments around the world to undertake infrastructure-building projects that would not otherwise have been possible. This chapter attempts to understand the theoretical framework utilised for the PPP concept globally and link that approach to the African context.

Numerous governments in the sub-Saharan region now understand that they must work with private partners to achieve their development goals. This has led to a shift towards the adoption of PPPs as the standard approach for implementing state infrastructure projects. As PPPs are founded on a relationship between the government and the private sector, any project that falls under this category must first be approved by the government. The public/private sector collaboration began in the sixteenth century in Europe when states began to partner with the private sector to achieve effective service delivery for the public good.

The application of PPPs is linked to outsourcing the external funding required to implement a project, which is important because large infrastructure projects are expensive. This chapter adopted John Stuart Mill's 1848 hypothesis that the 'state may own the canals and railroads, not exploiting them because they are almost always better exploited by private companies that take property on lease for a period' (Mill, 1848). This quotation indicates that the partnership between the state and private sector began a long time ago. John Stuart Mill was recognised as the first scholar to appropriate the concept of 'concession', which is the model for a PPP.

This chapter attempts to understand the theoretical development of the PPP concept globally and link that approach to the African context. Before adopting PPPs, governments constructed mega projects using government funding, which is now seldom the case. Global financial institutions such as the World Bank, the International Monetary Fund, the African Development Bank, and others recommend that governments enlist financial assistance from the private sector. The reason for the three spheres of government working with the private sector is that the latter has the means to raise the required funds. This chapter discusses the theoretical foundation for the public-private partnership and what such partnerships mean for infrastructure projects in Africa.

THEORETICAL FRAMEWORK FOR PUBLIC-PRIVATE PARTNERSHIPS

A public-private partnership is an open collaboration between a government institution or entity and a private sector enterprise for the implementation of a specific project. Scholars such as Harding (1998) explain that 'in any action which relies on the agreement of factors in the public private sectors, and which also contributes in some way to improving the urban economy and the quality of life'. The progress of a partnership between two bodies (government and private sector) requires understanding the various theories that are fundamental to such a partnership. This chapter presents a discussion of the theoretical foundation of the PPP concept, which requires an understanding of five theories, namely the theory of governance, the principal-agent theory (or agency theory), the network theory, the transaction cost economics theory, and the resource-based view theory. This is by no means an exhaustive list, as each researcher or expert must decide which theory will be most suited when conducting a study on PPP.

The Theory of Governance

The field of public administration has observed the changes that have occurred in government institutions over the past few decades. Civil servants cannot provide efficient service delivery solely through government entities. As a result, the approach has evolved to include private sector participation in delivering government projects. That is the key to the implementation of the theory of governance. Let us first define the concept of governance. Several scholars define governance as 'regimes of laws, administrative rules, judicial rulings, and practices that constrain, prescribe, and enable government activity, where such activity is broadly defined as the production and delivery of publicly supported goods and service' (Lynn, Heinrich & Hill, 2000).

Analysing the concept of governance requires us to understand how government institutions work with various stakeholders within the state to deliver public goods and services. The definition of governance can also be understood as political actions taken by the country's leadership during the course of performing their duties. This can be evaluated based on the government's various programmes, for example, social, economic, and environmental responsibilities. In this study's context, governance is the working relationship between the government and the private sector established for the implementation of a government project. PPPs require a strong relationship between a public entity and a private company throughout the project's negotiation and implementation.

The relationship between the two parties should remain stable to avoid any misunderstanding during the project's implementation. The two parties must always agree upon the contents of the contract because these are usually long-term partnerships that also serve as a strategy for the host government to attract investors. If the government demonstrates hostile behaviour, potential investors will shy away from investing in the country.

The Principal-Agent Theory (Agency Theory)

To comprehend the field of PPP requires an understanding of the science of policy, which explains the principle of delegation of power or authority to another institution or organisation. Guston (1996, p.1) explains that the analytical framework known as principal-agent theory is introduced to examine the problems of delegation. Many governments currently delegate large and expensive projects to third parties to implement on their behalf, which is where the private sector becomes involved. Guston (1996, p.2) posits that the principal-agent theory is also known as ideal contracting theory because of the implicit exchange in this delegation.

The understanding is that some of the tasks the government is failing to perform successfully are delegated to an agent to implement on behalf of the state. Roughly put, this theory, as applied to science policy, means that the state is the principal that requests the agent—science—to perform certain tasks because the principal is not capable of performing them directly. A PPP requires two major stakeholders for the implementation of the project to be executed, namely the government institution, which is considered to be the 'principal' and the private sector stakeholder, which is considered to be the 'agent'; this explains the applicability of the principal-agent theory, the former delegates the responsibility for implementing the project to the latter.

The principal must facilitate the agent's success in that project. Guston (1996, p.3) explains that 'executive agencies perform some of the requirements of the delegated authority directly, and they let grants and contracts to other performers, who in turn are their agents'. Gaston and De Palma, Leruth, and Prunier (2012, p.2) explain that 'in an agency relationship, one party, called the principal, delegate a portion of his/her power to another party, agent. Therefore, the agent makes decisions and acts on behalf of the principal'. This partnership—or delegation of authority—between a government department and a private sector enterprise is referred to as a PPP.

The government has several key reasons for wanting to be involved in a PPP. The first is to reduce the budgetary cost of the project, the second is that the private sector can construct or implement the project at a lower cost than the government can, the third is that the government can transfer the project risk to the agent and the fourth is that the private sector is much more efficient than the government. In a PPP, the cost of the project is calculated well and the target time to execute the project is respected. The aforementioned reasons are why the governments in developing countries want to work with the private sector to deliver infrastructure projects. The ensuing section presents a discussion of network theory in the implementation of a PPP. An effective project requires that the organisation should have a strong network with other partners.

The Network Theory

When a government awards or delegates an infrastructure project to a private sector company to implement, it implies that the public organisation lacks a suitable network to carry out the project or that the private company's experience has made them the preferred choice for the government project. Implementing a PPP project creates a strong network of ties between the different companies involved. Chowdhury, Chen and Tiong (2010, p.248) assert that 'The application of network theory to PPP structuring helps in understanding how many agreements a party participates in, how many parties are involved in an agreement and their influences on the structure'.

As explained above, every organisation brings experiences and competencies which will benefit the government project. A PPP is a complex arrangement that requires different entities' expertise to ensure the project's success. That is where the network theory performs a role. According to Kadushin (2012), a network is set based on the relationships, contains a set of objects (nodes) and a mapping or description of relations between the objects or nodes. A network is based on the relationship between two or more people, units, entities or organisations. Figure 1.1 presented hereunder represents the

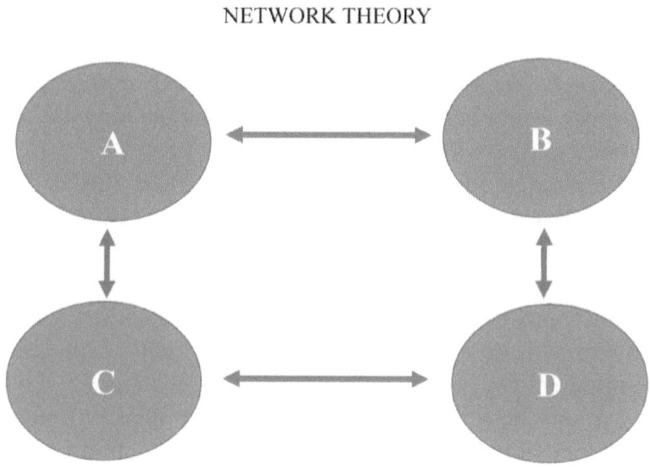

Figure 1.1 Network Theory. *Source*: Created by the author.

network an organisation can have. A PPP can involve numerous stakeholders in a contract signed between a government agency and a private sector entity.

The relationships between these organisations are based on trust and one of them must play a leading role. Furthermore, in terms of a PPP, these relationships are based on the expertise every company contributes to the project for its success. Chowdhury *et al.* (2010, p.252) explain that the network theory helps map out the relationships between people, thus identifying the opinion leader, who will be considered as the leading company in a PPP. According to the aforementioned authors, the growth of the business depends on identifying the opinion leader and how he/she can help in communication strategy.

The general understanding is that the main company that wins the government tender is the leading company that signs the PPP contract with the government agency or the local authority for the implementation of the project. Freeman (1979) states that network theory measures the centrality of the actors and events through three widely used measures, namely degree; closeness; and betweenness. The network relies on the trust each organisation has in the others for the benefit of the partnership. Currently, governments around the world want to work with the private sector to achieve public policy objectives and/or government programmes. The private sector has the expertise to build infrastructure in a limited amount of time and raise the financial capital required from various financial institutions.

The collaboration between the government and the various non-governmental organisations is part of the network theory. According to Wang, Xiong, Wu and Zhu (2017, 2), 'Many governments around the world are becoming more and more dependent on private actors for the implementation of public policies'. The relationship between the two (government and private companies) involves several stakeholders. Hodge and Greve (2007) explain that a PPP 'can be seen a cooperative institutional arrangement between public and private sector actors'. The foundation of the network theory is the closeness among partners for the execution of the project.

The broad argument advanced by Chowdhury *et al.* (2010) is that 'Network theory focuses on the importance of relationships between stakeholders. Through mapping the relationships, this method can identify position, power and influences of each stakeholder'. Integrating this statement with the field of PPP study implies that the company that is selected to sign the contract with the government entity must have sufficient work experience and the ability to implement the project successfully. Chowdhury *et al.* (2010) also went on to explain the importance of the network theory in more detail by saying 'The application of network theory on the structure of PPP projects addresses some important aspects, such as the distribution of power of related parties in PPP agreements and the sources'. The success of the host country when deciding to implement a PPP project should be based on the selection of an experienced private company to execute the project on the government's behalf.

Transaction Cost Economics Theory

When discussing the transaction cost economics (TCE) theory under PPP one must understand the financial transaction that occurs between the two parties—the government and the private sector.

The use of this theory in PPP transactions occurs when the companies partnering with host governments encounter problems. The TCE theory can provide a useful framework for understanding these issues. For instance, companies can use the theory to negotiate with the host country on matters such as tax payments and other financial arrangements related to project implementation. Ping Ho, Levitt, Tsui, and Hsu (2015) explain that:

> [W]hen PPP project are in distress, governments are often willing or compelled to negotiate and provide various aids, such as helping the concession firm to acquire more loans or to be relieved of some financial obligations, granting direct or indirect subsidies, and extending the concession duration.

This type of situation occurs across many projects in sub-Saharan Africa when a company claims to the host government that it is not making profits and demands an extended period of not paying some of the revenue to the host country. Another situation may be when the host country demands that the private company renegotiate the contract due to a change in political authority or some other reason. The realities of this kind of process are many. Any of the aforementioned situations can increase the project's transaction

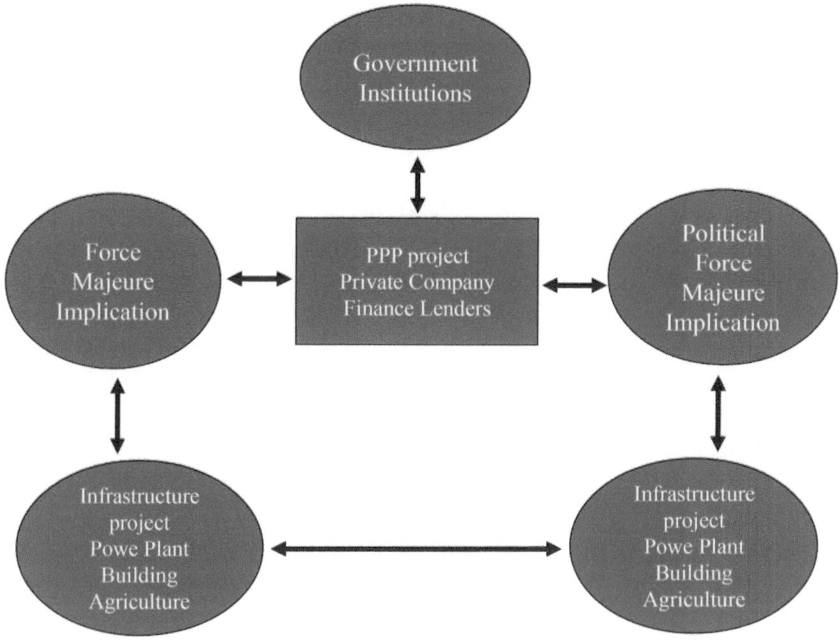

Figure 1.2 PPP Factor Implication. *Source*: Created by the author.

costs. Subedi (2019) posits that 'The host country can also act opportunistically and initiate renegotiation once the private concessionaire builds the roads and starts the operations'.

In this practice, the host government can request that the concessionaire revisit the toll road price because of the political pressure from various stakeholders within the country. A practical example in South Africa was the e-tolls project in Gauteng Province, where consumers refused to pay the e-toll fees. The provincial government is now investigating how to settle its debt with the investment company. Another argument is that the project was linked with corruption during former President Zuma's regime. Such projects are often undertaken to please the political constituency before an upcoming election in the country.

Erkan (2011) asserts that 'From the TCE perspective, government's opportunism through led renegotiation also causes substantial transaction cost regarding ex-ante and ex-post inefficiencies'. The investment companies, or private companies, involved in the project can face this kind of reality in the country if the legal system is insufficiently stable to protect the investors. To avoid this type of scenario, any PPP project should be implemented only after a discussion between the host country and the private companies, and legal guidelines must be in place before the final contract is signed. The party who fails to comply with the contract's stipulations should pay penalties to the other party. This will prevent opportunistic behaviour between the host government and the private sector, and enable a successful PPP project.

Resource-Based View Theory

The discussion of the resource-based view theory (RBVT) in PPP projects aims to assess the private company's ability to collaborate effectively with the government. In this context, the researcher is interested in determining if the private partner has skilled employees who can execute the project. This is the essence of the RBVT in PPP projects. Additionally, the company's funding or financial capacity to carry out the project delegated by government institutions is important. This study implies that PPPs require highly skilled personnel, and the company must meet specific requirements to implement a project on behalf of the government. The project cannot be awarded to a company that does not have the appropriate expertise to implement that project. That is where the resource-based view theory is needed; to explain the importance for any company involved in a PPP with any sphere of government to meet the requirements demanded by that project. Roumboutsos and Chiara (2009) explain that the RBVT in PPP can be possible when the following elements are in place:

- 'Goals are aligned with clear advantages for all parties;
- The alliance partnership contractual agreement builds on the assets of potential partners;
- Capacity is enhanced by compensating for each party's weaknesses'.

The performance of each company or organisation involved in the project must be taken into consideration. This theory demonstrates that each company involved in the PPP project needs to prove its capacity and performance to deliver that project. According to Lockett, Thompson, and Morgenstern (2009), 'This work implicitly assumes that in a competitive environment decision concerning the firm's activity set, will reflect the manager's attempts to use the resources at disposal in the interest of advancing the firm's performance'. Companies that wish to be involved in PPP projects must ensure that their performance is effective and efficient, as this will attract government agencies seeking a private sector partner for a PPP project. The private sector company should be able to show a sound financial report, and a history of completing projects on time is a selling point. A successfully delivered project will create more opportunities to be selected for other PPP projects.

The key to RBV theory in a PPP is the alliances or partnerships an organisation may enter into with other enterprises. Two companies combining their expertise to implement a PPP project can be referred to as an alliance.

Eisenhardt and Schoonhoven (1996, p.137) assert that 'Alliances as cooperative relationships driven by a logic of strategic resources needs and social resources opportunities'. Such alliances are entered into to ensure that the project is completed on time and that each partner's expertise brings an innovative approach to ensuring the project's successful implementation. Scholars such as Das and Teng (2000) 'considered strategic alliances an alternative to internationalization on the one hand and market exchanges on the other'. Entering an alliance with partners creates opportunities for the company to expand into other sectors of the economy. The PPP project must take into consideration the working relationship with other companies in a specific sector of the economy.

Entering into alliances with other companies can be profitable for international companies in terms of their resource base. Das and Teng (2000, p.37) explain that a 'company may use alliances or mergers to obtain resources possessed by other firms that are valuable and essential to achieving competitive advantage. In the international arena, multinational companies may enter foreign markets by acquiring a local company'. Under PPP, the strategy is for the international company to work with the local company for the latter to win the tender contract and the former provides skills transfer to the local partners. The advantage is that local companies promote international expertise. Most governments encourage international companies to work with local companies in a PPP arrangement. The local company provides the required facilities such as an office building, knowledge about the political network within the country, and contact with private companies involved in the sector. The local partners benefit from the innovation the international company brings in implementing the project.

Scholars have criticised the resource-based theory, stating that it has both strengths and weaknesses in terms of operation and that one should not only consider the strengths of the theory but also the weaknesses. Warnier and Weppe (2013, p.1365) opine that 'Former studies tackle the notion of resources mainly through their effects. "Strategic liabilities" are resources that destroy value, resource weaknesses can lead to the loss of competitive advantages or the emergence of a disadvantage and, finally, common resources are sufficient alone to create a competitive advantage'. The reality within any company is complex because the company's performance should be based on numerous conditions within a specific country. The resource-based theory should consider the context in which the company or organisation is operating. A PPP company's context must take the host country's rules and regulations into consideration.

The success of any company involved in a PPP project lies in its ability to deliver a specific project in accordance with the project contract awarded by the host government. In many countries in the sub-Saharan region, partnerships between private companies and the government are becoming increasingly popular for implementing various types of projects. PPP projects can be found in every sector across Africa, with each country aiming to achieve a mutually beneficial outcome whereby the host government benefits from the construction of infrastructure, while private companies generate good returns on investment.

The diversity of PPP projects in Africa is also a result of a lack of funding available from the host government to complete infrastructure projects. Poor budget planning by the government may also force reliance on the private sector for infrastructure development. Public enterprises' lack of financial capacity may also hinder their ability to invest in projects. To overcome these challenges, it is recommended that government officials at all levels understand the applicability of PPP. This understanding will help officials to negotiate with foreign investors or local financial institutions that have the financial capacity to undertake a PPP project.

Based on the sub-field of PPPs, this study notably observes that having a broad understanding of PPP theories is crucial. Discussing these theories helps readers to understand which theories can be applied in the field of public-private partnerships. A project's success can be linked to the theories discussed in this chapter. These theories must be linked to several models that the sub-field of PPP represents. The success of PPP is due to the various models that host governments and potential investors use to implement a project. Some states prefer a straightforward model such as build-operate-transfer, build-transfer or build-lease-transfer, while others prefer other models.

In order to study PPP in the field of Public Administration, there are several theories at the disposal of scholars. The selection of a specific theory (ies) will depend on the type of study a researcher embarks upon. As argued by Wang, Xiong, Wu, and Zhu (2018:299), 'there are three types of knowledge background to develop theoretical models to discuss about PPP'. Number one, a researcher can use PPP on analysing an economic background. For example, the Transaction cost theory discussed above looks on the transaction cost of PPP project. During a PPP project there is a lot of financial transaction cost involved in any PPP project implementation. In addition, Property right theory deals with the incompleteness of the PPP contract (Wang *et al.*, 2018).

In any PPP project there are two major players for the implementation of the project to be executed, the government institutions who is considered as "Principal" and the private sector is "Agent." This clarified the use of "Principal-Agent Theory," where one delegates the responsibility to the other company to implement the project on behalf of the state. Number two, PPP is also used in the field of Public Management and policy implementation. The approach of network theory and governance theory in the PPP is to understand the close cooperation between government institutions and the private sectors. The cooperation between the state and the private sector is to facilitate the implementation of the government programme to be achieved. It is also argued by Wang *et al.* (2018:299) that 'Public Choice theory and the New Public Management concern competition mechanisms for the provision of infrastructure and public service'.

CONCLUSION

The evolution of PPP in sub-Saharan Africa is growing every year due to the success of several infrastructure projects in different countries. This has become a mechanism for developing countries' governments to construct various projects. Understanding the theories of PPP makes it easy for scholars and practitioners in government institutions to implement PPP projects. This chapter discussed five different theories in the field of PPP, which provide a benchmark for every expert in the field to understand the theoretical framework that should be used to implement a PPP project. It is important to note that these five theories are not the only theories that scholars and practitioners should use to write about PPP. The use of PPP theories equips researchers, government officials, and private consultants with the necessary knowledge to comprehend this sub-field. It is important to recognise that the state or the government is the most significant stakeholder in any PPP project that takes place. All these theories on PPP discussed above are pertinent in the different infrastructure project. There is not specific theory for one PPP model, all the five theories discussed in this chapter is relevant in different model of PPP. It is advisable for government officials to understand the importance of the theories and linked it with PPP legislation in the country.

REFERENCES

Chowdhury, A.N., Chen, P.H., Tiong, R.L.K. (2010). Analysing the structure of public private partnership projects using network theory, *Construction Management and Economics*, Vol. 29(3), pp.247–260.

Davies, P and Eustice, K. (2005). Delivering the PPP promise: A review of PPP Issues and Activity, Price Water house coopers. Available from: https://ppp.worldbank.org/public-private-partnership/library/delivering-ppp-promise-review-ppp-issues-and-activity. Date of access: 12/07/2022

Das, T.K, and Teng, B. S. (2000). A resource- based theory of strategic alliances. *Journal of Management*. Vol. 26 (1), pp. 31–61.

De Palma, A, Leruth, L., and Prunier, G. (2012). Toward a principal—agent-based typology of risks in Public Private Partnerships. *Reflects et perspectives de la vie economique*. Vol. 51 (2), pp.57–73.

Eisenhardt, K.M, and Schoonhoven, C.B. (1996). Resource-based view of strategic alliance formation: Strategic and social effects of entrepreneurial firms. *Organisation Science*, Vol. 7(2), pp. 136–150.

Erkan, M. (2011). *International Energy Investment Law: Stability Through Contractual Clauses*, Kluwer Law International, BV; 27575th edition (December 21, 2010).

Freeman, L.C. (1979). Centrality in social networks: Conceptual clarification. *Social Network*, Vol. 1(3), pp. 215–239.

Guston, D.H. (1996). Principal-agent theory and the structure of science policy. *Science and Public Policy*, Vol. 23(4), pp. 229–240,

Harding, A. (1998). Public private partnership in the UK, in J Pierre (Ed), *Partnerships in Urban Governance-European and American Experience*. New York: ST Martins.

Hodge, G, and Greve, C. (2007). Public Private Partnerships: A comparative perspective on Victoria and Denmark. In: T. Christensen and P. Laegrid (Eds), *Transcending New Public Management: The Transformation of Public Sector Reforms*. UK: Ashgate.

Lynn, J. R., Heinrich, S. J and Hill, C. J. (2000). Studying governance and Public Management: Challenges and Prospects. *Journal of Public Administration Research and Theory,* Vol. 10(2), pp. 233–261.

Lockett, A., and Thompson, S. (2009). The development of the resource-based view of the firm: A critical appraisal. *International Journal of Management Review*, Vol. 11(1), pp. 9–28.

Kadushin, C. (2004). *Basic Network Concepts*, available at: Scribd.com/doc/12748 508/ Basic-Network-Concepts. Access: 06/01/2023

Mill, J.S. (1848). Principles of political economy with some of their application to social philosophy. Access date 09 February 2023. "The development of PPP concepts in economic theory. Alla, Mostepa Niul, *Journal Advance in Applied Sociology*. Vol. 6(11).

Roumboutsos, A., and Chiara, N. (2009). Public private partnerships: A strategic partnering approach in *Revamping PPPs. From `Revisiting and Rethinking` to `Revamping and Revitalising PPPs,* Centre for Infrastructure and Construction Industry Development The University of Hong Kong, Vol. 23, pp. 75–84.

Ping Ho S, Levitt, R., Tsui CW, Hsu, Y. (2015). Opportunism focused transaction cost analysis of PPP. *Journal of Management Engineering,* Vol.36 (6), pp. 1–11.

Subedi M. (2020) Public-Private Partnership and Bureaucracy. In: Farazmand A. (eds.) *Global Encyclopedia of Public Administration, Public Policy, and Governance*. Available at SSRN: https://ssrn.com/abstract=3861953. Date of Access: 20/11/2022

Warnier, V., and Weppe, X. (2013). Extending Resources-based theory: Considering strategic, ordinary and junk resources, *Journal of Management Decision*, Vol. 51(7), pp. 1359–1379.

Wang, H., Xiong, W., Wu, G. and Zhu, D. (2018). Public private partnership in public administration discipline: A literature review. *Public Management Review*, Vol. 20(2), pp. 225–316.

Chapter 2

Public-Private Partnerships and Public Procurement in Africa

Emmanuel Botlhale

As part of the age-old social compact between the government and the governed, the former has an obligation to provide a raft of goods and services, for example, education, health, infrastructure and other public works, to the latter. In most cases, the state procures these goods and services because; (i) either the market does not produce them; or (ii) it produces them in insufficient quantities. Due to either (i) or (ii), the government must procure certain goods and services. This practice is called public procurement. To provide expository clarity, the term 'public procurement' must be defined. It is notable that this term has been defined by many scholars, for example Arrowsmith (1998) and Warrillow (1995), and multilateral organisations such as the European Union, Organisation for Economic Co-operation and Development and World Trade Organization. Public procurement, or public sourcing, is the acquisition of goods or services by government organisations (OECD, 2023; Warrillow, 1995).

In a related vein, the European PPP Expertise Centre (2016, p. 5) defines public procurement as 'the process by which public authorities, such as government departments or local authorities, purchase works, goods or services from suppliers that they have selected for this purpose'. Private sector procurement is the opposite. As implied by the name, the private sector is made up of non-governmental, for-profit organisations (such as businesses, private enterprises, etc.). As a result, the two work in a variety of settings, including those subject to distinct legal regimes and requiring them to account to varied standards, including the general public and shareholders in the public and private sectors, respectively. Despite their differences, the two have one thing in common: value for money (VfM) and best value for money (BvM). Ceteris paribus, the two are frequently, if not always, easier to achieve in the private sector than in the public sector. The aforementioned framework allows governments and state-owned companies to collaborate with non-state actors to purchase commodities, works, and services. When this happens, such partnerships are called Public-Private Partnerships (PPPs).

PPPs do not have a single, commonly agreed definition (World Bank, 2018a). According to the International Monetary Fund (2004, p. 4), PPPs are described as 'arrangements where the private sector supplies infrastructure assets and services that historically have been provided by the government'. A growing number of countries have included a definition of PPPs in their legislation, each one adjusting it to take into account the unique institutional and legal conditions in that nation (World Bank, 2018b). For instance, according to South African law, a PPP is a contract between a public sector institution or municipality and a private party where the latter accepts significant financial, technical, and operational risk in the planning, financing, construction, and operation of a project (National Treasury [South Africa], 2018).

PPPs are increasingly being used as a competitive alternative to traditional public procurement. PPPs favourably enable governments to finance the purchase of goods and services off their balance sheets, therefore, freeing up resources that would be directed to other uses. Due to post-2007 fiscal strictures caused by the global financial crisis of 2007–2009, which were exacerbated and aggravated by the economic misery brought about by the COVID-19 pandemic, an increasing number of African countries are being forced to embrace PPPs (Botlhale, 2022). Either new PPP Acts are either being implemented or current PPP Acts are being amended because legal and institutional frameworks are essential. These Acts provide information on the methods, structure, and other elements of PPP regimes. They also detail how PPPs are to be carried out. They oversee the execution of PPPs as well. Additional PPP activities that go beyond PPP Acts include the creation of technical and regulatory advisory bodies, employee training, equipment upgrades, and skill upgrades.

Even though PPP outcomes vary across the African continent, it is imperative to use private resources and expertise to finance the delivery of public infrastructure and services while also creating a suitable, enabling, and conducive legal and institutional framework for the successful operation of PPP projects. Since this chapter's limited space will not allow it to cover all the reasons for the rising usage of PPPs, it will, instead, concentrate on two of them. These include (i) the post-2007 fiscal strictures: Global Financial Crisis (2007–2009); the global commodity crash of 2014–2015; COVID-19; and the Ukraine invasion; and (ii) concerns for Value for Money (VfM) and Best Value for Money (BvM), especially, given the consensus that, ceteris paribus, VfM and BvM are frequently, if not always, more readily achievable in the private sector than in the public sector. In this regard, it is claimed that PPPs provide better VfM and BvM (e.g., see Nwangwu, 2012).

The chapter is organised into five sections. Section 1 is the introduction which establishes the context for the discussion in the chapter. The justification for the use of PPPs is covered in section 2. Case studies of PPPs in Africa are discussed in section 3. The policy issues surrounding the operation of successful PPP projects in Africa are covered in section 4. Lastly, the chapter concludes in section 5 with summary thoughts and ideas.

THE JUSTIFICATION FOR THE ADOPTION OF PPPs

There are many and variegated justifications for the adoption of PPPs. For reason of economy, this chapter focuses on two. These are: (i) the post-2007 fiscal strictures; and (ii) concerns for Value for Money (VfM) and Best Value for Money (BvM), especially given the consensus that, ceteris paribus, VfM and BvM are frequently, if not always, more readily achievable in the private sector than in the public sector (e.g., see Nwangwu, 2012).

Post-2007 Fiscal Strictures

The most convincing justification for the introduction of PPPs comes from the post-2007 fiscal strictures. Global shocks have resulted in a smaller *fiscus*. This is especially true in resource-dependent developing nations, particularly, in sub-Saharan Africa. The following events constitute these shocks: (i) the Global Financial Crisis (2007–2009); (ii) the 2014–2015 global commodity crash; (iii) COVID-19; and (iv) the invasion of Ukraine [the Russo–Ukrainian War, which began in 2014, intensified on 24 February 2022 when Russia invaded Ukraine].

The early twenty-first century saw a catastrophic global economic calamity known as the Global Financial Crisis (GFC), which lasted from 2007 to 2009. Since the Great Depression, the GFC was the most serious financial catastrophe; hence, it is often called 'The Great Recession'. Cheap credit and loose lending rules, which created a housing bubble, were the root causes of the financial crisis of 2008 (Singh, 2022). The banks were left with trillions of dollars' worth of worthless investments in subprime mortgages after the bubble crashed and following the Great Recession, many people lost their homes, savings, and jobs (Singh, 2022). Although the GFC began in the United States, as vividly illustrated by the biggest bankruptcy in U.S. history—the collapse of Lehman Brothers in September 2007—the crisis was not limited to just the United States because of the interconnectedness of the world's economies.

Africa, particularly sub-Saharan Africa (SSA), disproportionately suffered the effects of the GFC largely due to monocultural economies. An economy that primarily depends on one product or resource for economic growth and development is referred to as a monocultural economy (Itumo, 2016). The idea could also be used in situations where a nation's budget is financed primarily (but not exclusively) to the tune of 70% of its total revenue by the sales or exports of a single product (Itumo, 2016). A country's dependence on a single basic product source for a greater proportion of overall national earnings and contribution to the gross domestic product is sometimes referred to as having a monocultural economy (Itumo, 2016). This phenomenon is called 'commodity dependence'.

A country is deemed to be commodity-dependent by UNCTAD (2021) if its principal commodity exports account for more than 60% of its total merchandise exports. Commodity dependency heightens a country's vulnerability to adverse commodity price shocks, which can have a detrimental impact on economic growth and welfare in the short and medium terms (UNCTAD, 2022a). This vulnerability is frequently made worse by the negative effects of shocks like the 2008–2009 global financial crisis, the 2019 coronavirus (COVID-19) pandemic, or the more recent geopolitical tensions in Eastern Europe (the 2022 war in Ukraine), which have the effect of disrupting global trade, raising financial volatility, and increasing food insecurity (UNCTAD, 2022b). The consequences of these crises highlight a long-standing problem with Africa's development: commodity dependence, which denotes a significant reliance of nations' exports on primary goods (UNCTAD, 2022b).

Monocultural economies disproportionately predominate in sub-Saharan Africa (SSA). Angola (oil), Botswana (diamonds), and Nigeria (oil) are a few examples [and Zambia's economy was heavily dependent on copper exports until the 1980s]. Due to the market's cyclical nature of price booms and busts, 45 of Africa's economies are dependent on commodities, and their earnings are extremely unstable (UNCTAD, 2022b). Due to monocultural economies, SSA economies disproportionately suffered the effects of the 2007–2009 GFC. Then, Africa's growth performance was impacted by then financial and economic crisis, and commodity prices and demand in Africa were diminishing, as were financial flows, and the projected boost in aid did not occur (African Development Bank, 2009). Botswana, which was then and still is largely dependent on the sale of diamonds, is a good example of how the GFC affected the government's balance sheet.

Prior to 2008, Botswana had 20 years of continuous budget surpluses (Jefferis, 2008), but its fortunes were reversed by the consequences of the GFC, which became particularly acute in November 2008 when it failed to sell a single diamond since it began selling diamonds in 1972 (Gaolathe, 2009). The effects of the worldwide financial and economic problems were acutely felt during the preparation of the 2009–2010 budget. To give an example, on 2 February 2009 when the late Baledzi Gaolathe, the then Minister of Finance and Development Planning, presented the 2009/10 Budget Speech to the National Assembly, he asked the House to approve a budget with a deficit of BWP [Botswana Pula] 13.4 billion [then, the equivalent of US$1.05 billion].

Post February 2 2009, the situation did not improve (see subsequent Budget Speeches). It is notable that Botswana was not exceptional; rather, it represented the prevailing situation on the continent then. For example, the GFC meant a reduced *fiscus* in South Africa. When the then Minister of Finance, Trevor Manuel, presented the 2009 Budget Speech on revenue estimates and tax proposals, he painted a gloomy picture of the *fiscus*. Inter alia, he said, 'Madam Speaker, the revised estimate of revenue for 2008/09 is R14.2 billion less than we in the 2008 Budget' and that 'for the year ahead, the main budget revenue estimate is R50 billion lower than we projected in February last year, against the background of slower growth, depressed trade and declining company profits' (Manuel, 2009). The overall result was a smaller *fiscus*, which resulted in the South African government buying fewer goods and services. This also meant that fewer developments were undertaken then.

The global commodity crash of 2014–2015 occurred when the world economy was still slowly recovering from the consequences of the 2007–2009 global financial crises. To put things in perspective, commodity price shocks are periods of quickly rising or declining commodity prices. Between June 2014 and February 2015, global commodities prices dropped by 38%. Many of the world's commodity-dependent nations are in Africa, notably in sub-Saharan Africa, and they were disproportionately affected by the commodity crash of 2014–2015. This meant further fiscal strictures that necessitated off-the-government balance sheet financing of public procurement of goods and services. Post-2015, the most catastrophic shock was COVID-19.

The fifth known pandemic since the 1918 flu pandemic was caused by the human coronavirus disease of 2019 (COVID-19), which was originally discovered in Wuhan, China, in 2019. On 30 January 2020 and 11 March 2020, respectively, the World Health Organization (WHO) declared the outbreak a public health emergency of international concern and a pandemic. The pandemic was one of the deadliest in history as adequately instanced by the fact that as of 27 January 2023, there were more than 670 million illnesses and 6.82 million confirmed deaths. The COVID-19 pandemic caused the worst global economic crisis in more than a century and sent shockwaves through the worldwide economy (World Bank, 2022).

Although household and business incomes were most directly affected by the crisis, the consequences of this large shock have repercussions for the entire economy through numerous mutually reinforcing channels that connect the financial health of households and firms, financial institutions, and governments (World Bank, 2022, p. 3). Even though it is difficult to estimate, the global COVID-19 (coronavirus) pandemic has had a profoundly damaging effect on the world economy (Statista Research Department, 2023). At US$84.54 trillion in 2020—Gross Domestic product (GDP) decreased globally by 3.4% (Statista Research Department, 2023). To put this amount into a vivid perspective, a 3.4% decline in economic growth resulted in nearly US$2 trillion of lost economic output (Statista Research Department, 2022).

The UN Department of Economic and Social Affairs' *World Economic Situation and Prospects 2022* listed several issues that were slowing down the economy, including fresh COVID-19 outbreaks, lingering labour market and supply chain issues, and escalating inflationary pressures (United Nations, 2022). The slowdown is anticipated to last throughout the following year (United Nations, 2022). Global output is predicted to expand by just 4% in 2022 and 3.5% in 2023 after a promising expansion of 5.5% in 2021, led by robust consumer spending and some uptake in investment, with trade in products approaching pre-pandemic levels (United Nations, 2022). In a similar vein, IMF (2022) paints a gloomy picture of the global economy due to the COVID-19 pandemic. According to the IMF (2022), global growth is expected to decrease from 6.0% in 2021 to 3.2% in 2022 and 2.7% in 2023. Except for the global financial crisis and the pandemic's acute phase, this is the weakest growth since 2001 (IMF, 2022). Heightened fiscal structures are one of COVID-19's most noticeable macroeconomic effects.

Despite the COVID-19 pandemic's worldwide reach, developing nations—particularly those in sub-Saharan Africa with resource-dependent economies—disproportionately felt its repercussions because of underlying structural issues. The pandemic has severely impacted Africa and, according to the African Development Bank's (2021) estimate, the continent's economic growth dropped by 2.1% in 2020. Southern Africa, one of Africa's sub-regions, is expected to have experienced the greatest economic growth decline in 2020, falling by an estimated 7.0% (Anyanwu and Salami, 2021). It was followed by West Africa (1.5%), North Africa (1.1%), Central Africa (2.7%) and East Africa, which relies the least on natural resources, expected to post a growth increase of 0.7% in 2020 (Anyanwu and Salami, 2021).

The demand for primary goods like metals (e.g., Botswana's diamonds), which are the economic foundation of the majority of developing countries, notably those in sub-Saharan Africa with resource-dependent economies, declined overall. Low demand resulted in low prices, which in turn led to lower export revenues and severe fiscal strictures. The three waves of the COVID-19 shock to African economies are as follows: (i) a short-term decline in trade and investment from China; (ii) a demand slump brought on by lockdowns in the European Union and OECD countries; and (iii) a continental supply shock that will have an impact on intra-African trade (OECD, 2020).

Resource-dependent economies of sub-Saharan African (SSA) countries crafted several COVID-19 economic recovery programmes, just like the rest of the world. For instance, Namibia's COVID-19 Socio-Economic Recovery Plan, Botswana's Economic Recovery and Transformation Plan (ERTP), and South Africa's Economic Reconstruction and Recovery Plan [the document lays out an economic recovery and reconstruction strategy for South Africa that aims to promote inclusive and fair growth]. To be funded, these economic recovery plans require hundreds of trillions of US dollars. The COVID-19 pandemic has left governments with little funds. Thus, it is necessary to use private capital to finance these expensive plans. Thus, PPPs will materially facilitate and aid the post-COVID-19 economic recovery in SSA countries.

The last global shock is the invasion of Ukraine. The Russo–Ukrainian War, which began in 2014, intensified on 24 February 2022 when Russia invaded Ukraine. While this is a Russo–Ukrainian war, its ramifications are felt all over the world due to the interconnectedness of the global economy. Since the beginning of the war in Ukraine on February 24, the outlook for the international economy has grown gloomier, leading World Trade Organization (WTO) economists to re-evaluate their predictions for global commerce over the next two years (WTO, 2022). The organisation has revised its projection for the growth of the merchandise trade volume to 3.0% in 2022 from its earlier forecast of 4.7%. For emerging and developing economies, there is less hope for a post-pandemic economic rebound because of the ongoing conflict in Ukraine. The aforementioned projection results in a reduced revenue envelope for developing economies, the bulk of which are reliant on natural resources. Thus, the use of PPPs as a means of leveraging private capital is very crucial.

Value for Money (VfM) and Best Value for Money (BvM)

The crucial concept, VfM, needs to be defined to provide expository clarity. VfM has been defined by numerous organisations, despite the fact that there are definitional issues and that there is ongoing uncertainty over how the concept should and may be applied (Governance and Social Development Resource Centre, 2010). Value for money is described as a benefit obtained from each and every purchase or amount of money spent (Karanja, 2021). Value for money is the effective, efficient, and economical use of resources (Asian Development Bank, 2021). To achieve this, relevant costs and benefits must be evaluated, along with risks, non-price features, and/or total cost of ownership as necessary (Asian Development Bank, 2021). Finding the best balance between the 'three E's' of economy, efficiency, and effectiveness is what VfM is all about (Jackson, 2012, p. 1). According to the Independent Commission for Aid Impact (2011), a 'fourth "E"—equity—is now also occasionally employed to guarantee that value-for-money analysis accounts for the importance of reaching disparate groups'.

Value for money is based on the highest efficiency and effectiveness of the purchase in addition to the minimal purchase price (economy) (Karanja, 2021). VfM has synonyms such as Optimal (optimisation), Return on Investment (ROI), things sold at a good price, where quality meets the price, quality-to-price ratio; and win-win (Karanja, 2021). VfM determination can be done using three main techniques: (i) Cost-Effectiveness Analysis and Cost-Utility analysis; (ii) Cost-Benefit analysis and social return on investment; and (iii) Rank correlation of cost vs. impact and Basic Efficiency Resource Analysis (Better Evaluation, 2022).

The successful implementation of the VfM principle may: (i) reduce risk and improve quality (risks, for example, are more effectively identified and managed through better design of the procurement arrangements); (ii) improve performance (suppliers may provide innovative and cost-effective solutions to address the identified needs); and (iii) improve performance (e.g., suppliers may offer cost-effective and innovative solutions to meet the identified needs) (Asian Development Bank, 2021). There will always be a trade-off between the advantages obtained and the expenses incurred in comparison to the advantages and expenses of an alternative method when decisions are made during the procurement cycle (Asian Development Bank, 2021). Opportunities exist for a project to utilise its resources more effectively, efficiently, and affordably throughout the procurement cycle, or to attain VfM (Asian Development Bank, 2021).

VfM considerations are key in procurement, be it public or private, hence, it must be ensured over the procurement cycle. According to CIPS (2022), there are 13 distinct steps in the procurement cycle. This cycle, which begins with the specification, progresses through the tendering process, and ends with asset management, is a transparent and reliable tool for all procurement and supply experts (CIPS, 2022). Key considerations during the Procurement and Supply Cycle are: Technology; Stakeholder engagement; Sustainability/CSR/Ethics/Security; Risk Assessment/Mitigation; Continuous improvement; People and skills; and Innovation (CIPS, 2022). The foregoing is key in both public and private sector procurement to ensure the attainment of VfM. Ceteris paribus, VfM is frequently, if not always, easier to achieve in the private sector than in the public sector. As noted earlier, the aforementioned framework allows governments and state-owned companies to collaborate with non-state actors to purchase commodities, works, and services. Because it is primarily motivated by profit, the private sector typically performs better than the public sector.

This leads to the question asked by Sarmad and Mohiuddin (1991), *Is the Private Sector more Productive than the Public Sector*? The idea to promote the private sector and limit the role of states (government) in running economies was primarily propounded in the 1970s by the Chicago school of economics, with Milton Friedman and George Stigler considered the leading scholars of the Chicago school. The idea got more impetus in the 1980s from the Bretton Woods institutions (World Bank and International Monetary Fund), mainly, through the imposition of Structural Adjustment Programmes. The last push came via the hand of Reaganomics (the neo-liberal economic policies of Ronald Reagan [U.S. President, from 1981 to 1989], Thatcherite economics [the neo-liberal economic policies of Margret Thatcher, the Prime Minister of the United Kingdom from 1979 to 1990] and the Washington Consensus (a list of 10 economic policy recommendations that are promoted for crisis-ridden developing nations by Washington, D.C.-based organisations like the International Monetary Fund, World Bank, and U.S. Department of the Treasury).

The 'Is the Private Sector more Productive than the Public Sector?' issue is not conclusively resolved as manifest in Sarmad and Mohiuddin (1991) and UNDP Global Centre for Public Service Excellence (2015). In this regard, the UNDP Global Centre for Public Service Excellence (2015) argues that the debate over whether the private sector is fundamentally more efficient than the public sector, however, has never been resolved. It strenuously refutes the notion that the private sector should take precedence. It argues that no type of ownership, whether public, private, or mixed, is intrinsically more efficient than the others and that the efficiency of service supply under all ownership models depends on elements including competition, regulation, autonomy, and broader issues of institutional evolution.

Notably, it contends that the literature shows that the effectiveness of service delivery is influenced by the nature of the service (health, education, etc.) and other unique contextual elements (such as market competition, regulation, etc.). The Public Services Privatisation Research Unit, based at the University of Greenwich, challenges the notion that privatisation or public-private partnerships (PPPs) can always deliver the same level and quality of service at a lower cost than the public sector (European Public Service Union, 2014). The study was updated with fresh data from a variety of public agencies since it was first released in 2014 to reflect those services. The paper looks at data from nine industries: power, water, waste management, transportation (including buses and trains), ports and airports, and health are just a few of the businesses that the study examined. The results repeatedly disproved the case for outsourcing and privatisation.

However, given the ascendancy of New Public Management and cogent reforms such as New Public Governance (see writings by Stephen P. Osborne, Jacob Torfing, Lotte Bøgh Andersen, Carsten Greve, and Kurt K. Klausen etc.) and tools such as privatisation, it can be argued a posteriori, there is a general response to the question: *Is the Private Sector more Productive than the Public Sector*? Thus, under the right circumstances, for example, competition, regulation, autonomy, and broader issues of institutional architecture, the private sector is more productive than the public sector. Arising from the above, VfM is frequently, if not always, easier to achieve in the private sector than in the public sector.

Given the primacy of VfM in public procurement, governments often partner with the private sector via the vehicle of PPPs to procure goods and services. In this regard, it is claimed that PPPs provide better VfM (e.g., see Nwangwu, 2012). However, it should be noted that PPPs, backed by private sector capital and management finesse, are not the fabled silver bullet. PPPs can be freighted with challenges (e.g., see Grimsey and Lewis, 2007; Hans and Koppenjan, 2001; Martin, 2008; Zhang, 2005). In this regard, Zhang (2005) identifies six barriers to PPPs in infrastructure development as: (1) social, political, and legal risk; (2) unfavourable economic and commercial conditions; (3) inefficient public procurement framework; (4) lack of mature financial engineering techniques; (5) problems related to the public sector; and (6) problems related to the private sector. A disabling legal and institutional framework for PPPs is cited by the World Bank (2018b) as a serious risk factor.

It is notable that to maximise returns on investment, it is not enough to only consider VfM in public procurement (Botlhale, 2020). Hence, there is a need to consider other ideals such as the Best Value for Money (BvM). Best value for money is defined as the most advantageous combination of cost, quality and sustainability to meet customer requirements (Gov.UK, 2023). In recent years, there has been a steady shift in how successful procurement is assessed in both the public and commercial sectors (Dimitri, 2013). Indeed, in terms of economic efficiency, judgements have moved away from using price alone as a criterion for success and towards a multi-criteria approach where many aspects of quality, in addition to price, are taken into account (Dimitri, 2013). The phrase 'best value for money' is the most popular way to describe this shift in emphasis (Dimitri, 2013).

BvM, therefore, refers to the best Return on Investment rather than the lowest financial cost (Dimitri, 2013). BvM leads to Best value Procurement (BvP), the opposite of lowest-bid procurement. The BvP approach is a method of purchasing construction works, services and so on (Designing Buildings Ltd., 2023). It considers criteria, such as quality, reliability and expertise, rather than just price to assess value (Designing Buildings Ltd., 2023). Ceteris paribus, BvP is frequently, if not always, easier to achieve in the private sector than in the public sector. Thus, under the right circumstances, for example, competition, regulation, autonomy, and broader issues of institutional architecture, the private sector is more productive than the public sector, hence, more BvP.

Therefore, the weight of the evidence would suggest that public projects be delivered through the PPP vehicle, using VfM at the very least or BvM at the very maximum. Thus, under the right circumstances, for example, competition, regulation, autonomy, and broader issues of institutional architecture, the private sector is more productive than the public sector, therefore, leading to more BvM and, cogently, more BvP. Ceteris paribus, BvM, like VfM, is frequently, if not always, easier to achieve in the private sector than in the public sector under the right circumstances. This, therefore, means that the public sector can partner with the private sector via the vehicle of PPP to ensure feasibly maximum BvM and, cogently, BvP.

PPP Projects in Africa

Many African countries have made significant investments in developing public-private partnership (PPP) legal-institutional frameworks to create an environment favourable for the implementation of PPP projects. In the post-COVID-19 pandemic era, PPPs are regarded as a viable alternative to address, amongst others, the infrastructure gap in Africa. This is the thinking at that continental level as instanced by the African Development Bank's support for PPPs projects in Africa. To exemplify, in a workshop held on 8 September 2021, representatives of the African Development Bank, governments, development finance institutions, the private sector, and professional associations discussed ways that the bank could strengthen its support for PPPs and direct more funding towards economic and social infrastructure (African Development Bank, 2020a). The bank hosted the event digitally under the title *Designing the African Development Bank's PPP Framework*.

The bank notes that the largest obstacle to raising the number of PPP investments in Africa is the lack of ability of the nations to find, create, structure, and sell bankable PPPs. In this regard, governments and nations with developing PPP markets are typically said to lack experience in overseeing the transaction stage of PPPs. Thus, the framework intends to address the foregoing problems and challenges. Amongst others, the PPP framework outlines the bank's responsibilities and priorities for supporting PPPs in Regional Member Countries and aims to foster a common understanding of PPPs both inside and outside the bank (African Development Bank, 2020b). From 2008 to 2018, successful PPP transactions were carried out in five African nations: South Africa, Morocco, Nigeria, Egypt, and Ghana (African Development Bank, 2020a). A brief discussion of successful PPP projects in selected African nations follows.

South Africa: according to the National Development Plan, infrastructure investment as a share of GDP must increase from 21% in 2015 to 30% in 2030 (National Treasury, 2017). To fund and develop infrastructure, the public and private sectors must collaborate. A greater reliance on PPP funding may result in more rigorous planning, discipline, accountability, and decision-making for infrastructure projects (National Treasury, 2017). Depending on the contractual arrangements, there are different types of PPP projects, such as (i) Design, finance, build, operate, and transfer (DFBOT) projects, (ii) Design, finance and operate (DFO) projects, (iii) Design, build, operate, and transfer (DBOT) projects, (iv) Equity partnership projects, and (v) facilities management projects (National Treasury, 2018). Hospitals, transportation and road developments, tourism initiatives, and projects for corporate headquarters are among these. The projects were supported by a combination of debt, equity, and, in certain cases, capital contributions from the government. SANRAL N4 East Toll Road (DFBOT, February 1998, 30 years), Gautrain Rapid Rail Link (DFBOT, September 2006, 20 years), and City of Tshwane Head Office Accommodation (DFBOT, March 2015, 25 years) are a few examples of PPP projects that have been done in South Africa (National Treasury, 2017).

Nigeria: achieving higher value and more inexpensive services is the cornerstone of Nigeria's whole PPP structure (Soyeju, 2013). The Infrastructure Concession Regulatory Commission (ICRC) was founded by the Federal Government of Nigeria in 2008 in accordance with the Infrastructure Concession Regulatory Commission (establishment, etc.) Act, 2005 (World Bank, 2021a). The ICRC was created to oversee Federal government Public-Private Partnership (PPP) efforts to alleviate Nigeria's physical infrastructure gap, which impedes economic progress (ICRC, 2023). It aims to facilitate the establishment and execution of efficient Public-Private Partnerships by the Federal Government of Nigeria and its Ministries, Departments, and Agencies (MDAs). The Infrastructure Concession Regulatory Commission Act (the ICRCA), which was enacted into law in 2005, provides the primary legal framework for Private Sector Participation in Infrastructure Development in Nigeria and is the principal legislation for PPPs in Nigeria (Nwangwu, 2012).

It is notable that PPPs are subject to a complex and conflicting web of legislation in Nigeria, and numerous organisations are also working to control the same transactions (Nwangwu, 2012). Examples are the Public Enterprises Privatisation and Commercialisation Act 1999 (Privatisation Act); the Public Procurement Act 2007; the National Planning Commission Act 1993; the Fiscal Responsibility Act 2007; and the National Policy on Public Private Partnerships (2009—this seeks to create an environment that will encourage private sector participation in the provision of infrastructure services in Nigeria).

Since its inception, the ICRC has overseen the implementation of many projects and some are currently ongoing. For example, in early July 2022, the then ICRC's acting Director General and Chief Executive Officer, announced that 53 qualified and bankable PPP projects, with a combined value of US$22 billion, were slated for publication by the Infrastructure Concession Regulatory Commission in 2022 (Punch, 2022). The announcement was made at the Africa Public Private Partnership Network Investment Summit 2022 held in Abuja. The then acting Director General and Chief Executive Officer also announced that, as of May 2022, there were 77 post-contract PPP projects in operation at the ICRC Projects Disclosure Portal (www.ppp.icrc.gov.ng or www.icrc.gov.ng), a portal which was created in cooperation with the World Bank and is the first disclosure portal ever (Punch, 2022). Some examples are: (i) DAGBOLU INLAND CONTAINER DEPOT (valued at 1207.16 million Nigerian naira/3.96 million US$, date; 2022/10/21); and (ii) LOLO INLAND CONTAINER DEPOT (valued at 989 million Nigerian naira/3.24 million US$, date; 2022/10/21) (ICRC, 2023).

Egypt: the primary legislative framework for PPP procurement in Egypt is provided by the Public Partnership Law of 2010 (Law 67), with subsequent changes, and the PPP Executive Regulations of Law No. 67 of 2010. Additionally, there is the Procurement Law of 2018 (Law 182). The provisions of the law apply to partnership contracts with the private sector and related advisory contracts concluded by the Administrative Authorities with the private sector to execute infrastructure projects, services and public utilities as well as in relation to the availability of related services (Arabic Republic of Egypt, 2010). Such contracts will not be subject to the provisions of Law no. 129 for 1947 concerning concessions of public utilities, and Law no. 61 for 1958 concerning concessions relating to the investment of natural resources and public utilities, as well as Public Tenders Law no. 89 for 1998 organising tenders and bids and any specific laws related to granting concessions of public utilities (Arabic Republic of Egypt, 2010).

The government is actively promoting PPPs across numerous industries, including education and rail transportation, as well as in emerging development fields such as climate control, seawater desalination, and dry ports, as part of Egypt's Vision 2030 (MENA forum, 2023). In 2022, the government rolled out PPP projects worth 16 billion Egyptian pounds ($860 million) in order to encourage PPPs across the nation. The PPP Unit is responsible for researching, using, and putting the PPP concept into practice, as well as coordinating with line Ministries and the private sector to create a clear policy framework and action plan (World Bank, 2021b). Making sure that PPP project proposals are supported by solid analyses of needs and value, acquire the requisite budget clearances, and that partner selection occurs as the result of a thorough and fair competition is a crucial responsibility of the Unit (World Bank, 2021b).

Botswana: although the Privatization Policy of 2000 and policy statements made in the 2002/2003 Budget Speech and National Development Plan 9

(2003/04–2008/09) might be credited with the birth of PPPs, post-2007 fiscal restraints provided the main impetus (Botlhale, 2022). PPPs are firmly based on a specified institutional and legal structure. The Public-Private Partnership Policy and Implementation Framework specifies the PPP's institutional and legal framework. The National Development Plan 11, 2016/17–2022/23 (NDP 11) acknowledges that having a decent infrastructure is one of the things that would help the nation's economy flourish (Olotch, 2021) To do this, the NDP 11 emphasises the government's resolve to employ PPPs more frequently as a method of acquiring and financing infrastructure projects (Olotch, 2021). A PPP Unit was established in the Ministry of Finance and Economic Development in 2016. Its principal mandate is to ensure the successful implementation of the PPP Policy.

Botswana does not have a PPP law, instead, it has a PPP Policy and Implementation Framework of 2009. The old Public Procurement Act was replaced with a new one in 2021. This is an Act to establish the Public Procurement Regulatory Authority; to provide for its functions; to provide for the management of the procurement of works, services and supplies; and for matters incidental thereto and connected therewith (Republic of Botswana, 2021). In terms of PPP projects, the longest-running and most lasting is Debswana which was established in 1969.

Policy Concerns Surrounding the Operation of Successful PPP Projects in Africa

It is one thing for one to say that PPPs are the way to go given post-2007 fiscal strictures and superior Value for Money (VfM) and Best Value for Money (BvM) that are associated with PPP projects and totally another to ensure the successful implementation of PPP projects in Africa. This is so because there is evidence that proves that PPP projects are faced with challenges. As mentioned earlier, PPPs, supported by private sector funding and management skill, should not be regarded as the fabled silver bullet. PPPs can be fraught with difficulties (see, for instance, Grimsey and Lewis (2007), Hans and Koppenjan (2001), Martin (2008, 2009), and Zhang (2005)). In this regard, Zhang (2005) lists some obstacles to PPPs in infrastructure development as follows: (1) social, political, and legal risk; (2) unfavourable economic and commercial conditions; (3) an ineffective public procurement framework; (4) a dearth of advanced financial engineering techniques; and (5) issues relating to the public sector and the private sector. According to the World Bank (2018b), a significant risk factor for PPPs is a restrictive legal and institutional environment. Therefore, there is an imperative need to resolve the foregoing challenges, through:

Commitment to PPPs: there is a need for a first office commitment to the PPP project. Anecdotal evidence demonstrates that the first office's commitment is key to many projects, for example, HIV and AIDS, SDGs, gender-based violence, etc. Thus, a PPP regime is potentially deliverable if it enjoys the support of the first office. In addition, it must be placed in the super Ministry; that is, Ministry of Finance (also called the Treasury).

Legal-institutional framework: an enabling legal-institutional framework is essential for the PPP regime to become entrenched. The UNCITRAL Legislative Guide on Privately Financed Infrastructure Projects emphasises this point. Therefore, there must be an unambiguous legal-institutional framework in the form of a specific PPP law. It is notable that some countries, for instance Botswana, have Procurement Acts but do not have specific PPP laws. PPP Acts are very crucial because they provide left and right of the PPP landscape and also provide for role clarity for the two parties.

Risk-sharing protocols: PPPs entail a lot of risks, therefore, there should be clarity on risk-sharing. That is, what risk should each party bear? The default position in many African countries is for the government to shift all the risk to the private partner. This has the effect of scaring away private investors. Thus, there must be equitable risk-sharing.

Results-based M&E framework: necessarily, PPP projects entail huge investments, therefore, there is a need for a results-based Monitoring and Evaluation framework. This should be accompanied by mutually agreed upon monitoring and evaluation indicators, both quantitative and qualitative. To be effective, M&E reports should not be a tick-box exercise but a mechanism that must be religiously used to ensure PPP projects' success.

CONCLUSION

PPPs have become one of the principal ways and means to overcome obstacles that developing nations, particularly those in sub-Saharan Africa (SSA), encounter when trying to build infrastructure like roads, schools, or hospitals. Mainly, this is caused by a lack of public funding and poor public project delivery. PPPs, therefore, enable governments to use the resources and innovation of the private sector to fund vital infrastructure, enhance project planning, execution, and management, and provide effective services to the public. They are, therefore, vital to overcoming the obstacles in fulfilling national aspirations such as National Visions and National Development Plans and supranational commitments such as Sustainable Development Goals (SDGs). Utilising PPPs is specifically addressed in SDG-17; *STRENGTHEN THE MEANS OF IMPLEMENTATION AND REVITALIZE THE GLOBAL PARTNERSHIP FOR SUSTAINABLE DEVELOPMENT*. The expanding use of PPPs is largely attributable to their increasing recognition as a competitive alternative to traditional public procurement. Due to post-2007 fiscal crises brought about by the global financial crisis of 2007–2009, which were made worse by the COVID-19 pandemic and latterly the Ukraine invasion by Russia, many African countries are being forced to implement PPP projects. Indisputably, again, PPPs are not the fabled silver bullet because they involve significant risk; as a result, a few essentials are crucial. Commitment to PPPs by the first office (President or Prime Minister as applicable) is one, along with a clear legal and institutional framework, risk-sharing protocols, and results-based M&E framework.

REFERENCES

African Development Bank. (2009). *Impact of the Global Financial and Economic Crisis on* Africa (Working Paper No. 96 March 2009), African Development Bank, Tunis, Tunisia.

African Development Bank. (2020a). *Supporting Public Private Partnerships in Africa: African Development Bank Ready to Scale Up* (8, September). Available from: https://www.afdb.org/en/news-and-events/press-releases/supporting-public-private-partnerships-africa-african-development-bank-ready-scale-37804. Date of access: 31, January, 2023.

African Development Bank. (2020b). *Designing the African Development Bank's PPP Framework Whitepaper for Discussion.* African Development Bank, Abidjan, Côte D'Ivoire.

African Development Bank. (2021). *African Economic Outlook 2021—From Debt Resolution to Growth: The Road Ahead for Africa.* African Development Bank, Abidjan, Côte D'Ivoire.

Asian Development Bank. (2021). *Value for Money Guidance Note on Procurement (December 2021).* Asian Development Bank, Manila, Philippines.

Anyanwu, J.C. & Salami, A.O. (2021). The impact of COVID-19 on African economies: an introduction. *Afr Dev Rev.*, Vol. 33 (Suppl. 1), pp. S1–S16. doi:10.1111/1467-8268.12531.

Arabic Republic of Egypt. (2010). *The Public Partnership Law of 2010.* Available from: https://ppp.worldbank.org/public-private-partnership/sites/ppp.worldbank.org/files/2021-12/Egyptian%20PPP%20law%2067%20for%202010%20English.pdf. Date of access: 26, January 2023.

Arrowsmith, S. (1998). National and International Perspectives on the Regulation of Public Procurement: Harmony or Conflict? In S. Arrowsmith & A. Davies (eds.), *Public Procurement: Global Revolution*, pp. 3–26. Kluwer Law International, London.

Better Evaluation. (2022). *Value for Money.* Available from: https://www.betterevaluation.org/methods-approaches/methods/value-for-money. Date of access: 28, January, 2023).

Botlhale E. K. (2020). Public-Private Partnerships as Alternative Public Procurement Instruments, in A. Farazmand (ed.), *Global Encyclopedia of Public*

Administration, Public Policy, *and Governance.* Springer International Publishing, Basel, Switzerland.

Botlhale, E.K. (2022). PPPs as Instruments of Public Procurement in Botswana post-2007. *International Journal of Procurement Management*, Vol. 15(4), pp. 488–505. doi.10.1504/IJPM.2022.123191.

CIPS. (2022). *Procurement and Supply Cycle.* Available from: https://www.cips.org/intelligence-hub/procurement/procurement-supply-cycle. Date of access: 28, January 2023.

Designing Buildings Ltd. (2023). *Best Value Procurement in the Construction Industry.* Available from: https://www.designingbuildings.co.uk/wiki/Best_value_procurement_in_the_construction_industry. Date of access: 21 January 2023.

Dimitri, N. (2013). "Best value for money" in Procurement. *Journal of Public Procurement*, Vol. 13(2), pp. 149–175. doi.org/10.1108/JOPP-13-02-2013-B001.

European PPP Expertise Centre. (2016). *PPPs and Procurement*; *Impact of the New EU Directives.* Available from: http://www.eib.org/en/attachments/epec/epec_ppps_and_procurement_en.pdf. Date of access: 21, August 2022.

European Public Service Union. (2014). *Public and Private Sector Efficiency.* European Public Service Union, Belgium.

Gaolathe, B. (2009). *2009/10 Budget Speech Delivered to the National Assembly on February 2.* Government Printing and Publishing Services, Gaborone.

Governance and Social Development Resource Centre. (2010). *Value for Money.* Governance and Social Development Resource Centre, London.

Gov.UK. (2023). *Definition of Best Value for Money.* Available from: https://www.finance-ni.gov.uk/articles/definition-best-value-money#:~:text=What%20is%20best%20value%20for,sustainability%20to%20meet%20customer%20requirements. Date of access: 31, January 2023.

Grimsey, D. & Lewis, M. (2007). Public Private Partnerships and Public Procurement. *Agenda: a Journal of Policy Analysis and Reform*, Vol. 14(2), pp. 171–88.

Hans, V.H. & Koppenjan, J. (2001). Building Public-Private Partnerships: assessing and managing risks in port development. *Public Management Review*, Vol. 3(4), pp. 593–616.

ICRC. (2023). *PPP Disclosure Framework.* Available from: https://ppp.icrc.gov.ng. Date of access: 26 January 2023.

IMF. (2022). *World Economic Outlook 2022 Oct International Monetary Fund; Countering the Cost-of-Living Crisis.* IMF, Washington, DC.

Independent Commission for Aid Impact. (2011). *ICAI's Approach to Effectiveness and Value for Money.* Independent Commission for Aid Impact, London.

International Monetary Fund. (2004). *Public-Private Partnerships.* International Monetary Fund, Washington, DC.

Itumo, V.N. (2016). Nigeria's Mono-Cultural Economy: Impact Assessment and Prospects. *European Journal of Interdisciplinary Studies*, Vol. 4(2), pp. 20–35.

Jackson, J. (2012). *Value for Money and International Development: Deconstructing Myths to Promote a More Constructive Discussion.* Available from: www.oecd.org/development/ effectiveness/49652541.pdf. Date of access: 28 January 2023.

Jefferis, K. (2008). *Why Botswana's Credit Rating Is Better than Japan*; *a Brief Economic History*. Proceedings of the Botswana Economic Forum conference, Gaborone International Conference Centre, Gaborone, Botswana, June 11.

Karanja, M. (2021). *Value for Money*. Available from: https://www.pwc.com/rw/en/publications/value-for-money.html. Date of access: 28 January 2023).

Manuel, T. (2009). *Budget Speech 2009 by the Minister of Finance, Trevor A Manuel*. Available from: https://www.gov.za/budget-speech-2009-minister-finance-trevor-manuel. Date of access: 26 January 2023.

Martin, L.M. (2008). Public-Private Partnerships' in K.V Thai (ed.), *International Handbook of Public Procurement* (1st edition) (pp. 703–724). CRC Press, Boca Raton, Florida.

MENA forum. (2023). *Exclusive Report on the Public-Private Partnership (PPP) Industry in Egypt*. Available from: https://pppmenaforum.com/google/?gclid=Cj0KCQiA8t2eBhDeARIsAAVEga1VS-5TygtL1v2Th8yfNuNDmM6wHXy2t-M4RlR_07HwjG3JgZnWo-UQaAjj5EALw_wcB Date of access: 26 January 2023.

National Treasury [South Africa]. (2017). *2017 Budget Review*. Available from: https://www.treasury.gov.za/documents/national%20budget/2017/review/annexure%20e.pdf. Date of access: 1 February, 2023.

National Treasury [South Africa]. (2018). *Public Private Partnership*. Available from: http://www.ppp.gov.za/Pages/whatisppp.aspx Date of access: 10 February 2022.

Nwangwu, G. (2012). The Legal Framework for Public-Private Partnerships (PPPs) in Nigeria. *European Procurement & Public Private Partnership Law Review*, Vol. 7(4): 268–277.

OECD. (2020). *COVID-19 in Africa*: *Regional Socio-Economic Implications and Policy Priorities*. OECD, Paris.

OECD. (2023). *Public-Procurement*. Available from: https://www.oecd.org/gov/public-procurement/. Date of access: 31 January 2023.

Olotch, C. (2021). *Public-Private Partnerships*: *How Does Botswana Fare*? Available from: https://blogs.worldbank.org/ppps/public-private-partnerships-how-does-botswana-fare#:~:text=Botswana%20does%20not%20have%20a%20PPP%20law (Date of access: 26 January 2023).

Punch. (2022). *ICRC Plans 53 PPP Projects Worth $22bn in 2022* (5th July). Available from: https://punchng.com/icrc-plans-53-ppp-projects-worth-22bn-in-2022. Date of access: 29 January 2023.

Republic of Botswana. (2021). *Public Procurement Act*. Government Printing and Publishing. Gaborone.

Sarmad, K. & Mohiuddin, Y. (1991). Is the Private Sector More Productive than the Public Sector? [With Comments]. *The Pakistan Development Review*, Vol 30(4), pp. 721–729. https://www.jstor.org/stable/41259496.

Singh, M. (2022). *The 2007–2008 Financial Crisis in Review*. Available from: https://www.investopedia.com/articles/economics/09/financial-crisis-review.asp. Date of access: 26 January 2023.

Soyeju, O. (2013). Legal Framework for Public Private Partnership in Nigeria. *De Jure* (Pretoria) [online], Vol. 46(3). Available from: [http://www.scielo.org

.za/scielo.php?script=sci_arttext&pid=S2225-71602013000300010&lng=en&nrm=iso>. Date of access: 26, January, 2023.

Statista Research Department. (2023). *Impact of the Coronavirus Pandemic on the Global Economy - Statistics & Facts* (23 January 2023). Available from: https://www.statista.com/topics/6139/covid-19-impact-on-the-global-economy/#topicOverview. Date of access: 30 January 2023.

UNCTAD (United Nations Conference on Trade and Development). (2021). *State of Commodity Dependence 2021*. UNCTAD, Geneva.

UNCTAD. (2022a). *Commodity Dependence: A Twenty-Year Perspective*. UNCTAD, Geneva.

UNCTAD. (2022b). *Rethinking the Foundations of Export Diversification in Africa: The Catalytic Role of Business and Financial Services*. United Nations Conference on Trade and Development, New York.

UNDP Global Centre for Public Service Excellence. (2015). *Is the Private Sector more Efficient? A Cautionary Tale; Singapore*. UNDP Global Centre for Public Service Excellence, Singapore.

United Nations. (2022). *World Economic Situation and Prospects 2022*. United Nations, New York.

Warrilow, C. (1995). Market-Oriented Public Procurement Systems. *International trade forum*, Vol. 3, pp. 24–29.

World Bank. (2018a). *What are Public Private Partnerships*? Available from: https://ppp.worldbank.org/public-private-partnership/overview/what-are-public-private-partnerships. Date of access: 10 February 2022.

World Bank. (2018b). *Legal Framework/Enabling Environment Assessment for PPPs*. Available from: https://ppp.worldbank.org/public-private-partnership/legislation-regulation/framework-assessment. Date of access:10 February 2022.

World Bank. (2021a). *PPP Unit Nigeria*. Available from: https://ppp.worldbank.org/public-private-partnership/library/ppp-unit-nigeria. Date of access: 29 January 2023.

World Bank. (2021b). *PPP Unit Egypt*. Available from: https://ppp.worldbank.org/public-private-partnership/library/ppp-unit-egypt. Date of access: 29 January 2023.

World Bank. (2022). *World Development Report 2022: Finance for an Equitable Recovery*. World Bank, Washington DC.

WTO. (2022). *Trade Statistics and Outlook; Russia-Ukraine Conflict Puts Fragile Global Trade Recovery at Risk*. Available from: https://www.wto.org/english/news_e/pres22_e/pr902_e.pdf. Date of access: 26 January 2023.

Zhang, X. (2005). Paving the Way for Public–Private Partnerships in Infrastructure Development. *Journal of Construction Engineering and Management*, Vol. 131(1), pp. 71–80. doi.org/10.1061/(ASCE)0733-9364(2005)131:1(71).

Chapter 3

Public-Private Partnerships in Africa's Electricity Markets

Alex Nduhura and Ivan Kiiza Twinomuhwezi

In past few decades, private sector involvement through public-private partnerships (PPPs) has become increasingly popular as a way of procuring and maintaining energy infrastructure and services. This has been due to liberalisation reforms in the electricity markets. The reforms were largely due to the structural adjustment programmes (SAPs) in the late 1980s through 1990s and early 2000s. The reforms were introduced and promoted largely by the World Bank and the International Monetary Fund across Africa and other developing countries. The aim of the reforms was to promote efficiency and effectiveness, ultimately resulting in the delivery of cost-reflective tariffs while enhancing private actor involvement.

To engage the private actors, the medium was through independent power producer (IPP) arrangements, technically operated as PPPs. This chapter reviews the general concept of PPPs as a policy issue in the electricity sector in Africa. The chapter offers a systematic and integrated approach on how PPPs have been and continue to be adopted in Africa's electricity market. It provides an analysis of the benefits and challenges of PPPs in Africa's electricity market while highlighting the misunderstandings, which undermine the value and success of the PPPs in the sector.

The chapter serves both as a structured introduction for those who are new to the subject of PPPs in electricity markets, whether in the academic, public, private or social sectors, investment, finance or contracting fields such as procurement and supply chain, and as an aide-mémoire for those developing PPP policies and negotiating PPPs in the electricity sector. No prior knowledge of PPPs is assumed or required to read and comprehend the concepts and issues discussed in the chapter.

BACKGROUND

Electricity is a vital input for inclusive economic growth and development. While other continents aspire to go to the moon and other planets, in Africa, access to electricity remains a key aspiration. In Africa, most households rely on dirty fuels for cooking (IRENA & AfDB, 2022). Citizens that thrive on agriculture lack electricity to plant, irrigate and harvest their crops. Besides, unreliable electricity limits citizens' ability to add values on the raw crop yields for safe storage and distribution. In the health sector, the hospitals and clinics, mainly health centers within the rural settings struggle to power the medical appliances and operating rooms for business sustainability owing to power outages. Besides, *adverse climate change* in the form of extreme weather events, rising temperatures and high variabilities in rainfall and water levels [in both lakes and rivers] is another big challenge affecting electricity sector. Arising from this context, governments in Africa have undertaken policy reforms that aim at making electricity available, efficient and more reliable through collaborative arrangements with potential private actors for the social and economic transformation of citizens.

Much of the first-phase electricity reforms started in the late 1980s through 1990s to early 2000s. During this period, most countries liberalised electricity markets with the passing of new policies and amending existing frameworks including reviewing, updating and establishing new legal, regulatory and institutional frameworks. The outcomes of the first phase of reforms were either new energy policy, amended acts, regulations, circulars, acts and national electricity regulatory agencies. Anchored on the liberalisation agenda, ushered in the second phase of reforms in the 2000s that continued with, firstly, the debundling of mandate of state boards or entities in electricity supply chain (generation, transmission, distribution), where the state remained largely with the regulatory function.

To perform the regulatory function, national electricity regulatory authorities/commissions were formed. This re-organisation further led to the establishment of state-owned companies (in essence, State-Owned Enterprises—SOEs) to perform the debundled tasks of generation, transmission and distribution as well as privatisation. For example, in Uganda, driven by the Power Sector Restructuring and Privatization Strategy (Uganda Bureau of Statistics, 2011), the vertically integrated state-owned company, Uganda Electricity Board (UEB), was unbundled to form the Uganda Electricity Generation Company Limited (UEGLC), Uganda Electricity Transmission Company Limited (UETCL) and Uganda Electricity Distribution Company Limited (UEDCL) to perform such mandates of generation, transmission and generation, respectively. Later UEDCL gave away part of its mandate through a lease to Umeme

Uganda Limited (Uganda Electricity Distribution Company Limited, 2005) under a management distributorship concession for 20 years. The reforms resulted in the establishment of the electricity acts such as the Electricity Act, 1999, in Uganda that in the year 2000 led to the creation and establishment of the Uganda Electricity Regulatory Authority (ERA). However, in some cases it is important to note that some countries like South Africa retained the vertically integrated model with the state-owned firm like Eskom manning the mandate of generation, transmission and distribution. It must be noted however that such models continue with time, to face reform.

The late 2000s ushered in the third wave of reforms and development in Africa's electricity markets. Key in this wave was the introduction of private participation engaging private actors to operate and maintain existing plants (brownfield projects). Additionally, private actors were also attracted to sign and execute concessions characterised by obligations to design, finance, build, own and transfer back to government non-existing plants (greenfield projects). Private actor participation was witnessed under the adoption of the Independent Power Producers (IPPs) model, where private actors technically known as Special Purpose Vehicles (SPVs) signed up concessions directly with the state/regulatory body or with the state-owned utility enterprises. These electricity concessions possessed features of PPPs (Koppenjan, 2015; Boardman, Greve & Hodge, 2015; Yescombe,2018; Nduhura, 2019a; Twinomuhwezi & Herman, 2020; Nuwagaba,2020; Nduhura, Tshombe, Molokwane, Twinomuhwezi & Nuwagaba, 2021; Verweij & van Meerkerk, 2021; Ahmed, Musonda & Pretorius, 2023).

Towards year 2010 to date, the fourth wave in the electricity reforms has ushered in additional developments. These developments are characterised by the demand for and increased investments in renewable energy by governments and private sector actors (Foster & Rana, 2020; Clark, Davis, Eberhard, Gratwick & Wamukonya, 2005). The driver for this trend has been largely the passing and implementation of UN Vision 2030 in the year 2015, which seeks to achieve a sustainable world manifested in the 17 Sustainable Development Goals (SDGs). The most influential SDG driving the renewable energy fad has been SDG 7 'Ensure access to affordable, reliable, sustainable and modern energy for all' (UNDESA, 2023). Other drivers exist, namely, the non-renewable nature of some sources of energy, the cost, adverse externalities on human life and environment. Based on this transition, governments are revamping electricity generation sources such as diesel, coal, and biofuel (wood) in search for clean and renewable energy sources such as solar, nuclear, wind, biogas, hydropower among other sources. In this pursuit, the public investment capacity in electricity supply chain in Africa has been weak, yet adequate finance, technology and expertise are required for successful and sustainable electricity transition.

Underlying the aforesaid, the context in the fourth wave in Africa's electricity market, governments have coopted neoliberal hybrid models in electricity markets where private actor involvement is now popular under the main public sector reform 'public private partnerships'. Private actor involvement through PPPs in Africa's electricity markets was traditionally adopted to access private finance at a time when most African governments are cash strapped. More recently, access to technology, efficiency and effectiveness are recognised as part of the drivers for PPP adoption in Africa's agenda to improve access to electricity. Therefore, private participation and PPPs are not new in Africa's electricity markets. What is new and perhaps not clear is the extent to which PPPs have been implemented, what needs to be done so that PPPs serve public interest, identifying challenges facing PPPs and what needs to be done to ensure fair operations of both public and private actors to serve better the current and future needs of the African electricity consumer. The next section discusses the concept of PPPs and how they have been applied, their challenges and their future in Africa's electricity markets.

THE CONCEPT OF PUBLIC-PRIVATE PARTNERSHIPS

The concept of PPPs has been traced back to different times in history by different scholars. For Yescombe, 2018, the term public-private partnership has been associated with the United States and in some cases, the United Kingdom. In the United States, PPPs are viewed to have associated with joint educational programmes between government and private actors in the early 1950s (*ibid*) and later joint cooperation between public and private actors for utilities in the 1960s. In the United Kingdom, PPPs originated under the code name Private Finance Initiative (PFI) under Margaret Thatcher's reformist government agenda. Under the reformist agenda, popularly known as new public management, Thatcher's government designed and passed a range of reforms that sought to make government more efficient and effective.

Among such reforms that were ushered in were public-private partnerships. Henceforth the term PPP has become a popular subject among several disciplines such as procurement and supply chain, project finance, public policy and governance. Significant contribution on PPPs is notable from scholars of procurement, engineering, finance and energy markets (Ahmed, Musonda & Pretorius, 2023).This may signify that stakeholders within the dockets of these professions need some grasp of the concept of PPP if they are to use PPP to serve their citizens or stakeholders much better. Over the last decades there has been significant debate on PPPs that has in turn led to the manifestation of a range of definitions. PPPs are defined as

> [A]n agreement between government and one or more private partners (which may include the operators and the financers) according to which the private partners deliver the service in such a manner that the service delivery objectives are aligned with the profit objectives of the private partners and where the effectiveness of the alignment depends on a sufficient transfer of risk to the private partner. (Organisation for Economic Cooperation and Development, 2008, p. 17)

> [C]ooperation between public-private actors in which they jointly develop products and services and share risks, costs and resources which are connected with these products and services. (Van Ham & Koppenjan, 2001, p.593)

Others have defined PPP as a 'combination of the deployment of private sector capital and, sometimes, public sector capital to improve public services or the management of public sector assets' (Gerrard, 2001, p.48). In defining PPPs some common words and concepts emerge, namely private and public actors, joint operations and working together, delivery of public services, risk, risk allocation and transfer and incentives. Therefore, where PPPs are applied, there is need to pay keen consideration to the key terms highlighted. While PPPs have been implemented across generation, transmission, and distribution across the world, in Africa, PPPs have been implemented largely in generation and distribution. It is important to note that in the energy market there reside diverse sources of electricity, namely: solar, wind, hydro, biomass as major energy sources.

In the development of PPPs at generation, most PPPs have been developed for the production of hydropower but most recently there has been increased interest in the deployment of PPPs for the generation and distribution of energy from solar as a source of electricity for lighting and cooking majorly across unconnected and rural settings in Africa (Awuku, Bennadji, Muhammad-Sukki & Sellami, 2022b). According to IRENA and AfDB (2022), the period between 2010 and 2020 attracted US$55 billion worth of private actor investment in Africa's electricity markets. Egypt, Kenya, Morocco and South Africa took the largest share at 75%. While countries such as Ethiopia, Uganda, Zimbabwe, Nigeria, Algeria, Senegal, Mauritania, Rwanda, Zambia and Mozambique shared 15% with each country having an average share of IPP investment within the range of 0.5 to 1.7%. While countries such as United Republic of Tanzania, Ghana, Libya, Sierra Leone, Burkina Faso, Gabon, Cameroon, Djibouti, Namibia, Angola, Mali, and Democratic Republic of Congo (DRC) each contributed less than an average of 5% (IRENA & AfDB, 2022). In the next section, we discuss the working of public-private partnerships and how they have been executed in electricity markets across Africa.

APPLICATION OF PPPs: CROSS-COUNTRY EXPERIENCE OF PPP ADOPTION IN AFRICA'S ELECTRICITY SECTOR

Uganda

Uganda is one of the countries that have made an attempt to deploy PPPs in the energy sector. Located in the heart of East Africa and a member of the East African Community, Uganda's quest for the adoption of PPPs in the energy sector can be traced from the year 2005 to 2012 and is recognised as the pioneer of private investment in energy markets in the sub-Saharan region (Tshombe, Molokwane, Nduhura & Nuwagaba, 2020). Prior to 2000 and largely up to 2012, Uganda faced enormous blackouts due to demand that had been outstripping supply of electricity. Additionally, the sector was characterised by low productivity [60MW of 150 installed], suppressed demand of over 200MW, poor and degenerating network, poor supply reliability [extensive load shedding], inadequate investments in the sector, poor commercial performance by the UEB, characterised by low connection rates, high technical and non-technical losses exceeding 30%, and high accounts receivables [9 months billings with about 50% being outstanding for more than 6 months (Electricity Regulatory Authority, 2020) .

In order to salvage the situation amidst budgetary constraints the Government of Uganda attracted private investors to invest in the energy sector. Prior to this call, the energy sector was nationalised with the state performing the function of regulation (Electricity Regulatory Authority) and state-owned enterprises such as Uganda Electricity Generation Company Limited (UEGCL) Company, Uganda Electricity Transmission Company Limited (UETCL) and Uganda Electricity Distribution Company Limited (UEDCL). During the period the state reviewed its operations to increase private actor involvement. It is during this period that the government of Uganda through a tendering process was able to attract and bring on board two important players Umeme Uganda Limited (distribution) and Bujagali Energy Limited (BEL) under PPP concession agreements (Nduhura, 2019b, pp. 1–203).

Build Own Operate Transfer (Bujagali Hydropower BEL Power Dam PPP)

Under this PPP arrangement in Uganda electricity sector, Bujagali Energy Limited (BEL) was contracted for a build-own-operate-transfer 30-year concession (now extended to 33 years). Under the concession, BEL was to build, own, operate and transfer a hydropower dam on River Nile at Jinja with installed capacity of 250MW. The aim was to increase production and supply of electricity that the dam has delivered. Empirical studies indicate that unlike in some instances where PPPs have failed to deliver as expected, BEL

PPP project has been able to successfully maintain the production capacity for which the dam was delivered. However, it is noted that why the state contracted BEL to deliver 250MW at times the plant has had to switch off turbines in order to reduce the cost of deemed energy costs to government due to inability to consume all the electricity produced in the country. Despite its success in providing required installed capacity of electricity through PPPs, the initial stages of the project were characterized by revolts from both environmentalists and politicians, who complained of the likelihood of social risks and adverse environment impacts if BEL project failed to comply with environmental social impact assessment (ESIA) standards.

Furthermore, among other arguments against the project was that PPP was inconsiderate of cultural heritage sites, that it would destroy the environment despite the environmental and social impact assessment reports approved by the National Environmental Management Authority (NEMA). While the objective of the PPP was to deliver additional installed capacity, post-implementation phase faced uproar on the cost of power being too high. To reduce risk on the part of the BEL, a Spanish Company, O & M Energy, was contracted to operate and maintain the dam observing the highest health and safety standards benchmarked to ISO 9001: 2018. Experience from the BEL PPP project indicates that by implementing social and environmental safeguards in the project, PPPs can support countries with electricity deficiency to increase installed power capacity. It is noted that while supply may increase tariffs can be high. To reduce the tariffs, governments can explore renegotiation of concessions period with the view to extend its tenure and also offer guarantees necessary for the special purpose vehicle (in such case BEL) to renegotiate structuring of loans and interest to support the achievement of the client's objective (in such case, reduction of tariffs).

Distributorship Management PPP Concession (Umeme Uganda Limited)

Another example of a 3P project in Uganda is the 20-year concession awarded to Umeme in 2005 which ends in 2025. Umeme Uganda Limited, a special purpose vehicle, incorporated in Uganda on 6 May 2004 for the purpose of entering and executing a 20-year electricity distribution concession was an outcome of a bidding process. During the process of bidding, it was revealed that most bidders that had submitted their bids to take up the concession pulled out. Several reasons are advanced for the pull outs, one being the distribution infrastructure was too old, with state agencies among the top defaulters. Under the concession Umeme was to buy electricity from supply chain tiers, and generation, transmission and distribution agencies. Umeme then sells the electricity to consumers categorised as domestic, commercial and industrial consumers.

The incentive framework for this concession is built into the tariff paid by the users of electricity with an allowable markup determined by the regulator that receives an application for tariffs or their change, reviews and based on analysis approves the end tariff charged by the concessionaire. The return on investment was agreed at 20%. The performance of Umeme based on regulator targets has been rated averagely at 80%. Distribution capacity improved from 1,900MVA in 2005 to 550MVA in 2021. The distribution network has expanded from 16,000 in 2005 to 44,000 in 2025. Over the years the number of transformers has also increased from 6,000 to 14,000 while energy losses reduced from 38% in 2005 to 16% in 2021.Unlike other SPVs Umeme was able to list on the stock market in Uganda in 2012 and was able to attract additional investments to improve its financial position and execute the shared value concept. Shared value is defined as a business sustainability concept whereby a firm seeks to address societal needs and challenges through the business itself, with a business model while making a profit (Porter, 2012, p.6)

Among the investors that bought shares Uganda's National Social Security Fund. By having the fund as shareholders and at the same time consumers of electricity, the Umeme transition from a private to a public listed company evidences the achievement of shared value benefit to society. The is considered to be the largest social security fund in East Africa by value and with over 1.5 million savers that double constitute of 1.7 million connected electricity user in Uganda. By implication as the savers consume electricity supplied largely by Umeme, they indirectly contribute to their dividend payout. According to audited financial report (Umeme, 2021), the firm has invested UGX 2.5trillion (approximately US$ 714 billion) in the distribution network that has resulted in safe, efficient and reliable electricity. It is revealed that distribution capacity increased from 50% to 85%. Additionally, consumer numbers increased from 292,237 to 1.52 million in 2021.In June 2012, Umeme became listed on the Uganda stock exchange market as a public company. The implication was that Umeme improved its financial position. The biggest shareholders are Ugandans under an institutional buyer status—the national social security fund (NSSF) owning a shareholding of 23.4%. Uganda presents an exemplary PPP utility investment model that combines finance and builds private actor roles in energy sector in Africa.

Notwithstanding the PPP private actors have been critiqued. For instance, while the number of connected consumers grew, they still represent a small number compared to a population of an estimated 44million (Uganda Bureau of Statistics, 2021). It is also revealed that the tariffs charged are unaffordable for many Ugandans; yet in some cases, the charge for Umeme (private actor) has in some cases represented only 2% of the tariff charged as 98% largely constituted costs with the electricity supply chain , that is, generation and transmission costs. It is revealed that while distribution has constituted percentages as low as 2% in some cases like for the industrial tariff, 98% tends to constitute generation and transmission costs where Umeme has no control. Besides any tariff charged must be forwarded to the regulator for review and approval. While Umeme has done largely its part, the government in the concession should play its role. The other challenge affecting Umeme has been demand generation. Experience indicates that combined effort is key to generate demand. While the private actor has a role to play government as the major player should be able to develop initiatives. Among its roles should be to ensure safety and security of transmission infrastructure from vandalism, sensitise citizens to the benefits of using electricity as a clean energy and provide any additional assistance to private actors for the mutual achievement of objectives.

Concession Agreements with Independent Power Producers (IPPs)

Across the country, the Ugandan government has also engaged private actors in the capacity of independent power producers (IPPs). Under this arrangement, private actors in the energy sector for lower installed capacities sign up power purchase agreements to sell electricity produced to the grid, while other IPPs secure licenses to generate, transmit and distribute electricity in approved territory. IPPs in Uganda have been contracted to generate, transmit and, in some cases, distribute electricity directly to consumers in some areas, for in instance in the West Nile region (WENRECO), and Kyegegwa (Ferdsult). Others include Kasese Cobalt Company Limited, Kilembe Investments, Tronder Power, and Kalangala Infrastructure Services, among others. The IPPs are concessioned to design and build plants for generation of electricity that is sold either to the grid with agreed feed-in tariffs or to end consumers with regulated tariffs. It is acknowledged that by engaging IPPs as part of the energy reforms post the year 2000 across the energy sector and country, Uganda has been able to benefit from cost-reflective tariffs; significant improvement in the quality of service and supply; improved collection rates; and supply surplus. While supply surplus is deemed to be a key benefit, the number of connected customers remains low as the surplus is deemed to be a liability to the country.

According to deemed energy is electricity that is availed for dispatch and consumption but not evacuated and consumed due to factors such as non-existent or weak grid infrastructure and or insufficient demand. The Office of the Auditor General (2021) indicates that Uganda pays UGX 87.7billion (approximately US$25million) as annual deemed energy in financial years 2019/2020 (Office of the Auditor General, 2021) and was slated to increase to UGX113billion (approximately US$32million) in the 2022. While there has been attempts to absorb deemed energy losses in the end tariff paid by consumers, this action raises the cost of electricity that further limits demand and reduces competitiveness of goods produced using expensive electricity. Experience shows that while private actors (IPPs) and state may focus on improving supply, it is important that initiatives to improve supply are in tandem with demand generation initiatives.

Upon recognising the challenge, the government of Uganda through the ERA has now embarked on several electricity demand generation initiatives aimed at rebalancing demand and supply of electricity in Uganda. Part of the demand generation initiatives has been subsidisation and reduction of connection fees in partnership with the World Bank. Another such initiative is codenamed Hybrid Electricity Connection Credit Framework. Under the initiative for a no pole requirement, the fee was reduced from connection of UGX 720,883 to UGX470,000; a customer pays UGX200,000 and applies to access a loan of UGX270,000 supported by the Uganda Development Bank (a national development bank). The mechanism for recovery is that as the customer pays for electricity units, a proportion of 15% is automatically deducted from the units paid to recover the loan facility. The loan is recoverable in eight years. In case of any bad debt it is considered as a subsidy to the customers, and is provided by the Global Energy Alliance for People and Planet (GEAPP) in partnership with Rockefeller Foundation (Electricity Regulatory Authority, 2023). The framework was implemented in January 2023 by Uganda Electricity Distribution Company Limited and Umeme Limited.

Operate and Maintain Concessions (Eskom at Nalubaale Dam)

The type of PPP for Nalubaale Hydropower Dam (Owen Falls Dam) has been the Operate and Maintain Concession. The concession has been adopted in Uganda but not been very popular due to the underperformance of Eskom. Considered a brownfield PPP, the Operate and Maintain concession involves licensing a private operator to operate and maintain existing electricity infrastructure (in such case a hydropower dam with installed capacity of 180MW owned by UETCL). In the year 2000, Eskom, a power utility firm from South Africa, was concessioned to operate and maintain Nalubaale hydropower dam situated on River Nile (longest river in Africa) at Jinja, in Uganda. Under the concession arrangement, Eskom is paid using availability incentive payment framework, where the government of Uganda through the Uganda Electricity Generation Company Limited (UEGCL) pays Eskom feed-in tariffs for the electricity produced and fed on the national grid. Under the concession agreement, Eskom is required to undertake repairs, procure for and install parts on the dam as per agreed schedule.

CROSS COUNTRY EXPERIENCE FOR ADOPTION OF PPPs IN AFRICA

Ghana

In Ghana the period between 2012 and 2016 marked a period of energy crisis resulting into both economic and social hardship (Awuku, Bennadji, Muhammad-Sukki & Sellami, 2022a). To salvage the energy crisis, private actor involvement has largely been PPPs that have been adopted in the energy sector. Like elsewhere PPPs have been popularly adopted due to several reasons in the sector. A lot of private sector-led investments have been made in off-grid where most actors are involved in the generation of electricity using solar-powered sources unlike other countries like Uganda where significant private actor involvement has been in the generation of hydropower electricity generation. The surge of private actor investment has largely been due to the benefits that solar-powered energy provides such as lower costs, ability to reach rural citizens and energy security. Other reasons that have favoured private actor involvement in Ghana solar have been subsidies, the need to avoid recurrent bills by rural communities, and favourable PPP regime and policies since the 1990s. The opportunities for PPPs have existed in Ghana's solar industry in three models illustrated as systems; off-grid solar systems, on-grid solar systems and hybrid (Awuku *et al.,* (2022b).

The key PPP players in Ghana's electricity sector have been private but largely not for profit actors (Awuku, *et al.,* (2022a). By implication, the operations of procuring hydropower on grid through PPP concessions reduce government's exposure to losses that normally result from conventional public-procurement agreements (PPA). Such effective forms of PPP concessions have been witnessed in some African countries like Uganda. These PPP models are said to be effective and efficient, because the private actors are largely responsible for demand generation, which reduces the burden of deemed energy losses on the part of government.

South Africa

South Africa has been part of the giants in Africa's electricity markets. According to IRENA and AfDB (2022), South Africa is the only country that produces electricity with nuclear power among the top three leaders in hydropower generation with installed capacity of 3479 MW, which is ahead of other African countries other than Ethiopia (4071MW) and Angola (3729MW) in terms of ranking with installed hydropower capacity generation in Africa. In terms of electricity from solar sources, South Africa accounts for 57% of the total 10431 MW of installed solar energy generation. Based on the aforesaid volume and nature of installed electricity capacities by source, it can thus be revealed that South Africa provides to a great extent some leadership (IRENA & AfDB, 2022).

Additionally, it is also revealed that Africa's largest industrial country South Africa is the largest consumer of electricity with electrification rate standing at 85% by 2020 (IRENA & AfDB (2022). Investments to deliver this relative success of electrification have been delivered through public investments by Eskom (national utility firm). The journey to engaging private actors in South Africa energy sector started as far the year of 2000 (Nel, 2018). The engagement of private actors was largely due to the emergence of feed in tariffs and partial liberalization of the electricity market in South Africa. These initiatives eventually attracted independent power producers (IPP) to invest in South Africa's electricity market. Under the IPP arrangement, Eskom the national energy utility company operating a vertically integrated models contracts independent power producers through a competitive tendering process to generate electricity and sale to Eskom using feed in tariffs. The concession agreements are usually up to 20 years. The global structure of IPPs has largely been financed by the sponsor to the tune of 75% and the other proportion of 25% provided by commercial debt. Thus, the financing structure is typically in the ratio of 75:25 by sponsor and commercial debt respectively. This financing structure helps to reduce the risk of bankruptcy that may transfer to government. Perhaps this explains why the PPPs have been attractive to global and solid financiers of PPP projects, which include the World Bank Group, IMF, German KfW Bankengruppe (development finance bank) and US-based Overseas Private Investment Corporation to finance PPP projects in South Africa's energy sector.

Nigeria

Considered one of Africa's biggest economies, Nigeria has made significant steps in the adoption of PPPs in the energy sector. Traditionally the state and tiered governments are argued to have monopolised the energy sector (Anyanwu, 2009). Vertically integrated utilities generated, transmitted and distributed electricity up to the 1990s. Like any other developing country weak financial constraints, deficiencies in energy infrastructure and an inadequate access to services have shown that governments (Federal, State, and Local) reduced the capability of Nigeria's government in electrifying the country. Additionally, vertically integrated state-owned companies were overstaffed, inefficient, characterised by corruption and considered vehicles of corruption (Anyanwu, 2009).

It was argued that approximately 100 million citizens were underserved with electricity and remained in the dark by then (Anyanwu, 2009). By 2021, Nigeria's national grid had been plagued with challenges in the transmission and distribution subsectors, which made it difficult to evacuate the available generation capacity through the grid. The Nigeria Electricity Regulatory Commission (NERC), based on data obtained in 2021, reported that power distribution in the year averaged 4,094.09 megawatt (MW), despite available generation capacity of about 8,000 MW[2]. Relatedly, average unutilised power generation increased year-on-year to 3,008.18 MW in 2021, from 1,030.80 MW in 2013, indicating an increase of 291% in the past eight years (KPMG, 2022, pp. 1, 2). The Nigerian Electricity Supply Industry (NESI), however, has undergone fundamental changes over the past few years with the implementation of the government's reform programme reputed to be one of the most ambitious privatisation exercises in the global power industry with a transaction cost of over three billion dollars ($3.0bn) (Nigerian Electricity Regulatory Commission, 2023).

Morocco

North Africa was the second-largest recipient of renewable energy investments. During 2010–2020, the region attracted USD 17.5 billion—or 32% of the total for the decade—concentrated in Morocco (USD 9.5 billion) and Egypt (USD 8.2 billion). Over time, investments followed a steady growth trajectory, peaking at USD 4 billion in 2018 before dropping in 2019 and 2020. Investments were concentrated in solar (PV and thermal) (67.5%) and wind (32%), with the remainder going to bioenergy and small hydropower. According to IRENA and AfDB (2022) Morocco's electricity production indicates that the electricity production in the country reached 37,293 GWh in December 2018, compared with a record low of 31,056 GWh in December 2012. This was partly attributed to the renewable energy PPP and finance initiatives of MENA (Middle East and North Africa) countries. In 2009, Morocco designed a new national strategic plan to attract private investment, and adopt renewable energy sources (Othman & Khallaf, 2022). This plan resulted in featuring Morocco as one of the top six destination countries for the adoption of renewable energy PPP projects with 5.6% of the total investment in this sector between 2013 and 2015. Besides the aforesaid governmental strategic plan, political stability and the rule of law were emphasised in order to attract more PPPs and other forms of private investments in renewable energy projects. Thus, strategic planning, political stability and the rule of law are the three factors that have mainly enhanced and supported the successful implementation and management of renewable energy PPP projects in Morocco.

Egypt

Energy is one of the impediments which Egypt used to experience in her efforts towards inclusive and sustainable growth. It is argued that before the twenty-first century, Egypt used to experience episodes of significant power shortage mainly in rural areas, where power supply and the grid quality were lower; and there was too much dependence on non-renewable fossil energy sources such as coal, gas and oil (Vagliasindi, 2013). However, with continued soaring demand for energy associated with high population growth and energy-intensive consumption, Egypt adopted some laws and decrees to support liberalisation policy and private sector participation in the energy sector prior the year 2000 and after the economic crisis that the country had experienced (Vagliasindi, 2013).

The aim of reforms was to promote renewable energy generation since it has enough natural and renewable energy sources for sustainable energy production. While the state opted for directly investing into renewable energy projects it also sought the attraction of private actor involvement in the form of IPPs that are operationalised as PPPs. With the onset of PPP policy in energy, electricity consumption in Egypt continued to increase rapidly from 85 TWh in 2004/2005 to over 140 TWh in 2012/2013, with a corresponding increase in electricity generation from 101 TWh to 164 TWh, representing an average annual growth rate of 7%. Furthermore, electricity production for Egypt has increased from 4,386 GWh in 1977 to 20,300 GWh in 2022 (CEIC DATA, 2022).

Thus, with private sector participation in the energy sector, more than 99% of the population has access to grid electricity and clean cooking fuels in Egypt (World Bank, 2021; WHO, 2021; IRENA & AfDB, 2022, p. 54). The Egypt government prefers privately developed and owned PPP initiatives, for instance build-own-operate-transfer energy projects (BOT or BOOT), to ensure that growth is inclusive and sustainable, incorporating productive capacities that create employment and livelihoods for the poor and excluded (Allam, Saaf & Dawoud, 2003). Notably some PPP projects have been executed.

Kenya

In Kenya, PPPs have been evidenced as well (Aitken, 2014; IRENA & AfDB, 2022). Most of the projects in Kenya, like countries such as Cameroon and South Africa, have been of the Greenfield nature. Greenfield projects are energy infrastructure–related projects that involve putting in place infrastructure that was non-existent. Applied to Kenya's Thika Power Plant, the project involved the development, design, construction and operation of a Greenfield 87 MW heavy fuel oil (HFO) diesel power plant on a 20-year concession. A power purchase agreement was signed with Kenya Power and Lighting Company (KPLC) (the national transmission and distribution company) and Thika Power (a subsidiary of Melec PowerGen Inc., and an affiliate of the Matelec Group of Companies from Lebanon); the cost of the concession was US$150 million (Kabeyi & Olanrewaju, 2020). Other notable private electricity plants include Iberafrica (10.5MW), Tsavo (74MW), Gulf (80.32MW), Rabai (90MW) and Triumph (83MW) (Kabeyi & Olanrewaju, 2020).

The study revealed that privately concessioned electricity plants outperformed publicly owned plants in terms of efficiency, availability, capacity load factor and reliability. The reasons for being outperformance by privately concessioned dams were associated with delayed procurement of technical services and spare parts for publicly owned dams (Kabeyi & Olanrewaju, 2020).

By being able to perform better, it can be argued that PP dams in Kenya are doing well and contributing to the growth of Kenya's economy. In assessing the contribution of the IPPs/PPPs in Kenya's electricity supply chain, Eberhard, Gratwick and Kariuki (2018) reveal that by 2015 IPPs investments in Kenya had reached over US$2.3billion and had delivered 28% (equivalent 1,106 MW) installed capacity of electricity. The contribution is more than the current installed nationwide capacities in countries such as Benin, Comoros, Rwanda, Malawi, Burundi, Gabon, Madagascar, and Mauritius among others (IRENA & AfDB, 2022). IPPs have performed equally well like publicly owned dams including the national generator KenGen. Like in the countries where PPPs are applied, operators seek to meet their targets in order to avoid penalties contained in concession agreements. Since electricity is considered as a catalyst for social and economic development, it implies that IPPs/PPPs given the example of Kenya have significant potential to contribute to nations' development.

OTHER PPPs PROJECTS IN AFRICA

Countries like Mozambique have also adopted PPPs (Maia, 2022)—starting in the 1990s, and largely driven by IMF's reformist agenda of privatisation and liberalisation of economies. This era is deemed to have also ushered in PPPs with early steps in the roads, waterways, and customs management area. Gradually the adoption spread to other sectors such as energy. For instance, the Mozambique government signed a PPP with Aggreko and Shanduka

Group to open and deliver power from a 107.5MW gas-fired power plant. In this tri-party power purchase agreement, Aggreko, Eskom (the South African power utility) and Electricidade de Moçambique (EDM) (the Mozambique power utility) are the offtakers and represent public governments' interests (Vagliasindi, 2013). According to Maia (2022), the power plant is situated in Ressano Garcia on the Mozambique/South African border, 90 km north-west of Maputo at Gigawatt Park. This natural gas-fired plant is a development of Gigawatt Mozambique with an initial investment of US$250 million.

CHALLENGES FACING PPPs IN AFRICA'S ELECTRICITY MARKET

Although PPPs have delivered to some extent benefits for governments and their citizens, challenges exist. Although PPPs have been adopted in Africa to increase access to electricity, access has improved but remains low. Several challenges have been identified and need to be addressed. Firstly, the feed-in tariffs are deemed to be too high exerting burden on the final consumer of electricity. The reasons that tend to arise for the high feed-in tariff have been varied. For instance, investors decry the high cost of finance for both capital and operating expenses. This is because investors of PPPs have to borrow from foreign markets yet make collections in local currency that is usually weaker and at times faced with currency convertibility. This is exacerbated with fluctuations in the value of the local currency.

Allegations of corruption remain a major challenge in PPP electricity markets. Corruption is alleged to occur during procurement, determination of tariffs, negotiation of concession terms (through incompleteness or design of terms to favour private rather than public interest) and monopolisation. Additionally, the opaque nature of PPP concessions in energy further enhances the allegations of corruption. In an era of increasing distrust of governments, this creates room for citizens to think that the PPP game in which the public and private actors are engaged is rigged in favour of the private actor's interests and not the citizen's interests. This not only results into resentment of PPPs from the onset but expose existing PPP concessions to early termination, making citizens lose out on the benefits that PPPs may deliver.

There is increasing trend of vandalized infrastructure. This has been a common practice in Uganda. This has resulted in most times blackouts due to the disruption in the supply of electricity across the supply chain. While governments commit to take on the risk of vandalism, when blackouts occur due to vandalism, usually the special purpose vehicles tend to take on the blame from the public making PPPs unpopular. However, it may not be feasible to provide security for the whole length of electricity infrastructure investment in technology to detect in real-time acts of vandalism and provide an audit trail of vandalism as well as the persons involved. If this is done, it should be made known to the governments so that such becomes a cost that should be factored in the end tariff of electricity. Notwithstanding, this approach may cause further increases in electricity tariffs. This could be controlled by adoption of some suitable demand generation strategies and incentives in order to bring down any increases in tariffs due to investments in technologies to detect real-time acts of vandalism.

While PPPs in the electricity sector have delivered increased installed capacities of electricity (Kabanda, 2014; Nduhura, 2019a), quality of electricity (Nduhura, Lukamba &Nuwgaba, 2020) and reliability (Nduhura, 2019a), dependable and high-end consumer tariffs remain a constraint. The end user tariffs are considerably deemed to be high and unaffordable. This can be explained by some factors. There are several reasons that have been explained but what is rarely mentioned is that most African countries have sought to adopt PPPs under the motivation for gaining access to project finance without undertaking independent value for money assessments. The other reason is the absence of mini-grids and focus on national grid (generation and consumption locations are located far from each other).

Limited autonomy and stability of legal, regulatory, and institutional framework renders PPP concessions to politicisation. For example, members of parliament woke up one day and vote to terminate a PPP concession of Umeme. Yet such procedure may not be defined within the PPP concession termination clause neither in the Uganda's PPA policy framework 2010, PPA Act 2015 and regulations 2019. Such actions disfavour private sector investment in PPP markets not only in Africa but the rest of the world. It has severally been opined that despite the increase in installed capacities that Africa has witnessed over the years from 2000–2021 (IRENA & AfDB, 2022) in some countries like Uganda (Office of the Auditor, 2019) unlike South Africa, Nigeria and Egypt (IRENA & AfDB, 2022) there exists low industrialisation capacity (Ganda & Ngwakwe, 2014). This has resulted into high deemed energy costs. Deemed energy is power produced but not evacuated for use by offtakes due to either lack of infrastructure to evaluate or lack of demand.

In Uganda in FY 2019/2020 UGX87.7billion (approximately US$25 million) and above are paid out as deemed energy costs annually (Office of the Auditor, 2021). Low industrialisation capacity limits demand as the amount of electricity that is produced cannot be evacuated for use. Focus on off-grid IPPs has provided as traditional feed in tariffs regimes. In some cases, such FiTs have not been standard and largely favour the private actor and in most case not government interests. The reasons provided have been that most private actors have varying return on investments and costs in parity of others based on public and governments complaints over high user fees. Additionally, perhaps the ills of agency theory (information asymmetry) may partly be responsible. The outcome has been a grievance of high user fees prompting at times early termination of PPP concessions. Notable examples have been in Uganda where it is deemed that the return on investment of 20% by an electricity concessionaire was deemed to be too high from both public and government perspectives yet the concessionaire. While room for negotiation was allowed by Umeme, the company opined that the ROI was at that time arrived at based on the risk that resided in Uganda's electricity sector. The absence of a competitive approach such as use of auctions to determine feed-in tariffs tend to render tariffs (user fees) uncompetitive reducing the government's plan to electrify their countries.

In the early years of adoption of PPPs, there was limited focus on mini-grids and off-grid models. The absence and limitation of such models increase transmission costs and deemed energy costs paid to producers of electricity when deemed energy is not evacuated from the dams either due to infrastructure or demand. Yet concessions for mini-grids that sell electricity to the customer may not attract deemed energy costs for governments and reduce transmission costs that are a significant cost in the tariffs paid by consumers of electricity, discouraging first-time optimal and sustainable consumption for consumers that have connected.

CONCLUSION AND FUTURE OF PPPs IN AFRICA'S ELECTRICITY MARKETS

Most African countries have set out to increase access to electricity. Realising their incapacity to deliver this aspiration, they have coopted private actors through public-private partnerships in electricity markets. The motivation for adoption of PPPs has been primarily to access project finance and not independent value for money assessment before taking private finance. The popular types for PPP adoption have been operate and maintain, build-operate-transfer and management concessions. The incentive models have been feed-in tariffs (FiTs) in the form of availability payments for actors that produce and sell electricity to the grid. Other actors have been incentivised through regulated end tariffs paid by electricity consumers. Whilst this is a case, it is noted that private actor costs constitute a significant percentage of the tariffs yet significant contribution to the tariffs has been contributed by costs by state-owned enterprise. These charge generation and transmission costs (in some instances contributing up to 98% of the tariff).

Additionally, some other factors contributed to by the state deprive the successful performance of private actors under PPPs; yet in public domain such is untold. While PPPs have and resonate with a potential to deliver Africa's electrification dream, they are constrained by challenges that need to be addressed. Corruption can be reduced through requirement to list on the stock exchange since listing helps to improve transparency of firm's operations. Additionally, publishing of concession agreements is key using the World Bank public disclosure framework. Drivers for the adoption of PPPs should move from just access to private capital but focus more on value for money assessment and benefit using public sector comparator approach. The need for increased autonomy and stability of legal, regulatory and institutional framework in electricity markets can be enhanced by depoliticising implementation of PPPs concessions in electricity markets. The benefits of non-politicisation of PPP affairs help to reduce the exposure of the state to early termination liabilities. Additionally, depoliticisation helps to consolidate investor trust and confidence in electricity PPP markets. This aids timely financial closure as well.

While electricity markets in Africa are risky at the time of entry of PPP actors, as time progress the risks reduce. Therefore, the return on investment clause should contain some flexibility to adjust return on investment rates to match with the dynamic market realities and industry risk profiles over the tenure of the concessions.

While installed capacities through PPPs have increased, access to electricity has not grown at a level required to achieve national and global access rates. Therefore, interventions to reduce electricity tariffs, that remain hindrance to access and optimal utilisation of electricity, should be designed and implemented. Some may include the use of auctions to secure competitive feed in tariffs from private actors (bidders), promote mini grids to reduce transmission costs since power is generated, transmitted, distributed and consumed in close proximity. Promote off-grid solutions such as solar home systems and vertically integrated private models under a mini-grid initiative. Fiscal and monetary policies need to be formulated and implemented to improve the stability and strength of local currency in order to reduce exchange risk and currency convertibility challenges that largely contribute to tariffs since debt finance is acquired in foreign currency. The need to establish PPP fund is critical as a source of debt for special purpose vehicles in the country.

There is also a need to promote PPPs in renewable energy space. This is because most investors and financiers are increasing shifting focus on execution and funding for renewable energy projects. To attract investors in renewable electricity solutions, governments need to provide incentives; for example in Uganda, solar products have received tax incentives that have made off-grid access surpass access to electricity rates via the grid. By doing so, African governments are likely to attract able PPP investors and achieve timely financial closure for PPPs in electricity.

REFERENCES

Ahmed, A. B., Musonda, I., & Pretorius, J. H. C. (2023). Dynamics of PPP investment in energy and country governance: evidence from sub-Saharan Africa. *Built Environment Project and Asset Management*, Vo. 13(1), pp.172–184.

Aitken, R. (2014). Case studies on PPP frameworks based on energy sector experience in sub-Saharan Africa. *Restio Energy*.

Allam, A. R., Saaf, E. J., & Dawoud, M. A. (2003). Desalination of brackish groundwater in Egypt. *Desalination*, Vol. 152(1–3), pp.19–26.

Anyanwu, J. C. (2009). Public-private Partnerships in the Nigerian Energy Sector: Banks Roles and Lessons of Experience. *Joint Ventures, Mergers and Acquisitions, and Capital Flow Nova Science Publishers, New York*.

Awuku, S. A., Bennadji, A., Muhammad-Sukki, F., & Sellami, N. (2022a). Public-private partnership in Ghana's solar energy industry: The history, current state, challenges, prospects and theoretical perspective. *Energy Nexus*, 100058.

Awuku, S. A., Bennadji, A., Muhammad-Sukki, F., & Sellami, N. (2022b). Promoting the solar industry in Ghana through effective public-private partnership (PPP): Some lessons from South Africa and Morocco. *Energies*, pp.15 (1), p.17.

Boardman, A. E., Greve, C., & Hodge, G. A. (2015). Comparative analyses of infrastructure public-private partnerships. *Journal of Comparative Policy Analysis: Research and Practice*, Vol.17 (5), pp.441–447.

CEIC DATA (2022). *Egypt Electricity Consumption*. https://www.ceicdata.com/en/egypt/electricity-consumption. Accessed May 3, 2023 16:05. EAT.

Clark, A., Davis, M., Eberhard, A., Gratwick, K & Wamukonya, N. (2005). *Power Sector Reform in Africa: Assessing the Impact on Poor People,* A study managed by the Graduate School of Business, University of Cape Town for ESMAP/World Bank.

Eberhard, A., Gratwick, K., & Kariuki, L. (2018). Kenya's lessons from two decades of experience with independent power producers. *Utilities Policy*, Vol. 52, 37–49.

Electricity Regulatory Authority. (2020). Structure of Uganda's electricity sector, *Uganda Electricity Sector Overview*. Available from: https://www.era.go.ug/index.php/sector-overview/uganda-electricity-sector. Date of Access: 15, April, 2023

Electricity Regulatory Authority. (2023). Government reduces electricity connection fees, Government Reduces Customer Connecting Fees, Date of Access: 02 February 2023.

Foster, V and Rana, A. (2020). *Rethinking Power Sector Reform in the Developing World*, International Bank for Reconstruction and Development / The World Bank, Washington, DC.

Foster, V., Eberhard, A., and Gabrielle, G., (2021) .The evolution of electricity sectors in Africa: ongoing obstacles and emerging opportunities to reach universal targets. *Handbook. 595–568. Future Africa Labs.*

Ganda, F., & Ngwakwe, C. C. (2014). Problems of sustainable energy in sub-Saharan Africa and possible solutions. *Mediterranean Journal of Social Sciences*, Vol. 5(6), p.453.

Gerrard, M. (2001). Public-private partnerships. *Finance and development*, Vol. 38(3), pp.48–51.

IRENA and AfDB. (2022). Renewable Energy Market Analysis: Africa and Its Regions, International Renewable Energy Agency and African Development Bank, Abu Dhabi and Abidjan. Available: www.irena.org/publications

Kabeyi, M. J. B & Olanrewaju, O. A. (2020). Performance analysis of diesel engine power plants for grid electricity supply. AIIE, 31 Proceedings, 5–7 October 2020, Virtual Event, South Africa, pp. 1–17.

Koppenjan, J. F. (2015). Public–private partnerships for green infrastructures. Tensions and challenges. *Current Opinion in Environmental Sustainability*, Vol. 12, p.30–34.

KPMG. (2022). Power Sector Updates, *Power Sector Watch*, Edition 2022—Q2, KPMG in Nigeria, pp. 1, 2.

Maia, D. A. D. (2022). Financialization and reprimarization in the African context: the case of Mozambique, Instituto Superior de Economia e Gestão.

Nduhura, A. (2019a). *Public Private Partnerships and Competitiveness of the Hydroelectricity Sub-Sector in Uganda: case of Bujagali and Karuma Dam Projects* (Doctoral dissertation, North-West University (South Africa).

Nduhura, A. (2019b). *Public Private Partnerships and Competitiveness of the Hydroelectricity Sub-Sector in Uganda: Case of Bujagali and Karuma Dam Projects*, Published Ph.D. Thesis, North-West University, pp. 1–203.

Nduhura, A., Tshombe, L. M., Molokwane, T., Twinomuhwezi, I. K., & Nuwagaba, I. (2021). Public private partnerships and continuity of government service delivery in the era of COVID-19 outbreak in Sub-Saharan Africa. *International Journal of Procurement Management*, Vol. 14(4), pp.505–530.

Nel, D. (2018). An assessment of emerging hybrid public-private partnerships in the energy sector in South Africa. *International Journal of Economics and Finance Studies*, Vol. 10(1), pp.33–49.

Nigerian Electricity Regulatory Commission. (2023). NESI, Nigerian Electricity Regulatory Commission. Available from: https://nerc.gov.ng/index.php/home/nesi. Date of access: 15, April 2023.

Office of the Auditor General. (2019). Annual Report. Republic of Uganda.

Office of the Auditor General. (2021). Annual Report. Republic of Uganda.

Organisation for Economic Cooperation and Development. (2008). Public-private partnerships: In pursuit of risk sharing and value for money, OECD, Paris, France.

Othman, K., & Khallaf, R. (2022). Identification of the Barriers and Key Success Factors for Renewable Energy Public-Private Partnership Projects: A Continental Analysis. *Buildings*, Vol. 12(10), p.1511.

Porter, M. E. (2012). The new competitive advantage: Creating shared value. In *Presentation at the HSM World Business Forum CSV. Retrieved August*, Vol. 21, p. 2016.

Tshombe, L. M., Molokwane, T., Nduhura, A & Nuwagaba, I. (2020). An analysis of public-private partnerships in the East Africa, *Research in World Economy*, Vol. 11(5), Special Issue, Sciedu Press, Canada, pp. 152–163.

Twinomuhwezi, I. K., & Herman, C. (2020). Critical success factors for public-private partnership in universal secondary education: perspectives and policy lessons from Uganda. *International Journal of Educational Administration and Policy Studies*, Vol. 12(2), 133–146.

Uganda Bureau of Statistics. (2021). *2021 Statistical Abstract.* Available from: https://www.ubos.org/wp-content/uploads/publications/01_20222021_Statistical_Abstract.pdf. Date of Access 10, January, 2023.

Uganda Electricity Distribution Company Limited. (2005). Umeme. Available from: https://www.uedcl.co.ug/umeme/. Date of access 14, April, 2023.

UNDESA. (2023). Goals 7 Ensure access to affordable, reliable, sustainable and modern energy for all', Department of Economic and Social Affairs Sustainable Development. Available from: https://sdgs.un.org/goals/goal7). Date of access, 27 March, 2023.

Vagliasindi, M. (2013). *Revisiting Public-Private Partnerships in the Power Sector.* World Bank Publications.

Van Ham, H & Koppenjan, J. (2001). Building public-private partnerships: Assessing and managing risks in port development. *Public Management Review*, 4, 593–616.

Verweij, S., & van Meerkerk, I. (2021). Do public–private partnerships achieve better time and cost performance than regular contracts? *Public Money & Management*, Vol. 41 (4), pp. 286–295.

WHO (2021), "Global Health Observatory data repository", World Health Organization, Geneva, Switzerland, https://apps. who.int/gho/data/view.main.HHAIRFUELSCLEANCOUNTRYv (Accessed February 3, 2023).

World Bank (2021), World development indicators. https://databank.worldbank.org/source/worlddevelopment-indicators. (Accessed February 3, 2023).

Yescombe, E. R. (2018). Public-private partnerships in Sub-Saharan Africa. *Dar es Salam: UONGOZI Institute.*

Chapter 4

Public-Private Partnership Legal Frameworks in Selected African Jurisdictions

Trends and Future Prospects

Gosego Rockfall Lekgowe

Despite criticisms that PPPs have failed to meet expectations in developing countries (Leigland, 2020), their popularity as a policy instrument for addressing the challenge of infrastructure deficit is gaining momentum in Africa (Leigland, 2020). PPPs are even seen as vital in the achievement of Sustainable Development Goals (SDGs) (Leigland, 2020). It is not at all surprising that they are gaining popularity in Africa. At a time when traditional business models for infrastructure development are failing, as an alternative, PPPs offer African governments the needed versatility and flexibility to design arrangements that fit their needs in terms of capital requirements, extent of private sector involvement and duration. Despite these benefits, there have been costly PPPs failures in Africa (Yescombe, 2018). Literature attributes some of these failures to lack of sound and clear regulatory framework (Bayliss, 2003).

As PPPs entail long-term engagements, involve high level of risk and make use of public goods, literature recognises the need for clear legislative framework for their success. As a result, African governments have put in place legislative frameworks which specifically regulate the implementation of PPPs. This chapter examines legislative frameworks for PPPs in selected jurisdictions in Africa. For a fair spread, the chapter focuses on four African countries selected from three Regional Economic Communities in Africa: Kenya from the East African Community (EAC), Ghana from the Economic Community of West African States (ECOWAS), and Tanzania and Zambia, both from the Southern African Development Community (SADC). There is extensive literature from Organization of Economic Co-operation and

Development (OECD), UN and the World Bank that establishes guidelines for a model PPP legislation. Using such frameworks as a guide, the chapter evaluates the content of PPP legislation in these countries, and notes deficiencies and developing trends. Whilst these findings are specific only to the selected countries, they may hold some lessons for other countries as they develop their legislative frameworks.

AFRICA AND PPPs

Africa's Infrastructure Deficit

Despite Africa being seen as a land of opportunity and an emerging destination of choice for investors (African Union, 2015), Africa faces grave predicaments. Along with political instability, rising levels of poverty, high sovereign debt, poor education and disease, infrastructure deficit remains one of the main stumbling blocks to economic growth and improved living standards in Africa (Wheeler, 1984). In 2018, sub-Saharan Africa, which houses one-seventh of the world's population, ranked at the bottom of all developing regions across virtually all dimensions of infrastructure performance (Calderon, Cantu, & Chuhan-Pole, 2018). Africa's infrastructure gap has been attributed to rapid population growth, fast urbanisation, climate change and colonial legacy (African Union, 2015).

Poor infrastructure stalls economic progress by cutting productivity growth (Calderon, 2009). Gil, Stafford, and Musonda (2019, p.7) capture the deleterious impact of poor infrastructure:

> [L]ack of transport infrastructure complicates the flow of goods and people, making it harder for individuals and organisations to coordinate action, cooperate and trade; an unreliable power supply deters private investment and undermines productivity; lack of basic social infrastructure makes it harder to develop and retain talent, tackle gender inequality and poverty, and so build local capabilities. This raises transactional costs, reduces business competitiveness and hinder governments from achieving the goal of service provision to their populations which worsens poverty and inequality. To derive high economic benefits, Africa needs larger stocks of infrastructure.

Both nationally and regionally, the problem of poor infrastructure in Africa has sparked the need for active policies and leadership, to identify the challenges and create solutions to Africa's infrastructure deficit. At the continental level, the African Union Programme for Infrastructure Development in Africa (African Union, 2015) provides 'a common framework and roadmap for Africa to build infrastructure in priority areas such as transport, energy, Information Communications and Technology and Transboundary networks'.

This is expected to boost trade and trigger economic growth. The Regional Economic Communities have institutions responsible for policy formulation and identification of regional infrastructural needs. The SADC Regional Indicative Strategic Development Plan 2020–2030 identifies infrastructure development as one of the strategic pillars that serves as an enabler for regional integration, economic development and poverty reduction (Southern African Development Community, 2020). The operationalisation of this pillar is implemented through the SADC Regional Infrastructure Development Master Plan, approved in 2012. SADC aims to deliver interconnected, integrated, and quality seamless infrastructure and networks, including cross-border infrastructure. To address infrastructure deficit in Africa, these PPPs are emerging as a preferred tool in these policies.

PPPs in Africa

For conceptual clarity, it is necessary to define PPPs. Loosely defined, public-private partnerships (PPPs) involve a commercial partnership between the public entities and private entities for the procurement of public infrastructures or services. The commercial partnership is typically characterised by transfer of risk to the private party or sharing of risk, over a long term (United Nations, 2007). As PPPs cover a continuum of operations that involve service provision to the public, they may be confused with privatisation and public procurement. This is especially so as there is literature that claims that PPPs are a language game designed to conceal and camouflage the more pejorative and controversial schemes such as privatisation.

Thus, it is necessary to draw a distinction amongst these concepts. PPPs differ in privatisation and public procurement. Generally, accountability for delivery of the service under PPPs remains on the public sector whereas under privatisation it moves to the private sector (UNECE, 2008). Under privatisation, the private sector delivers the service independently of the public sector, regulated by general laws. Under PPPs, generally, ownership of public goods is not transferred to the private entity. In public procurement, the public entity purchases or leases goods or services under competitive conditions from a number of bidders in order to contain costs. The transaction is usually a one-off arrangement.

Across developed (UNECE, 2008), emerging and developing economies, PPPs are 'enjoying a global resurgence in popularity' and becoming the dominant apparatus to bridge the infrastructure deficit. Multilateral institutions such as the World Bank and the International Monetary Fund are giving PPPs attention. In Africa, regional bodies and governments have recognised PPPs as a vital tool for development of sound infrastructure development. The African Union Programme for Infrastructure Development in Africa acknowledges that countries must 'mobilize their own public and private domestic resources and attract foreign private investment' (African Union, 2015). The three main African Regional Economic Communities have also identified PPPs as the model for infrastructure development. The 2012 SADC Regional Infrastructure Development Master Plan (Southern African Development Community, 2012), the 2021 ECOWAS Regional Infrastructure Master Plan (Economic Community of West African States, 2021), and the 2020 East African Community Investment Guide (East African Community, 2020) also identify PPPs as one of the viable funding mechanisms for infrastructure projects. In fact, PPPs have become the established means of delivering infrastructure services in Africa.

The accelerated spread and acceptance of PPPs in Africa hinge on their acclaimed benefits. Traditionally, debt financing for infrastructure development used to occur through credit support from project financiers, international and national credit agencies and governments. These sources are no longer able to meet the needs of fast-paced growth of infrastructure markets (United Nations, 2001). Crucially, PPPs offer governments the opportunity to tap into various sources of capital. Infrastructure development requires high level of investment and in most African countries, the public purse alone cannot adequately finance it. Through access to alternative sources of capital, PPPs offer governments the ability to develop new infrastructure services even when faced with fiscal constraints.

In poorer countries with limited public finance, PPPs allow governments to develop new infrastructures which require significant capital expenditure. However, these benefits go beyond private capital acquisition. Through the concept of value for money, PPPs deliver improved infrastructure at lower cost compared to public sector provision. As risks are transferred to the private sector, the private sector is incentivised to mitigate it. The pooling of resources, which results in the private sector bringing its expertise to the projects, helps drive costs down in the long run (Yong, 2010). Further, compared to governments, the private sector has been shown to deliver projects on time and without cost overruns (Yong, 2010).

Not only do PPPs offer benefits in terms of timely delivery and cost, they also offer a fertile opportunity for innovation and high-quality outputs. PPPs offer the right incentives to private sector, which are absent in public services; this competitive combination of specialised expertise and motivations of the public sector creates high potential for creativity and innovation. There are other non-financial benefits that arise from PPPs. As PPPs involve participants from the local communities, this form of community participation lends legitimacy for policymaking and implementation. This allows PPPs to be used to achieve various social objectives such as citizen economic empowerment. Lastly, by resorting to PPPs, governments gain the time and space to focus on the core mandate of policymaking and regulation.

However, PPPs are not all glory. They are complex and demand highly skilled public sector. To deliver on their acclaimed benefits, PPPs need public officials who understand their operations. In most African nations, there is the challenge of capacity gaps—the lack of fully competent officials who understand the operations of PPPs (Worch, Kabinga, Eberhard, Markard & Truffer, 2019). This has led to negligence of procedures, poor planning and management, failure to appreciate and account for projects' fiscal risks (Hellowell, 2019). Weak bargaining positions resulting from lack of understanding of PPPs can create room for profit-motivated private parties to increase prices unfairly (Farnam, 2005) or drive hard bargains. The result is project delays, political interference, corruption and cost overruns leading to PPP failures. In addition, due to their complex nature, PPPs can be costly to finance and implement leading to excessive budgetary commitments. The close and ongoing monitoring increases costs for the public sector.

In addition, political support is critical to the success of PPPs (Yescombe, 2018). Political support is required to ensure that civil servants who do not support PPPs do not sabotage the process. Involvement of opposition political parties, organised labour and civic society groups is critical to allay any fears by the investors in case of change of government. Where labour and civic society organisations are unpersuaded, that the profit motive of private entities can be harnessed in the public interest, opposition from these groups can make it difficult for PPPs to achieve their goals.

WHY ENABLING LEGISLATION FOR PPPs?

Building an effective legal framework is identified as one of the integral elements for the success of PPPs (UNECE, 2008). According to the African Union Programme for Infrastructure Development in Africa, absence of enabling legislative frameworks and lack of expertise in understanding PPPs constitute some of the bottlenecks in unlocking the benefits of PPPs (Organization of Economic Co-operation and Development, 2013). Weak PPP culture and poor institutional and regulatory frameworks in many sub-Sahara African economies have been identified as the biggest risks that jeopardise foreign investment in Africa (Owolabi, Oyedele, Alaka, Ebohon, Ajayi, Akinade & Olawale, 2018). For instance, Hamukoma and Levy (2019) have shown that the inability to attract private investment in new electricity generation in South Africa was a result of the failure to put in place a credible regulatory framework. A PPP law offers great advantages for African governments.

First, like any other market of goods, infrastructure and associated goods encounter market failures in the form of information asymmetries (which causes inefficient market outcomes), externalities, monopolistic features and inequalities (Marques, 2017). Legislation ensures access to information to transaction parties, mitigates externalities by allocating costs and responsibilities and introduces fair play in engagements between public entities and private sector. Second, as PPPs involve multiple parties, large up-front financial investments, and tremendous risks from both private and public entities, there is need for a stable, clear and predictable regulatory environment that establishes the expectations of the parties, validity of transactions and remedies for breach. Compared to policies—which may be subject to frequent changes, and often are drafted in vague and general language, legislation offers such a certain environment. Third, PPP laws reduce transaction costs. This is because PPP law contains terms of contracts including risk allocation, costing, breach and remedies and the roles and obligations of the parties.

This obviates the need for long, extensive and complex negotiations which may require expensive expertise. This is an advantage in Africa where there is still lack of expertise on these matters. Fourth, PPPs involve the provision of essential services which affect collective needs of the public which makes them prone to abuse and corruption by politicians who are guided by the political cycle and patronage (Marques, 2017). Endemic corruption is one of the daunting challenges in infrastructure projects in Africa. By providing a transparent and predictable regulatory system, legislation can deter and minimise risk of conflicts of interest, regulatory capture, corruption, and unethical behaviour (Organization of Economic Co-operation and Development, 2012). Lastly, a PPP law adds to maintaining a certain, predictable and stable regulatory system and signals to investors the willingness by a State to respect the Rule of Law in its engagements with the private sector. This increases the prospects of foreign investor attraction and the viability of PPPs. To derive these benefits, a PPP legislation must contain core ingredients of a model PPP law. The next section addresses this point.

THE CORE INGREDIENTS OF A PPP LAW

Having demonstrated the need for a sound legislative framework for the success of PPPs, this section moves to consider the ingredients of a sound PPP law. A sound and suitable legislative framework is one that contains core ingredients of a PPP law. A large and growing body of literature has investigated ingredients of a model legislative framework (UNECE, 2008). These literatures, such as the United Nations Commission on International Trade Law (UNCITRAL) Legislative Guide on Privately Financed Infrastructure

Projects, the UNECE Guidebook on Promoting Good Governance in Public-Private Partnerships and OECD Principles for good public governance of Public-Private Partnerships, are based on data drawn from international best practices, experiences and lessons gained from past projects.

Whilst findings from these literatures cannot be extrapolated to all countries due to different legal systems and contexts, they provide evidence-based frameworks that are helpful to consider in promulgating PPP legislation. Below, this section evaluates PPP legislation in selected African countries using five core indicators derived from these literatures—namely: legal definition and recognition of PPPs in a legal system; institutional mechanisms; clarity of PPP implementation process; dispute resolution schemes; and lastly, transparency and accountability. These five core indicators do not represent the gold standard of successful PPP law; the law operates in a broader context with a multiplicity of factors that may influence its application and success. However, these core indicators play a critical role in ensuring that, at minimum, a PPP law will deliver on the promises of PPPs—value for money and risk-sharing. What follows is an examination of selected legislation under the core indicators stated.

Definition and Recognition

To situate PPPs in a legal system, a PPP law must define and recognise PPPs as a vehicle for infrastructure development. As PPPs are a new phenomenon and legal concept in African countries, a PPP law must define PPP and recognise it as a valid instrument and grant public entities the competence to utilise in infrastructure development (United Nations, 2001). Partners such as contractors, investors and lenders need clarity on this. By doing so, PPPs will become part of the legal culture, while providing clarity and predictability in PPP operations. Defining and recognising PPPs in a PPP law also allows governments to choose the types of PPPs that advance their strategic goals. Thus, defining PPP is not a matter of semantics, it can determine the success or failure of a PPP (Fourie & Burger, 2000).

In general, a broad definition that specifies the general features of a PPP is preferred. The UNCITRAL Legislative Guide provides a simple, clear and flexible model definition for a PPP. A PPP is defined as 'an agreement between a contracting authority and a private entity for the implementation of a project, against payments by the contracting authority or the users of the facility, including both those projects that entail a transfer of the demand risk to the private partner (concession PPPs) and those other types of PPPs that do not entail such risk transfer (non-concession PPPs)' (United Nations, 2001). This broad definition allows flexibility in designing and choosing the best structure for a PPP arrangement. It achieves clarity in that it specifies the permissible contractual forms. The World Bank's PPP Reference Guide (World Bank, 2017) introduces duration, and defines PPP as a long-term contractual arrangement between one or more contracting authorities and a private partner for providing a public asset or service, in which the private partner bears significant risk and management responsibility, and remuneration may be linked to performance.

The Ghana Public Private Partnership Act of 2020 does not contain a specific definition for a PPP. The Act applies to commercial arrangements carried out through partnership arrangements in respect of contracting authorities including the security services (Republic of Ghana, 2020). Even though the scope of the Act distils the nature of the subject it applies to, it is not easy to identify the nature of the PPPs to which the Act is intended to apply. The Act does not apply to the outsourcing of government services without the transfer of financial and operational risks to a private party, which leads to the conclusion that where there is risk-sharing, the Act will apply. This approach is neither desirable nor recommended.

The Zambia Public Private Partnership Act, No. 4 of 2009 (Republic of Zambia, 2009) is one the earliest PPP laws in Southern Africa. It adopts a short definition of a PPP, which is defined as an investment through private sector participation in an infrastructure project or infrastructure facility. This definition is too broad and fails to specifically indicate the essential elements of a PPP. However, the features of a PPP can be distilled from the definition of a PPP agreement under Section 2 which includes the requirement that the private party 'assumes substantial financial, technical and operational risks in connection with the performance of the institutional function or use of State property' and receives consideration for performing a public function or utilising State property, either by way of a fee from any revenue fund or a Ministry's budgetary funds or user levies collected by the concessionaire from users or customers for a service provided by it.

Like the Zambia PPP Act, the Tanzanian Public Private Partnership Act of 2010 (Republic of Tanzania, 2010) adopts a short definition of a PPP. A PPP is defined as an investment through private sector participation in a project undertaken in terms of this Act. The definition is too wide to capture all contractual arrangements entered into between the public sector and private sector in relation to infrastructure development. It is only through the use of the phrase 'investment through private participation' that one can infer that the law may be aimed at long-term projects. There is no indication of risk-sharing or transfer to the private party. This can also be garnered from the objectives of the Tanzanian PPP under Section 4 which includes 'to promote private sector participation in the provision of public services through public-private partnership projects in terms of investment capital, managerial skills and technology' (Republic of Tanzania, 2010). As it strived for simplicity, both the Zambia and Tanzanian definitions may have sacrificed clarity.

Kenya has used PPPs since 1996 across telecommunications, energy, transport, water and sewerage. In 2011, it enacted a 2011 PPP Policy (Republic of Kenya, 2011), which was followed by its first Public Private Partnership Act, No. 15 of 2013 (Republic of Kenya, 2013), putting Kenya in the list of the first eastern countries to enact a PPP law. The current law regulating PPPs is the Public Private Partnership Act, No. 14 of 2021 (Republic of Kenya, 2021). The Kenya PPP Act's inclusive definition of a PPP is more detailed. A PPP is defined as 'a contractual arrangement between a contracting authority and a private party under which a private party undertakes to perform a public function or provide a service on behalf of the contracting authority; receives a benefit for performing a public function by way of—compensation from a public fund; charges or fees collected by the private party from users or consumers of a service provided to them; or a combination of such compensation and such charges or fees'.

The definition introduces the element of risk-sharing and indicates that the private party 'is generally liable for risks arising from the performance of the function in accordance with the terms of the project agreement'. Further, the definition requires that the private party transfers the facility to the contracting authority. Whilst it remains broad in terms of its scope, the Kenyan definition is clear and contains the essence of a PPP. Public entities have the authority to enter into PPPs. The Public Private Partnership Committee, created under Section 6, approves negotiated contract terms, the cancellation of procurements or termination of project agreements, and the variation of project agreements. Under Section 20, public entities are authorised to enter into PPPs and to designate their properties for use.

What can be clearly seen from this analysis is that most laws recognise the importance of defining PPPs. However, not all laws achieve clarity in their definitions. Apart from the Kenya PPP Act, other laws adopt general definitions. These definitions are not helpful models of clarity. In some laws, the essential ingredients of a PPP are not contained in the statutory definitions. The UNCITRAL Legislative Guide and the World Bank's PPP Reference Guide declare risk and term essential elements of a PPP. The Kenya PPP Act provides a definition of a PPP that should be used as a guide.

Institutional Mechanisms: Roles and Competences

Another core ingredient of a PPP law is a clear, predictable and legitimate institutional framework supported by competent and well-resourced authorities (Organization of Economic Co-operation and Development, 2012). Recommendation 6 of the Legislative Guide on Privately Financed Infrastructure

Projects recommends that institutional mechanisms should be established to coordinate the activities of the public authorities responsible for issuing approvals, licences, permits or authorisations required for the implementation of PPP. The institutional mechanisms should have competence, autonomy and be independent from political interference. As PPPs involve various partners with different roles and responsibilities a PPP law needs to clearly set out the roles of the public entity and private sector in the execution of the PPP. Consumers and the private sector ought to know where to go with proposals, requests or complaints. Clarity in this respect avoids overlapping of duties, unnecessary confusion and conflict.

It may also help reduce room for opportunistic behaviour. All PPP laws examined create enabling legal and institutional framework to guide PPPs. An examination of the institutional mechanisms follows. The analysis below shows that generally, institutions are spread along three core roles: policy formulation, PPP screening and approval and financial and risk assessment. There is a clear definition of roles and simple institutional framework. The Tanzanian PPP Act creates the Public Private Partnership Coordination Unit (PPP Coordination Unit) and the Public Private Partnership Finance Unit (PPP Finance Unit). The PPP Coordination Unit is responsible for promoting and coordinating all matters related to PPP projects undertaken within the Mainland Tanzania. It assesses projects, approves proposals and feasibility studies and makes recommendations to the PPP Finance Unit, which seats at the Ministry of Finance. The Unit also advises government on policy. On the other hand, the PPP Finance Unit ascertains whether the project is affordable, provides value for money and whether it presents any risks. When the projects involve pubic finance, the proposal is forwarded to the Ministry of Finance, which initiates funding.

The Kenyan PPP Act establishes the Public Private Partnership Committee (PPP Committee) and Directorate of Public Private Partnerships. The PPP Committee is composed of principal secretaries from ministries of planning, infrastructure and finance, and the Solicitor General. Three persons may be appointed from outside the public service. Like Tanzania's PPP Coordination Unit, the Committee formulates policies; oversees implementation of PPPs; approves proposals; and conducts feasibility studies. The Directorate of PPPs is the implementation organ for PPPs. It is headed by a Director General appointed by the Public Service Commission. It coordinates selection of PPP projects from contracting authorities, keeps a national list of projects, supervises contracting authorities on feasibility studies, leads contracting authorities on negotiations, reviews and approves project proposals, and creates public awareness on PPPs.

Like the Kenya PPP Act, the Ghana PPP Act establishes the PPP Committee. The PPP Committee examines, considers and approves PPP requests from contracting authorities or makes recommendations to mandated approving authorities, such as Cabinet or Parliament. The PPP Committee also considers unsolicited proposals. Its members are appointed by the president, and the membership entails individuals from various sectors of the economy. In addition, there is the Technical Committee of Fiscal Commitments and the PPP Office. The Technical Committee of Fiscal Commitments identifies fiscal commitments and contingent liabilities associated with PPPs, and considers affordability in light of budgetary commitments and makes recommendations to the PPP Committee on fiscal risk. The Public Private Partnerships Office, within the Division responsible for public investments and assets in the Ministry, serves as the secretariat to the PPP Committee and The Technical Committee of Fiscal Commitments. Institutional mechanisms are also set up for local authorities. For local authorities, the Executive Committees are considered to be PPP Committees (Republic of Ghana, 2020).

Lastly, the Zambia Act establishes the PPP Council and the PPP Technical Committee. The Council is composed of ministers and other members, who are all appointed by the president. This does not achieve the required degree of independence. The Council formulates policy, approves preliminary award of agreements, and supervises contracting authorities on PPP projects. The Act requires the Council to approve or reject a proposal within 21 days after receiving a recommendation from the Technical Committee. Following submission of proposals to it from contracting authorities, the Technical Committee evaluates and selects projects for award, and recommends to the Council.

As stated above, the institutions are spread along three core roles: policy formulation, approval of proposals, and implementation of PPP, and in some laws, financial and risk assessment. The advantage of separating the policy formulation and implementation roles serves to ensure that specific roles are assigned to competent individuals. Setting up a technical or finance unit ensures that risk assessment receives adequate attention. The constitution of the bodies is mostly made up of public officers. In the Zambian case, the institutions are not independent from the president which creates a risk of political interference. Other affected economic players such as trade unions and business organisations have not explicitly been given any representation in these institutions. There is a case to be made for including these players as they represent important sectors in the economy.

The PPP Processes: Project Identification and Appraisal

Without a clear and well-defined implementation process stipulating the criteria for project selection and stages for PPP approval, there will be confusion in PPP implementation and projects will suffer from delays and cost overruns. The criteria for selection of PPPs must make feasibility studies a requirement. According to UNCITRAL Legislative Guide, a feasibility study is required. The study identifies national infrastructure needs linked to national priorities and establishes if PPP offers value for money—that is, the project is expected to deliver higher net economic benefits if done as a PPP. It must also assess fiscal risk. The selection of private entities must be based on a transparent, efficient and competitive procurement process. This minimises political manipulation and risk, and ensures that PPPs deliver optimum outcomes. Whilst traditional procurement legislation may meet this requirement, some adjustments may be required to meet the needs of PPPs.

The Kenyan PPP Act requires that an up-to-date national list of projects be maintained, and made transparent. This ensures that PPP projects are based on established national needs. Contracting authorities are required to carry out feasibility studies. The list of factors to be considered in conducting a feasibility study includes affordability and value for money. There is no mention of fiscal risk amongst these factors. Even the definition of feasibility study does not mention risk. Under Part V, the Act lays down a procurement process for PPPs which makes some adjustments to traditional procurement law. It stipulates procurement methods applicable to PPPs, and requires that principles of transparency, cost effectiveness and equal opportunity be applied.

A clearly defined process is made for privately initiated proposals. This incentivises the private sector to be innovative and identify infrastructure needs. The government benefits from innovative ideas of the private sector. The PPP Act stipulates rigorous requirements to be met by privately initiated proposals. The proposed projects must be linked to national priorities and subject to due diligence and feasibility assessment. The Act does not adopt the 'Swiss-challenge' where third parties are invited to match the privately initiated proposal. To avoid inefficiency, which discourages investors, there are time frames for decision making and completion of certain procedures. For instance, the Directorate has to evaluate the proposal within 90 days. Apart from the failure to explicitly make risk part of factors of a feasibility study, all in all, the Kenya PPP Act meets the essential requirements of a clear and sound process for PPPs.

The Ghana PPP Act requires a feasibility study, and lists factors to be considered including value for money and risk. Contracting authorities are required to ensure that value for money is obtained from PPPs. The PPP Act contains a detailed procurement process for PPPs. The Act requires the process to be open, competitive, transparent, cost effective, equitable and fair. Provision is made for unsolicited proposals. Unsolicited proposals are required to demonstrate innovation and be consistent with national development and infrastructure policies. Further, the proposals must offer value for money and be affordable. However, unlike the Kenya PPP Act, there are no time frames for decision making which may introduce inefficiencies in the process.

Under the Zambia PPP Act, a feasibility study is a requirement (Republic of Zambia, 2009). However, the Act does not list the factors to be considered in conducting a feasibility study, which is left to secondary legislation. The procurement process for PPPs is required to be fair, equitable, transparent, competitive and cost effective. There is a public invitation for proposals. Also, provision for direct negotiation is made where certain conditions are met such as where there is an urgent need. Clear provision is made for unsolicited proposals. These proposals are required to be beneficial to the public. A preliminary evaluation must be made within 14 days of receipt of the proposal. The Act adopts the Swiss Challenge, and requires the contracting authority to advertise the proposal for the purpose of receiving competitive proposals and if the originator of the proposal matches a competing proposal, the project will be awarded to it.

Under the Tanzania PPP Act, contracting authorities are required to conduct a feasibility study which must demonstrate amongst other things, fiscal risks, affordability, value for money and comparative advantage. In contrast to other legislation examined above, the Tanzania PPP Act does not contain provisions on procurement of PPPs; instead it requires procurement of PPPs to be done under the Public Procurement Act. Whilst provision has been made for unsolicited proposals, no guidance has been provided in the Act on the procedures and timeframes. It would have been preferable to have such procedures in the law that specifically govern PPPs.

In summary, in most cases, the essential components of a PPP are included in the PPP process—feasibility study, the goal of achieving value for money and risk-sharing. As regards procedures for PPPs, the majority of the jurisdictions studied include public procurement procedures in their legislation. In addition to making the law on PPPs readily accessible, it allows for one-stop consolidated procedures with necessary adjustments for PPPs. Provision for unsolicited proposals is included in most laws with clear procedures. Efficiency measures have been incorporated in the legislation in the form of time frames for execution of roles.

Efficient and Impartial Dispute Resolution Mechanisms

Inefficient dispute resolution mechanisms add costs to PPP execution and may dissuade investors from funding PPP projects. Clear, predictable and transparent rules for dispute resolution during the bidding process and post-contract stages are critical for an effective PPP law. As PPPs are complex, involve high risks and are long term, disputes are likely to arise. Investors need to be assured that their rights will be protected under the law. The

UNCITRAL Legislative Guide requires that disputes between the contracting authority and the private partner be settled through the dispute settlement mechanisms agreed by the parties in the PPP contract. However, the Guide also recognises that the State may provide dispute settlement mechanisms in its legislation that are best suited to the needs of PPPs.

The dispute settlement mechanisms must be open to customers and users of infrastructure facilities and other parties to resolve their disputes. There are various systems of dispute settlement: judicial system which uses national courts and quasi-judicial means ranges from conciliation, mediation, recourse to sector regulator and arbitration (national or international). Each system has its own merits and demerits. National courts can be inefficient, lack technical expertise, have corrupt judges and generally lack support by investors with concerns that local courts favour the public partner. In addition, the adversarial nature of the proceedings can be damaging to the relationship of the parties. Quasi-judicial means offer less confrontational resolution methods, allow for disputes to be resolved by individuals with technical expertise and can be efficient.

Generally, PPP Acts adopt a flexible system on dispute resolution which is favourable for PPPs. The Kenya PPP Act, the Ghana PPP Act and Zambian PPP Act all adopt a flexible dispute settlement system recommended under the UNCITRAL Legislative Guide. This system grants the parties the freedom to agree on a suitable method of dispute settlement. This approach has some advantages. By not making the judicial system mandatory, it caters for the interests of the investors who look for efficiency and neutrality. It also allows parties to tailor a dispute settlement system to the practical needs or circumstances of a PPP. The Tanzania PPP Act requires that disputes be resolved through negotiation, mediation or arbitration. It does not give the parties any other options which may create difficulties where parties may be desirous of considering other means such as judicial means especially in urgent cases.

Giving users of infrastructure recourse to a dispute settlement system does not appear to be a common feature of these laws. Apart from the Kenya and Tanzania PPP Acts, the Ghana and Zambian PPP Acts create an obligation for concessionaires who provide services to the public to establish simplified and efficient mechanisms for handling claims submitted by its customers or users of the infrastructure facility. It is unclear whether customers have recourse to the courts in the event they are dissatisfied with the decisions from such mechanisms. To ensure that concessionaires can be held accountable, there must be recourse to review or appeal by a higher body otherwise user rights remain hollow. In countries where there are public consumer protection authorities, instead of establishing new systems, users should have the right to refer disputes to such bodies.

CONCLUSION

Putting in place enabling legislation contributes to the successful implementation of PPPs. It ensures that, at the barest minimum: PPP projects address pressing societal needs, private entities are selected on a competitive basis, and public servants are able to factor in risk transfer and value for money in the conception and preparation of PPPs. With these comes the certainty and predictability much admired by investors.

African governments are realising the need to enact PPP laws to harness these benefits. However, effective PPP laws need to contain some of the core ingredients of PPP laws—such laws need to properly define and recognise PPPs as valid and acceptable policy instruments, create independent institutional mechanisms for executing separate roles, contain clear PPP process, have efficient, fair and transparent procurement systems and lastly, provide for flexible dispute settlement systems.

Whilst the majority of PPP laws examined contain these ingredients, some PPP laws fail to properly define PPPs, provide for a clear procurement system and ensure the independence of institutions from political interference. Lastly, what stands out from this analysis is that the involvement of organised labour organisations and civic society is not seen as a vital component of an effective PPP process. For policymakers looking to enact PPP laws, it is worth giving this attention.

REFERENCES

African Union (2015). Programme for infrastructure development in Africa. *Addis Ababa: African Union.*

Bayliss, K. (2003). Utility privatisation in Sub-Saharan Africa: a case study of water. *The Journal of Modern African Studies*, *41*(4), 507–531.

Calderon, C., Cantu, C., & Chuhan-Pole, P. (2018). Infrastructure development in Sub-Saharan Africa: a scorecard. *World Bank Policy Research Working Paper*, (8425).

Calderon, C. (2009). Infrastructure and growth in Africa, Policy research working paper 4914. The World Bank, African Sustainable Development Front Office, April 2009.

Gil, N., Stafford, A and Musonda, I. (2019). Duality by design: The global race to build Africa's infrastructure. In N. Gil, A. Stafford, & I. Musonda (Eds.), *Duality by Design: The Global Race to Build Africa's Infrastructure* (pp. 1–30). Cambridge: Cambridge University Press.

East African Community (2020). *East African Community Investment Guide*. Available from: East African Community (2020). East African Community Investment Guide.

Economic Community of West African States. (2021). ECOWAS Regional Infrastructure Master Plan, SOFRECO, pp. 1–794.

Farnam, P. (2005). Assessing public–private partnerships in Africa. *The South African Institute of International Affairs.*

Fourie, F., & Burger, P. (2000). An economic analysis and assessment of public-private partnerships (PPPs). *South African Journal of Economics*, *68*(4), 305–316.

Gil, N., Stafford, A., & Musonda, I. (Eds.). (2019). *Duality by Design: The Global Race to Build Africa's Infrastructure*. Cambridge University Press.

Hamukoma, N., & Levy, B. (2019). When the quest for electricity reform and the need for investment collide: South Africa, 1998–2004. In N. Gil, A. Stafford, & I. Musonda (Eds.), *Duality by Design: The Global Race to Build Africa's Infrastructure* (pp. 69–96). Cambridge: Cambridge University Press.

Hellowell, M. (2019). Delivering healthcare infrastructure and services through public–private partnerships: The Lesotho case. In N. Gil, A. Stafford, & I. Musonda (Eds.), *Duality by Design: The Global Race to Build Africa's Infrastructure* (pp. 203–226). Cambridge: Cambridge University Press.

Leigland, J. (2020). *Public-Private Partnerships in Sub-Saharan Africa: The Evidence-based Critique*. Oxford University Press, USA.

Marques, R. C. (2017). Why not regulate PPPs? *Utilities Policy*, *48*, 141–146, 142.

Owolabi, H. A., Oyedele, L., Alaka, H., Ebohon, O. J., Ajayi, S., Akinade, O & Olawale, O. (2018). Public private partnerships (PPP) in the developing world: Mitigating financiers' risks. *World Journal of Science, Technology and Sustainable Development.*

Organization of Economic Co-operation and Development. (2013). *Public-Private Partnerships in the Middle East and North Africa: A Handbook for Policy Makers.*

Organization of Economic Co-operation and Development. (2012). Recommendation of the council on principles for public governance of public-private partnerships. *Paris: Organization for Economic Cooperation & Development (OECD).*

Republic of Ghana. (2020). Public private partnership, 2020. Available from: https://mofep.gov.gh/sites/default/files/acts/PPP-ACT-1039.pdf.

Republic of Kenya. (2021). Public private partnership act, Act No. 14 of 2021 Available form:http://kenyalaw.org/kl/fileadmin/pdfdownloads/Acts/2021/ThePublicPrivatePartnershipsAct_No.14of2021.pdf.

Republic of Kenya. (2013). Public private partnership act, Act No 15 of 2013. Available form: http://www.parliament.go.ke/sites/default/files/2017-05/PublicPrivate_Partnerships_ActNo15of2013.pdf

Republic of Kenya. (2011). *Policy Statement on Public Private Partnerships.* National Treasury, Public Relations. Nairobi.

Republic of Tanzania. (2010). Public private partnership act, 2010. Available from: https://media.tanzlii.org/files/legislation/akn-tz-act-2010-18-eng-2019-11-30.pdf

Republic of Zambia. (2009). Public private partnership act, Act No. 4 of 2009. Available from: https://www.mofnp.gov.zm/?page_id=3396#:~:text=The%20PPP%20Act,effective%20delivery%20of%20social%20services.

Southern African Development Community. (2012). SADC *Regional Infrastructure Development Master Plan: Executive Summary*, Gaborone, Botswana.

Southern African Development Community. (2020). *Regional Indicative Strategic Development Plan (RISDP) 2020–2030*, Gaborone, Botswana.

UNECE. (2008). *Guidebook on Promoting Good Governance in Public-Private Partnerships*, United Nations Economic Commission for Europe, United Nations Publications, New York & Geneva, pp. 1–91.

United Nations. (2001). *UNCITRAL Legislative Guide on Privately Financed Infrastructure Projects,* United Nations Commission on International Trade Law, United Nations Publications.

Wheeler, D. 1984. Sources of stagnation in Sub-Saharan Africa. *World Development 12*: 1–23.

Worch, H., Kabinga, M., Eberhard, A., Markard, J., & Truffer, B. (2019). Why the lights went out: A capability perspective on the unintended consequences of sector reform processes. In N. Gil, A. Stafford, & I. Musonda (Eds.), *Duality by Design: The Global Race to Build Africa's Infrastructure* (pp. 33–68). Cambridge: Cambridge University Press.

World Bank. (2017). *Public-Private Partnerships: Reference Guide Version 3.* World Bank.

Yescombe, E. R. (2018). Public-private partnerships in Sub-Saharan Africa: Case studies for policymakers 2017.

Yong, K. (ed.) (2010). *Public-Private Partnerships Policy and Practice: A Reference Guide*, Commonwealth Secretariat, London.

Chapter 5

The Politics of Managing Public-Private Partnership Projects to Ensure Value for Money in Africa

A Contextual Analysis of the Uganda National Roads Authority

Innocent Nuwagaba

This chapter explores the politics behind managing public-private partnership (PPP) projects in Africa to ensure Value for Money (VFM) in the roads sector, focusing specifically on the context of Uganda National Roads Authority (UNRA). Dealing with changes in the political, policy and legal aspects is one of the key concerns in the use of PPP projects to ensure VFM (Rana, Ghassan & Malak, 2023). PPPs are agreements where public bodies enter into long-term contracts with private entities for the construction or management of public sector facilities, or to provide services to the community (Hadi & Erzaij, 2019). VFM is therefore 'a measure of the extent to which cost savings are achieved when delivering a public service via PPP Projects compared to conventional public procurement' (Matti, 2014). This is because what drives most African governments to provide services to their citizens through PPPs projects is the belief that PPPs lead to more VFM than conventional public procurement. Optimal risk allocation is one of the core VFM drivers in any PPP arrangement. A project is a temporary organisation that is created for the purpose of delivering one or more business products according to an agreed business case.

Organisations set up and invest in projects in order to introduce change into their day-to-day business as usual activities. That is why effective monitoring of the execution of PPPs is very essential when it comes to ensuring VFM (Matsumoto, Monteiro, Rial & Sakrak, 2021). Some scholars, however, argue that implementing infrastructural development projects using the PPP contractual arrangements makes such projects to be executed in a hurry when at times, there is limited funding to finance such large-scale projects especially in the development of transport infrastructure (Reidolda, Berzhanova, Azylkanova, 2022). In this regard, African countries should stand up for their own economic priorities by walking firmly on their own political feet if they are to effectively implement their own PPP projects (Janebová, Dostál, Plenta, & Végh, 2019). Following the adoption of PPP projects by most African countries mainly to construct and maintain road infrastructure, PPP policies have been passed by the ruling politicians to use them in the roads sector. It should also be noted that, a well-designed, detailed and clear legal framework is often noted as a prerequisite for all types of PPP activities, since they are becoming an emerging trend on the African continent (Mouraviev & Koulouri, 2018).

To illustrate, sub-Saharan Africa has seen the rehabilitation of road networks, as well as building the countries' institutional and financial capacity for their continued maintenance using PPP arrangements in order to overcome the most critical challenges confronting transport planners and policymakers (Solomon, Srinath, Chika, & Lei, 2014). However, some scholars wonder whether the use of PPP projects can cater for the low-income earners especially in the health sectors since healthcare is a very essential social service that needs to be availed by every citizen in any country (Republic of Botswana, 2009). PPPs come in the following models: design-build (DB); design-build-maintain (DBM); design-build-finance (DBF); design-build- operate (DBO); lease-operate-maintain (LOM); design-build-operate-maintain (DBOM); design-build-finance-operate (DBFO); design-build-finance-operate-maintain (DBFOM); build-own-operate-transfer (BOOT); build-own-operate (BOO) (Borole, 2022). The United States and the United Kingdom are among some of the first countries to use and implement PPPs for development projects. Other countries that have a rich history in the use of PPPs to ensure value for money include the Netherlands and Ireland (Mswaili, 2022).

In the United Kingdom, PPPs were adopted for developing strategic and very crucial infrastructure in the various sectors of telecommunications, housing, energy, railways, manufacturing, education, health, ports, roads, courts, mining and agriculture to boost her economic growth and development (Assel, Yelena, Sanim, Lyailya & Orazkul, 2022). Actually, the PPP projects in the UK are common especially in the health sector as it is the same case in Italy, Canada and France (Stasevich, Fatikhov & Saidov, 2023). In Africa, West African countries such as Nigeria have earmarked power and transport as the major sectors that can use PPPs for infrastructural development in order to stimulate the country's economic growth and development (African Development Fund, 2010). In Ghana, PPPs are widely regarded as paramount to the delivery of better quality services in the roads sector (Mahamadu, Mahdjoubi, Booth & Fewings, 2015). In Southern Africa, since 1994, South Africa has been implementing over 50 PPP-related projects in development or implementation at national and provincial levels, and 300 projects at municipal level (Genberg, 2016; Borole, 2022). In East Africa, countries such as Kenya, Tanzania, Burundi, Rwanda and Uganda are venturing into PPPs to develop infrastructure such as the standard gauge railway (Barigaba, 2023).

In Uganda, the Uganda National Roads Authority (UNRA) is planning to use such PPP projects to develop new and refurbish its already existing infrastructure. For example, the Jinja Expressway is one of the proposed PPP projects yet to be implemented by UNRA (African Development Bank, 2018). Although the Uganda National Roads Authority has been using contracting out PPP model, other PPP models such as build-operate-transfer are now in use to construct roads such as the Kampala-Jinja Expressway and management contract for Kampala-Entebbe Expressway in Uganda (African Development Bank, 2018). However according to the government newspaper *New Vision* of 10 October 2019, the Kampala-Jinja Expressway PPP project faced procurement delays and political confrontation as the Executive seemed to favour a PPP from the start other than an Engineering Procurement Contractor, then PPP toll management design (*New Vision*, 2019, p.1). The objectives of the study are: To find out the role of political framework in the use of PPPs by Uganda National Roads Authority (UNRA) to ensure VFM in the roads sector; and to find out the role of the legislative framework in the use of PPPs by UNRA to ensure VFM in the roads sector.

LITERATURE REVIEW

PPPs are an effective mechanism of financing many developmental projects in different parts of the world (Aitkaliyeva, Zhanabayeva, Kussainova, Kulubekova, & Kadyrbergenova, 2022). With PPP projects, government leverages its project specifications, laws, limited financing, monitoring and evaluation skills and assets to realise Value for Money (Mutegi, 2023). PPPs are a mode of procurement that public sector uses through collaborating with private sector to provide essential services to the citizens (Ali & Timuçin, 2023). However, selecting the most suitable PPP project to ensure VFM is a serious debate in a number of research studies (Zhao, Yu & Gao, 2023). The rationale for use of PPPs in projects is that, they are essential in the revamping of key sectors of the economy (Girish & Adolf, 2023). In this regard, a PPP is a very important avenue for realisation of sustainable development goals since it is a basis for developing better social and economic infrastructure (Hassan & Fatile, 2022). One of the weaknesses of using PPP however is that, there is lack of vivid and candid evidence pertaining to effective stakeholder involvement in the use of PPP projects to ensure VFM (Uddin, S., Ong, S & Matous, 2023).

The Theoretical Framework for PPP Projects in Africa

This study is guided by the stakeholder management theory. With regard to PPPs in the roads sector in Africa, there are multiple stakeholders with varying influences based on their interests, legitimacy and power in its implementation. Politicians are some of the PPP stakeholders with more power and influence especially when it comes to formulating policies that govern the implementation of PPPs in the African Union member states (Freeman, 2010). This means that the success of any PPP project mainly depends on the nature of the relationships that partners develop with some key PPP stakeholders who have more political power, influence and control in implementing certain important decisions that affect the implementation of PPP projects since a good political environment enables effective implementation of different PPPs (Verger & Moschetti, 2016).

PPP Projects as a Financing Mechanism for Infrastructural Development in Africa

The evolution of PPPs is currently a matter of debate in Africa (Trotsenko, 2019). Governments in Africa are cash stricken and finding it hard to access the funds required to develop the necessary infrastructure in different sectors such as the roads sector so as to effectively provide essential services to their citizens. This is because the road transport provides a fundamental support for the socio-economic development in these countries (Miklinska, 2019). One way of funding roads sector is through the involvement of key stakeholders in both the public and private sectors to come up with feasible policies that are aimed at promoting PPP projects (Santos, 2019). However, because financing road projects using private equity involves a lot of political risks, the stakeholders of both public and private partners need to come up with policies that will aid them in managing such risks effectively. That is why funding road sector in Africa is one of the major constraints that political leaders face when it comes to implementing PPP policies (Bonvino, 2019).

PPP Projects as a Strategy for Ensuring Value for Money

Many governments in Africa view PPP projects as a strategy for ensuring VFM through improving provision of quality of service delivery to their citizens in a more efficient, effective and economic manner. Most African countries are currently focusing on using PPPs as a financing mechanism for implementing developmental projects so as to revamp their failed economies (Aidan, 2018). That is why some countries within Africa such as Zimbabwe are currently focusing on the use of PPP projects in the development of its road infrastructure in most of its towns such as Ruwa Town. Nevertheless, the major constraint hindering projects in the African Union member states is that the contributions governments are supposed to make when implementing PPP projects are usually more than what was calculated initially leading to public budget deficits and subsequent failure of such PPP projects (Liu, Liao, Guo, Mulugeta, D, Wang & Jian, 2019).

Although many governments are relying on the use of PPP projects to ensure VFM, there are instances where some PPPs have been affected by some unethical practices especially where they have not been effectively managed (Misael, 2022). In fact, the ethical issues with most PPP projects tend to be more complex than what some experts and researchers can imagine (Mohammad, Kin, Victor & Feng, 2023). In addition, a number of PPP projects in different parts of the globe have been terminated before achieving their intended objective due to sudden change of ownership, increased operational cost and delays in the execution of such projects as a result of failure to effectively handle certain political, policy and legal issues especially those pertaining to dispute resolution. This makes a number of PPPs to be associated with some risks since the different stakeholders of both public sector and private sector have varying interests, motives and aspirations when adopting such PPP projects (Yan & Xinyu, 2023).

The Use of PPP Project by Political Leaders to Improve Service Delivery

In Africa, PPPs have been initiated by some political leaders as a strategy to develop better infrastructure so as to improve delivery of services to the public (Yergali, Kasiya, Kemel, Assel, Almagul & Ismailova, 2019). In Africa, although most scholars and practitioners have criticised PPPs for inflating the profits of private partners at the expense of the public sector, they have not fully analysed the potential PPPs that are aimed at supporting the economy of African countries through provision of public services (Peeter & Vinnari, 2019). That is why there is increasing debate that PPPs must mainly focus on delivery of essential services to the citizens. As a result, supporters of PPPs are arguing that governments in Africa should consider Sustainable Development Goals (SDGs) when designing PPP policies (Baxter, 2019). The conventional beliefs for PPPs were embedded in the concept of weakening government's involvement in doing business so as to encourage private sector investments based on well-designed economic reform policies (Farris, 2019).

Politics gives a platform for the implementation and sustainability of PPPs in different nations all over Africa. Politicians and government agencies usually use PPPs to avoid tax increases in African countries where debt and taxes are already high (Krol, 2018). Literature illustrates that there is lack of in-depth analysis on how and why political processes and lobbyism combine to promote wrong projects (Albalate, Bel & Gragera, 2018). Due to the amount of resources involved in the implementation of PPPs, they can be susceptible to corruption (Estache & Saussier, 2013). Politicians often change the PPP guidelines to suit their personal interests. There are also instances where some PPPs have failed because of lack of support from certain political leaders. At times, political leaders do not consult and involve the citizens when implementing such PPP projects, which subsequently lead to their failure (Ypi, 2016).

Implementing an Effective PPP Policy

A robust PPP policy supports the use of PPPs in the roads sector in Africa. The advent of the private sector meant that there was need for a PPP implementation policy, which coherently stipulates the emergence of the private sector and reduced public sector responsibilities (Demisse, Awulachew, Adenew & Mengiste, 2011). Studies indicate that policy provides a clear operational arrangement, which not only facilitates a cordial relationship between partners but also aids VFM from the PPPs being implemented. Policies provide the platform for effective implementation of PPPs in the roads sector in all countries. It is therefore, necessary to undertake a thorough needs assessment as a basis for developing a better PPP policy framework under which infrastructural projects can be hinged for their successful implementation (Osei-Kyei, Chan, Yu, Chen & Dansoh, 2018).

It is also crucial to critically analyse and determine which PPP policies are relevant to the successful development and implementation of infrastructural projects so that only such policies are formulated (Feder, Birner & Anderson, 2011). It is therefore vital that we comprehend the factors that affect policy development to come up with better policy approaches that can be used to successfully execute a number of infrastructure projects (Feder *et al.*, 2011). However, unfavourable political environment is one of the factors that affect formulation of better policies for implementing different PPP models. Weak political institutional capacity creates uncertainties about the quality of policies leading to higher country risk, and decreases the incentives for private investors to participate in PPPs (Lee, Han, Quising & Villaruel, 2018).

A Legal Framework as a Prerequisite for Successful PPP Adoption

An effective PPP legal framework provides a starting point for effective implementation of PPPs in the African roads sector. A well-designed, detailed and clear legal framework is often noted as a prerequisite for all types of PPP activities, since they are becoming an emerging trend among the African Union member states (Mouraviev & Koulouri, 2018). The Economic Intelligence Unit (2015) contends that although PPPs may be implemented without a specific PPP law, the enactment of such laws is very critical in order to bring about consistent PPP legal frameworks in all government ministries, departments and agencies. This means that adoption and implementation of PPPs cannot be well streamlined unless institutions, processes, frameworks and procedures under and through which such PPPs can be adopted and implemented are developed (Rankin, Nogales, Santacoloma, Mhlanga & Rizzo, 2016).

Therefore, the PPP legal framework is very fundamental in determining successful implementation of any PPP project (Asian Development Bank, International Agency Development Bank and World Bank, 2014; Economic Intelligence Unit, 2015). Depending on the prevailing circumstances, different approaches are used when developing the legal framework for PPPs in any sector. For instance, the legal framework for developed countries within Africa may differ from that of developing economies (KPMG, 2015). This means that the initiators of the PPP legal framework should be careful when inserting certain important PPP clauses within it so that such clauses can always be relied upon to ensure successful implementation of PPP projects (Mouraviev & Kakabadse, 2015). That is why PPP experts insist that one of the very important things that governments must do before involving a private sector partner in implementing any PPP project is to first develop a robust PPP legal framework that can be used to enforce PPP contracts and provide room for arbitration among private sector actors (Mouraviev & Kakabadse, 2015).

METHODOLOGY

This study adopted a qualitative approach under the exploratory study design (Creswell, 2013). Data was collected through documents analysis (Joubish, Kharram, Ahmed, Fatima & Haider, 2011). The technique involves a review of relevant documents, which contain existing information related to the proposed study. A document review checklist was used to critically examine the literature on key issues pertaining to the role of political, policy and legal frameworks in the use of PPP projects by UNRA to ensure VFM in the roads sector (Saunders, Lewis & Thornhill, 1997).

An in-depth literature on the role of political, policy and legal frameworks in the use of PPP projects by UNRA to ensure VFM in the roads sector was identified and critically analysed from peer-reviewed journal articles and different documents pertaining to PPPs and VFM in the roads sector. The review captured all the relevant information from scholarly and practitioner writings that were in line with the study objectives. Guided by a document review checklist, the researcher reviewed diverse project reports, academic journals and policy documents. However, a critical review of literature reveals that most of the existing information identified provided a generic overview of the above issues (Rotter & Özbek, 2010).

The review supported the development of the conceptual framework by guiding an inquiry into the appropriate theory, the role of political, policy and legal frameworks in the use of PPP projects by UNRA to ensure VFM in the roads sector (Saunders *et al.,* 2012). Data was analysed using narrations and descriptions of the study phenomena (Schutt, 2011). In the process of getting the answers in line with study objectives, attention was paid to ensure that personal biases were minimised. Personal opinion was also reduced during data collection and analysis by being neutral. To ensure reliability, the researcher made sure that the data was critically examined (Golafshani, 2003).

RESULTS AND DISCUSSION

As to whether the political environment and approach affects the PPP projects used by UNRA in ensuring VFM in the roads sector, the findings revealed that politicians are some of the PPP stakeholders with more power and influence especially when it comes to formulating policies that govern the implementation of PPP projects that are suitable for ensuring VFM in Africa (Freeman, 2010). Evidently, strong commitment and support from political leadership leads to effective ad option, implementation and sustainability of PPP projects that are used as channels delivering essential services to the public.

In addition, the control and ambition of many political leaders normally determines the success of PPPs (Verhoest, Petersen, Scherrer & Soecipto, 2015). Scholars and practitioners argue that political leadership support is very crucial in implementing any PPP project. The current trend of PPPs, therefore, calls for unique management and governance by public and private sector actors (Verger & Moschetti, 2016). Some PPP experts note that the performance of any PPP project greatly depends on the existing conducive political climate which paves way for effective PPP management (Vadali,

Tiwari & Rajan, 2014; Verhoest *et al.*, 2015). Literature also shows that PPPs can easily prevail where there is good harmony between the political leaders, project financiers, implementers and beneficiaries (Brinkerhoff & Brinkerhoff, 2011). Brinkerhoff and Brinkerhoff (2011) argue that for PPP projects to achieve their objectives, they need to adopt a multi-structural approach that involves a concerted effort of all political leaders, government technocrats, development partners, implementing partners and project customers.

KPMG (2015) believe that good political governance and commitment form the bedrock for successful implementation of any PPP project. Therefore, a good political framework is fundamental in attracting serious private partners to invest in the development of infrastructure using PPP financing mechanisms since they know that there are limited political risks (Javed, Lam & Chan, 2013; Osei-Kyei & Chan, 2015). This implies that political leadership commitment is very crucial for the public and private partners especially when investing their productive resources such as money, time, technical expertise, land, equipment and good will in the implementation of PPP projects (European PPP Expertise Centre, 2015). This finding conforms to the debates by scholars and development partners such as Albalate *et al.* (2018), Krol (2018), Lee *et al.* (2018). Feder *et al.* (2011) and Rankin *et al.* (2016) who argue that politics provides the context for PPP implementation and sustainability in all countries.

The Role of Policy Framework in the Use of PPP Projects by UNRA to Ensure VFM in the Roads Sector

With regard to whether the policy framework and enforcement affect the PPP projects used by UNRA in ensuring VFM in the roads sector, findings illustrate that financing and asset ownership are separated in PPPs, increasing the potential for misalignment of incentives and the likelihood that the public party can use its powers to alter certain policies after the PPP contract is signed, and thereby hold up the private party once existing network assets are sunk (Howell & Sadowski, 2018). Various studies point to the fact that a well-designed policy framework is very crucial for effective adoption of PPPs in Africa (Chan, 2010). That is why such countries tend to face role conflicts as one of the constraints when implementing PPP projects since they lack policy guidelines to base on for streamlining PPP implementation modalities (Zou, Kumaraswamy, Chung, & Wong, 2014). The use of PPPs to implement road construction and maintenance projects in Uganda is at a very small scale compared to other sectors such as agriculture, education and energy, because

PPP policies particularly for the roads sector are not yet fully developed by the government (Asian Development Bank, 2008).

This finding sustains debates by scholars and development partners such as Howell and Sadowski (2018), Lee *et al.,* (2018), Chan, Lam, Chan and Cheung (2010), Tion (1990), Akintoye *et al.* (2005), Farlam (2005), Feder *et al.* (2011), Yong (2010), United Nations Economic Commission for Europe (2008), and Rankin *et al.* (2016). All affirm that a sound policy framework is necessary for developing sustainable relationships in PPPs since it articulates the intent to deliver public services and provides the broad picture for design and implementation that are critical in managing stakeholder expectations in addition to guiding monitoring progress of PPPs.

The Role of the Legislative Framework on PPP Projects by UNRA to Ensure VFM in the Roads Sector

As to whether the legislative framework affects the PPP projects used by UNRA in ensuring VFM in the roads sector, the findings revealed that poor legislative framework is also a constraint that affects different PPP models. Poor governance, insufficient legal capacity, and weak legal framework can hamper the implementation of PPPs (Lee *et al.,* 2018). Strong legal institutions and effective rule of law, as well as perception of a country's level of corruption and democratic accountability, are essential for securing PPP arrangements and successful outcome of a PPP project (Lee *et al.,* 2018). Although PPPs in the roads sector are becoming a common trend in many developing countries like Uganda, most of these developing countries are failing to deliver services to the public because most stakeholders involved in the management of such PPPs are not fully compliant with the existing legislative frameworks (Yong, 2010).

The Economic Intelligence Unit (2015) asserts that some countries in sub-Saharan Africa are implementing PPPs in the roads sector without hinging on a specific PPP law, and yet enacting such laws brings harmony across different ministries, departments and agencies. This means that the conception, initiation, design, planning, financing, development, implementation, maintenance, monitoring, management and sustainability of PPPs are not well streamlined and require developing institutions, structures, systems, processes, frameworks and procedures to successfully implement such PPPs in the roads sector (United Nations Economic Commission for Europe, 2008). The Economic Intelligence Unit (2015) further notes that failure to upgrade, standardise and harmonise PPP laws brings about disruptions, confusion, role conflicts and lack of confidence within government ministries, departments and agencies involved in the implementation of PPP projects in the roads sector.

Sometimes, failure to standardise PPP laws may lead to suspicion from some key PPP stakeholders as to whether really the government is fully committed to ensuring the success of PPPs in certain sectors (Farquharson, de Mästle, Yescombe & Encinas, 2011). Although PPPs are adopted to improve delivery of services to the citizens, at times the citizens themselves are not fully aware of their rights and obligations embedded within the existing PPP legal framework in terms of participating in decision making on matters that directly affect them and demanding for better services (Zou, 2014). The key PPP implementing partners may at times fail to account to the citizens since the beneficiaries of the PPP projects do not have access to PPP laws that they can use in demanding for such accountability.

A well-developed PPP legal framework should as such always be used to empower PPP project beneficiaries in getting to know what their rights are in terms of demanding for accountability from the PPP implementing partners based on existing PPP laws (United Nations Economic Commission for Europe, 2008). This finding is in line with the debates by scholars and development partners such as Lee *et al.* (2018), Yong (2010), Rankin, *et al.* (2016), Economic Intelligence Unit (2015), Mouraviev and Kakabadse (2015), Yong (2010), Rankin *et al.* (2016), Farquharson *et al.* (2011), KPMG (2015), United Nations Economic Commission for Europe (2008), and Asian Development Bank, International Agency Development Bank and World Bank (2014). All these scholars argue that the partnership agreement is protected by a legal framework and will be upheld amidst all the challenges encountered during PPP implementation. However, developing countries are implementing PPPs without a specific PPP law although passing such laws can harmonise practices and establish consistent frameworks across government ministries, departments and agencies.

CONCLUSION AND RECOMMENDATIONS

Study findings reveal that politics highly influences the adoption of PPP projects in the roads sector in African Union member states. This confirms that the political environment and approach indeed affect the PPP projects used in the roads sector. Secondly, findings revealed that policy framework also influences the adoption of PPPs in the roads sector in African Union member states. This proved that the policy framework really affects the PPP projects used in the roads sector of Africa. Finally, the findings revealed that a legal framework indeed effects PPP projects to be adopted in in the roads sector.

There is therefore need for the governments within Africa to ensure a conducive political environment for realising the success of PPPs. In this regard, the political commitment, political control and political ambition should all be geared towards creating a conducive environment for effective implementation of different PPP models in order to ensure VFM in the roads sector. Governments of African countries should ensure that strong political commitment is used to support different PPP models being implemented in the roads sector to improve service delivery. In addition, governments of African Union member states should ensure that political control and political ambition are well used as a basis for the success of planning and implementation of different PPP models being used in the roads sector.

African countries should also know that the evolution of PPPs is demanding for exceptional but challenging forms of governance to both public and private sector actors. African countries should ensure that their PPPs are used to nurture a cross-sectorial relationship where the public and private sectors work towards commitment and competence that creates a synergy which recognises that the whole is more than the sum of the parts. Governments of African countries should also ensure that strong political commitment is used to support different PPP models being used to improve service delivery. African governments further need to have a robust PPP policy for the roads sector projects in place because the policy provides a clear operational arrangement which not only facilitates a cordial relationship between partners but also aids VFM from the PPPs.

Such policies will provide the platform for effective implementation of PPPs in the roads sector. In this regard, it is recommended that policy preparation be followed by an assessment of the political context as it determines which policies are developed and implemented. In the same breath, technical expectations of given policies should also be well aligned. African countries should understand that failure to harmonise the technical and political expectations at design, implementation, monitoring and evaluation stages will restrain PPP project sustainability. African countries need to ensure that they use an effective PPP legal framework because for PPPs to blossom there should be a landscape which offers transparency, participation and promotion of the rule of law. This will attract and build confidence among private sector actors to invest in the roads sector knowing that their investments will be protected and channelled towards planned activities.

In addition, the partnership agreement should be protected by a legal framework and upheld in spite of all the challenges encountered during PPP implementation. In order to ensure that PPPs thrive successfully in the roads sector, African countries must ensure that they establish legislative frameworks that support quick and transparent decision making, allow for competitive bidding and develop regulations that specifically apply to each type of

PPP. Therefore, African countries should ensure that the legal and regulatory frameworks take a centre piece in developing, shaping and controlling the adoption, implementation, sustainability and management of different PPP models used to ensure VfM in the roads sector.

REFERENCES

Aitkaliyeva A. M., Zhanabayeva, Z. K., Kussainova, L. I., Kulubekova, A and Kadyrbergenova, A. K. (2022). Assessment of the Effectiveness of PPP Projects on the Example of the Transport Infrastructure of the Republic of Kazakhstan. *Journal of Public Policy and Administration*, Vol. 21, No. 5, p. 653–664.

African Development Fund. (2010). Project Appraisal Report of Capacity Building for PPP Infrastructure (Cb4pppi) in Nigeria.

African Development Bank Group (2018). Uganda - Kampala Jinja Expressway PPP Project—RLRAP Summary. Available from. https://www.afdb.org/en/documents/document/uganda-kampala-jinja-expressway-ppp-project-rap-summary-102687.

Ali, O. R. M. & Timuçin, H. (2023). Identifying Critical Success and Risk Factors of Airport Projects in Turkey Based on Public-Private Partnership.

Assel, U., Yelena, F. Sanim, Z., Lyailya, Z. & Orazkul, D. (2022). Stages and Features of the Implementation of Public-Private Partnership in Kazakhstan. *Journal of Public Policy and Administration*, Vol. 21, No. 5, P. 556–568.

Asian Development Bank. (2008). *Public-Private Partnership Handbook*. Available from: https://www.adb.org/documents/public-private-partnership-ppp-handbook.

Asian Development Bank, International Agency Development Bank and World Bank (2014). Public Private Partnerships Reference Guide. Vol. 2.

Aidan, B. (2018). China, Japan, India and the East Africa Blue Economy. Policy Insights, 61, South African Institute of International Affairs, South Africa.

Albalate, D., Bel. G & Gragera, A. (2018). When Politics and Lobbyism Combine to Promote White Elephants by Using PPPs. Research Institute of Applied Economics, Working Paper 2018/23 1/25 pág.

Barigaba, J. (2023). Uganda, Tanzania Standard gauge Railway line clear as Kenya derailed Sunday January 15 2023. https://www.theeastafrican.co.ke/tea/business/uganda-tanzania-sgr-line clear-as-kenya-derailed-4086104.

Baxter, D. (2019).Trends that will drive global Public Private Partnerships (PPPs) in 2019, World Bank. Available from: https://blogs.worldbank.org/ppps/trends-will-drive-global-ppps-2019.

Bonvino, G. (2019). Funding Public Transport with Transit Oriented Development Land Value Capture, in: Knowles, R.D. and Ferbrache, F. (ed.) *Transit Oriented Development and Sustainable Cities*, Edward Elgar, pp. 1–13.

Borole, T. (2022). *The Effectiveness of Public-Private Partnerships in the Development of Road Infrastructure: The Case of Toll Concessions in South Africa* (PhD Thesis). North West University, South Africa.

Brinkerhoff, D. W. & Brinkerhoff, J. M. (2011). Public–Private Partnerships: Perspectives on Purposes, Publicness, and Good Governance. *Public Administration and Development,* Vol. 31(1), pp.2–14. DOI: 10.1002/pad.584.

Chan, A. P. C., Lam, P.T.I, Chan, D. W. M. & Cheung, E. (2010). Critical Success Factors for PPPs in Infrastructure Developments: Chinese Perspective. *Journal of Construction Engineering and Management,* Vol. 136(5).

Mahamadu, A., Mahdjoubi, L., Booth, C., & Fewings, P. (2015). Integrated Delivery of Quality, Safety and Environment Through Road Sector Procurement: The Case of Public Sector Agencies in Ghana. *Journal of Construction in Developing Countries*, Vol. 20(1), pp. 1–24.

Matsumoto, C., Monteiro, R., Rial, I & Sakrak, O. A. (2021). Mastering the Risky Business of Public-Private Partnerships in Infrastructure. *International Monetary Fund.* Vol. 2021 (10). Available from: https://www.elibrary.imf.org/view/journals/087/2021/010/article-A001-en.xml.

Creswell, J.W. (2014). *Research Design: Qualitative, Quantitative and Mixed Methods Approaches.* Boston: Sage Publications.

Creswell, J. W. (2013). *Qualitative Inquiry and Research Approaches: Choosing among Five Traditions* (2nd Ed.). Thousand Oaks. California: Sage.

Demisse, B., Awulachew, S.B., Adenew, B. & Mengiste, A. (2011). *Creating Extension Service Delivery through Public-Private Partnership*. In: International Water Management Institute Conference Papers organised.

Economic Intelligence Unit. (2015). *Evaluating the Environment for Public–Private Partnerships in Africa: The 2015 Infrascope*. EIU, London.

European PPP Expertise Centre. (2015). *PPP Motivations and Challenges for the Public Sector: Why (not) and how*, European PPP Expertise Centre. Available from: https://www.eib.org/attachments/epec/epec_ppp_motivations_and_challenges_en.pdf.

Farris, J. (2019). Competing Interests of Government Appointed PPP Board of Nonprofit Corporation. *Delaware Journal of Corporate Law*, Vol. 43(3), pp. 551–573.

Feder, G., Birner, R. & Anderson, J.R. (2011). The Private Sector's Role in Agricultural Extension Systems: Potential and Limitations. *Journal of Agribusiness in Emerging Economies*, Vol. 1(1), pp. 31–54.

Farlam, P. (2005). *Working Together Assessing Public-Private Partnerships in Africa,* South African Institute of International Affairs.

Farquharson, E., de Mästle, C.T., Yescombe, E. & Encinas, J. (2011). *How to Engage with the Private Sector in Public-Private Partnerships in Emerging Markets.* World Bank.

Freeman, R. E., Harrison, J. S., Wicks, A. C., Parmar, B. L. & De Colle, S. (2010). *Stakeholder Theory. The State of the Art.* Cambridge: Cambridge University.

Girish, C. G. & Adolf, K. Y. N. (2023). Public Private Partnerships and Port-Land Interface Projects. *Journal of Blue Economy and Smart Sea Transport Systems.* pp. 41–47.

Golafshani, N. (2003). Understanding Reliability and Validity in Qualitative Research. The Qualitative Report, 8(4), 597–606. https://doi.org/10.46743/2160-3715/2003.1870

Hadi, A. H. and Erzaij, R. E. (2019). Determination a Reasonable Concession Period for PPPs, *Civil Engineering Journal*, Vol. 5 (6). doi:10.1061/9780784480267.037.

Genberg, H. (2016). The Role of Institutional Investors in Financing Development in Asia and the Pacific. Discussion Paper First High-Level Follow-up Dialogue on Financing for Development in Asia and the Pacific, MPFD Discussion Paper No. DP/11, UN-ESCAP.

Howell, B. & Sadowski, B. (2018). Anatomy of a Public-Private Partnership: Hold-up and Regulatory Commitment in Ultrafast Broadband. *Telecommunications Policy*, Vol. 42, (7), pp. 552–565.

Zhao, H., Yu, G & Gao, J. (2023). Operation Mode Selection of Offshore Wind Power PPP Project: A Case in China, Research Square, School of Management Engineering, Qingdao University of Technology, Qingdao 266520, China (Preprint). DOI: 10.21203/rs.3.rs-2391897/v1.

Janebová, P., Dostál, V., Plenta, P. & Végh. Z. (2019). *European Union (EU) Elections 2019: What do the Central European Political Parties stand for?* Association for International Affairs (AMO), Friedrich Naumann Foundation for Freedom, Bonn, pp. 1–32.

Javed, A.A., Lam, P.T. & Chan, A.P. (2013). A Model Framework of Output Specifications for Hospital PPP/PFI Projects. *Facilities*, Vol.31 (13/14), pp.610–633.

Joubish, M. F., Kharram, M.A., Ahmed, A. & Fatima S.T. (2011). Paradigms and Characteristics of a Good Qualitative Research, *World Applied Sciences Journal*, Vol. 12(11), pp.2082–2087.

Khadka, R. (2018). Management Control in Public Private Partnership: A Comparative Case Study of Norwegian and Australian Road Projects, NORD, Universitet, pp. i–89.

Hassan, K. I & Fatile, J. O. (2022). Public Private Partnership and Educational Infrastructure in Nigeria, *Journal of Public Administration, Finance and Law,* (26). doi .org/10.47743/jopafl-2022-26-13.

KPMG. (2015). Public-Private Partnership - Emerging Global Trends and Implications for future Infrastructure development in Australia. Available from: https://assets.kpmg.com/content/dam/kpmg/pdf/2015/06/public-private-partnerships-june-2015.pdf.

Krol, R. (2018). Highway Infrastructure: Issues Concerning Private-Sector Participation: Mercatus Research, George Mason University, Arlington, VA, July 2018.

Osei-Kyei, R.O., Chan, A.P.C., Yu, Y., Chen, C & Dansoh, A. (2018). Root Causes of Conflict and Conflict Resolution Mechanisms in PPPs: Comparative Study between Ghana and China, *Cities*, Vol. 87, pp. 185–195.

Lee, M., Han, X., Quising, P. H. and Villaruel, M. L. (2018). Hazard Analysis on Public Private Partnership Projects in Developing Asia, ADB Economics Working Paper Series, No. 548, Manila.

Liu, Q., Liao, Z., Guo, Q., Mulugeta, D. D., Wang, S & Jian, F. (2019). Effects of Short-Term Uncertainties on the Revenue Estimation of PPP Sewage Treatment Projects, *Water*, Vol. 11(1203).

Matti, S. (2013). Is There a Distinctive Canadian PPP Model? Reflections on Twenty Years of Practice. The Canadian Council for Public-Private Partnerships. Available at: https://www.pppcouncil.ca/web/P3_Knowledge_Centre/Research/Is_There_a_Distinctive_Canadian_PPP_Model__Reflections_on_Twenty_Years_of_Practice.aspx.

Mutegi, D. G. (2023). Applicability of Public-Private Partnerships in the Development of Affordable Urban Housing in Kenya, *BOHR International Journal of Social Science and Humanities Research*, Vol. 2(1), pp. 24–33.

Misael, A. (2022). Crossroads of Public and Private—The Ethical Management of Public-private Partnerships. A dissertation for Masters of Public Administration in Non-profit Sector Management and Leadership.

Mswaili, N. V. (2022). Public Private Partnership and Implementation of Affordable Housing Projects in Mombasa County. Kenya Master thesis in Public Policy and Administration at Kenyatta University. *Journal of Social Science and Humanities Research*, Vol. 2, No. 1, pp. 24–33.

Miklinska, J. G. (2019). (Planned) Public Private Partnership Projects for the Development of Polish Inland Waterways, Economic and Social Development: Book of Proceedings, Lisbon, pp. 351–360.

Mohammad, H. Kin, K. Victor, S. & Feng, X. (2023). Public Health Risk Evaluation through Mathematical Optimization in the Process of PPPs. *International Journal of Environment, Research and Public Health*, Vol. 20(2).

Mouraviev, N. & Kakabadse, N.K. (2015). Legal and Regulatory Barriers to Effective Public-Private Partnership Governance in Kazakhstan. *International Journal of Public Sector Management*, Vol. 28(3), pp. 81–197.

Mouraviev, K. & Koulouri, A. (2018). Enabling Green Energy Production: Implementing Policy by Using Public–Private Collaboration.

New Vision. (2016). Reported Cases of Alleged Corruption among UNRA Officials and Its Private Partners: Ugandan Government's Official News Paper, p. 5 &27.

Stasevich, A. U., Fatikhov, R, F & Saidov A. S. (2023). Concept of Outpatient Urology Development in the Process of Restructuring using the Experience of Public-Private Partnership According to Scientific Publications, *Journal of Pharmaceutical Negative Results,* Vol. 14(1).

Nwangwu, G. (2022). Utilizing Public Private Partnerships to improve Nigeria's Healthcare, *Law and Social Justice Review,* Vol. 3(2).

Osei-Kyei, R & Chan, A.P. (2015). Review of studies on the Critical Success Factors for PPP projects from 1990 to 2013. *International Journal of Project Management*, Vol. 33(6), pp. 1335–1346.

Peeter, P & Vinnari, E. (2019). The Discursive Legitimation of Profit in PPPs' Service Delivery. *Critical Perspectives on Accounting*, Vol. 69.

Rana, H. C., Ghassan, C. & Malak, M. A. (2023). Avoiding Disputes in PPP Road Contracts: Quantifying Impacts of Increased Allowable Truck Loads, *Journal of Legal Affairs and Dispute Resolution in Engineering and Construction*, Vol.15 (2).

Rankin, M., Gálvez Nogales, E., Santacoloma, P., Mhlanga, N. & Rizzo, C. (2016). *Public–Private Partnerships for Agribusiness Development: A Review of International Experiences.* Food and Agriculture Organisation, Rome, Italy.

Reidolda, S. A. M., Berzhanova, S. A. & Azylkanova, L. N. (2022). Analysis of the Effectiveness of PPP Projects in the Akmola Region. *Economic Series of the Bulletin of the L.N. Gumilyov ENU*, (4). https://doi.org/10.32523/2789-4320-2022-4-11-25.

Republic of Botswana. (2009). Overview of PPPs in Botswana, Ministry of Finance, Government of Botswana. Available from: https://www.finance.gov.bw/index.php?Itemid=401&option=com_content&view=article&id=259&catid=13. Date of Access: 23, February 2023.

Rotter, J. P & Özbek, N. (2010). Private-Public Partnerships (PPP): Collaborating for a Sustainable Business in Sweden. Swedish University of Agricultural Sciences Faculty of Natural Resources and Agricultural Sciences Department of Economics (Master's Thesis), Uppsala.

Saunders, M.N., Lewis, P. & Thornhill, A. (2012). *Research Methods for Business*, 6th Edition, Pearson Professional Limited, UK.

Santos, G. (2019). Road Transport Infrastructure Funding through Use of Public-Private Partnerships, *Transport Reviews,* Vol. 35(2), doi: 10.1080/01441647.2015.1017025.

Estache, A & Saussier, S. (2014). Public Private Partnerships and Efficiency: A Short Assessment, Economics of Public-Private Partnerships Chair Institute of Business Administration, EPPP DP No. 2014-06.

Schutt, R. K. (2011). *Investigating the Social World: The Process and Practice of Research*, 7th Edition, SAGE Publications, pp. 320 - 357.

Uddin S, Ong S, Matous P. (2023) Stakeholder Engagement Variability Across Public, Private and Public-Private Partnership Projects: A Data-Driven Network-based Analysis. *PLoS ONE* Vol. 18(1), e0279916. doi: 10.1371/journal.pone.0279916.

Solomon, O. B., Srinath, P., Chika, U & Lei, Z. (2014). Challenges of Implementing Infrastructure Megaprojects through Public-Private Partnerships in Nigeria: A Case Study of Road Infrastructure.

Trotsenko, O. (2019). Digital mechanization of PPPs in the Russian agro-industrial complex. *Advances in Intelligent Systems Research*, Vol. 167. International Scientific and Practical Conference "Digital agriculture - development strategy" (ISPC 2019), Atlantis Press.

United Nations Economic Commission for Europe. (2008). Guidebook on Promoting Good Governance in Public-Private Partnerships. Geneva - Switzerland: United Nations Publications. Date of Access: 10th June 2017.

Vadali, N., Tiwari, A.P. & Rajan A, T. (2014). Effect of the Political Environment on PPPs Projects: Evidence from Road Projects. *Journal of Infrastructure Development*, Vol. 6(2), pp.145.

Verger, A. and Moschetti, M. (2016). Public-Private Partnerships as an Education Policy Approach: Multiple Meanings, Risks and Challenges. *Education Research and Foresight Series*, No. 19. Paris, UNESCO. https://en.unesco.org/node/268820.

Verhoest, K., Petersen, O.H., Scherrer, W. & Soecipto, R.M. (2015). How Do Governments Support the Development of Public Private Partnerships? Measuring and Comparing PPP Governmental Support in 20 European Countries. *Transport Reviews*, Vol. 35(2), p.118–139.

Yan, L. & Xinyu W. (2023). Game Analysis of Social Capital Violations and Government Regulation in Public–Private Partnership Risk Sharing. January 2023. doi: 10.1002/sys.21657.

Yergali, A., Kasiya, K., Kemel, M., Assel, U., Almagul, N. & Ismailova, D. (2019). Innovative Development of Entrepreneurship in Kazakhstan within the Framework of the PPPs, *Revista Espacios*, Vol. 40(20), p. 7.

Yong, H. K. (2010). *Public-Private Partnerships Policy and Practice: A Reference Guide*. London, Commonwealth Secretariat.

Ypi, L. (2016). Political Commitment and Value of Partisanship. *The American Political Review*, Vol. 110 (3), pp. 601–613.

Zou, W., Kumaraswamy, M., Chung, J., & Wong, J. (2014). Identifying the Critical Success Factors for Relationship Management in PPP Projects. *International Journal of Project Management*, 32(2), 265–274. doi:10.1016/j.ijproman.2013.05.004

Part II

THE DYNAMIC WORLD OF PUBLIC-PRIVATE PARTNERSHIPS

Chapter 6

Public-Private Partnerships in Botswana

Thekiso Molokwane

Countries in Africa south of the Sahara continue to face daunting service delivery and infrastructure challenges. Africa is lagging behind in infrastructure development, with 60% of its population lacking access to modern infrastructure (African Development Bank, 2018). Many governments and public administrations still operate in an old development paradigm and do not have the capacity to mobilise the full range of stakeholders and introduce the wide spectrum of policies (Glemarec & Puppim De Oliveira, 2012, p. 201) permitting for innovative financings of public services and infrastructure. The lack of service delivery differs from one country to another and is evident in different sectors such as access to water, electricity, sanitation and roads.

The picture in Africa is however not all doom and gloom. There are success stories that have been documented. Sub-Saharan Africa enjoyed relatively rapid growth over the decade leading to the 2009 global financial crisis. After many years of poor performance, it grew faster than developed countries between 1995 and 2005 (Robinson, Gaertner & Papageorgiou, 2011, p. 21). Following deep shortfalls in national budgets, African governments are turning to public-private partnerships (PPPs) to bridge the financing gap. Foreign investments supported by collaborative co-financing with development finance institutions offer the prospect of necessary capital to finance industries, build infrastructure, provide social amenities and create jobs (Africa Renewal, 2018, p. 7). South Africa and Nigeria may be Africa's biggest economies, according to the International Monetary Fund, but thanks to public-private partnerships (PPPs), Morocco, Rwanda, Côte d'Ivoire and a few other smaller countries can boast world-class infrastructure (Africa Renewal, 2018, p. 4).

An important factor for the success of PPPs is good governance with regard to transparency in procurement. Furthermore, governments should put in place appropriate legislative frameworks, incentive frameworks and guarantees to investors, as well as regulations to protect projects' end users and/or consumers (African Development Bank, 2018). By 2018, the African Development Bank estimated that Africa's infrastructure funding gap had grown to reach USD 170 billion annually (Bavier, 2018). Narrowing sub-Saharan Africa's infrastructure gap could have a big effect on growth. Closing the infrastructure gap relative to the best performers in the world could increase growth of GDP per capita by 2.6% per year (Africa Renewal, 2018, p. 3).

PPP refers to an arrangement where the public and private sectors enter into a contract, where the private sector finances, designs, builds and operates an infrastructure for a period. After the concessional period, the facility may or may not be transferred back to the public depending on the PPP model adopted (Osei-Kyei, Tam & Ma, 2020; Osei-Kyei, Chan & Trinh, 2019; Tshombe & Molokwane, 2016, p. 72). However, even as PPPs continue to change the face of Africa through mega projects, experts are urging African governments to be careful and learn from failed PPPs when signing on to new partnerships (Africa Renewal, 2018, p. 3). To determine which procurement method is best for government, a comparison of the procurement options is undertaken in the early stages of the procurement process. The criterion used to select the optimal procurement method is known as Value for Money (VFM) although the criteria used to ascertain which method or which bid offers the best deal for government are determined under PPP policy and this varies significantly between nations (Regan, 2014, p. 8).

The aim is to generate greater efficiency and synergies; to increase financial revenues; and to reduce deficits (Tshombe & Molokwane, 2016, p. 73). Botswana is widely reputed for its transparency, openness and overall good governance. The 2020 Ibrahim Index of African Governance ranked Botswana 5th out of 54 countries in overall governance, the best-scoring country in Southern Africa. The African Development Bank's 2021 Country Policy and Institutional Assessment ranked Botswana 2nd out of 13 countries in Southern Africa under the governance cluster with a score of 4.8. The government has consistently committed itself to undertaking some of its projects through the PPP mode as evidenced in the budget speeches by the Ministers of Finance over the past few years.

For instance, in the budget speech delivered by the Honourable Minister of Finance Peggy Serame on 6 February 2023, the minister mentioned that in the 2023/2024 financial year the government of Botswana would significantly increase the development budget as it strives to fill infrastructure gaps and implement projects that are necessary to unlock constraints to economic growth. She indicated that the budget would continue to address expenditure inefficiencies and weaknesses in revenue collection by strengthening tax audit capabilities, and leveraging on the PPP and Development Manager

Model approaches (Republic of Botswana, 2023a). Despite the above-mentioned strong governance record, Botswana's economy remains largely undiversified. Over the past decades, the country has followed a natural resource-based growth model that is highly dependent on the diamond mining industry and a large public sector (African Development Bank, 2022, p. 1). This chapter seeks to answer specific research questions. These include: (a) What is Botswana's development strategy? (b) Is Botswana's institutional framework for development still beneficial to the country? and (c) Are the country's PPP processes and institutional responsibilities relevant to the current economic challenges?

PUBLIC-PRIVATE PARTNERSHIPS

Cyclical economic downturns and scarcity of finance experienced by governments compelled them to seek alternative ways of financing economic development. Consequently, the public and private sectors began to form partnerships to fund economic and social infrastructure projects. The process and justification for using PPPs for economic infrastructure is relatively straightforward as there is a bankable revenue stream, yet this is not necessarily the case for social infrastructure also for economic infrastructure which built in suburb or remote area which not generate feasible demand yet (Maryoui, 2013). A PPP, refers to a contractual arrangement between public (national, state, provincial, or local) and private entities. Under this arrangement, there is technology transfer predominantly from the private to the public sector. Risk is also allocated to the partner who is best placed to handle it (Asian Development Bank, 2012, p. 2) although preference in developing countries is to allocate more risk to the private party.

A PPP aims to deliver improved services for customers and better VFM for taxpayers through optimal risk allocation, management synergies, encouragement of innovation, efficient asset utilisation, and asset management with a whole-of-life-cycle approach (Asian Development Bank, 2012, p. 3; Delmon, 2010). The private sector will seek a secure revenue stream to ensure repayment of debt/ investment (and hence lower interest rates) and profitability over time. PPPs involve both construction and maintenance of new infrastructure (Greenfield) assets as well as management of existing public sector assets (Brownfield) (Asian Development Bank, 2012, p. 3). In a typical PPP, the private sector brings its capital and technical capabilities to accomplish specific public sector infrastructure project in association with related public sector agencies, thus sharing the project risks and benefits. The benefits for the private sector are usually in the form of toll collected from users of furnished facilities or in the form of payments directly from the government or public sector client (Soomro and Zhang, 2011, p. 62).

There is no universal norm as to the most appropriate approach to PPP. That analysis needs to be made on a country-by-country, sector-by-sector and project by-project basis. The model is therefore not meant to be normative; that is, it does not identify which PPP option would be the most appropriate, most efficient or most effective nor does it try to be comprehensive (nor uncontroversial). Instead, it serves three key purposes. It:

- facilitates the task of practitioners when seeking to identify relevant lessons learned from other projects, sectors, countries, legal systems and cultures;
- helps mapping, referencing and analytical studies by providing a practical, descriptive nomenclature; and
- assists in the description of a given PPP structure, e.g. for policy or decision makers without the confusion of political, nationalistic or cultural labels often associated with other terminology (Delmon 2010, p. 5).

Despite the many proven successes, practical experience has shown that establishing PPPs is not as easy as it was considered by many governments and thus history is full of hundreds of failure cases representing almost every nation and every sector. PPPs are complex institutional arrangements and public and private sectors are not the only stakeholders in real (Soomro and Zhang, 2011, p. 62).

PPP Mechanisms

There are various PPP mechanisms that have been established by both the public and private partners over the years. Scholars in the field of PPPs have equally analysed these mechanisms. This study discusses selected mechanisms that include: VFM; risk-sharing; financing and contract term. The mechanisms discussed below are not exhaustive.

Value for Money

Contemporary researchers in the area of PPPs accentuate VFM as a core component in PPPs (Molokwane, 2015, p. 40). Value for money does not simply equate to selecting the cheapest bid or lowest price for an asset; it means opting for the best long-term solution for service delivery. It involves analysing the total long-term costs (life-cycle costs) of service delivery and evaluating the concomitant benefits to the public at large (Partnerships Kosovo, 2009m p.8). Explaining this analysis further the Economist Intelligence Unit (2014, p. 56) asserts that VfM analysis refers to an analysis that compares the benefits of contracting infrastructure projects through PPP with the benefits of traditional public sector procurement and investment. A relatively broad assessment of whether a project is good VFM takes into account factors such as urban design outcomes and the impact on the environment and communities (p. 26). According to Hayford and Utz (2006, p. 3, 4), VFM drivers for privately financed projects (PFPs) are typically stated to be the following: risk transfer; whole-of-life costing; innovation and asset utilisation.

Risk Allocation

The primary objective of any contract is to allocate the risk between the parties (Molokwane, 2015, p. 43). Risk allocation refers to the distribution of proportional risk to parties in a contract (Economist Intelligence Unit, 2014, p. 56). Among the most important benefits of PPPs are the achievable efficiency gains and substantial risk allocation to the private sector rather than just access to private finance (Asian Development Bank, 2012, p. 27). It is critical to allocate responsibility for dealing with the consequences of each risk to one of the participants in the contract, or agreeing to deal with the risk through a specified mechanism that may involve sharing of risk (p. 28). Risks generally borne by the public sector in traditional construction or turnkey contracts are distributed between the public and private partners. Notwithstanding, PPP projects are arguably more efficient than standard government forms of procurement because certain risks in which the private sector has expertise, such as design construction, allocation of capital or industrial relations management, are transferred to the private sector contractor (Quick, 2003, p.2). However, a PPP does not necessarily mean that the private partner assumes all the risks, or even the major share of risks linked to the project. The most important principle of risk allocation arrangements in PPPs is that risks are disaggregated, quantified, and allocated to the party best able to manage each risk (Asian Development Bank, 2012, p. 28).

Project Financing

Over the years, PPPs have developed a distinctive form of debt financing termed ‘project finance’ that is ideally suited to providing the kind of funding needed for new, large, long-term, single-purpose assets described. The first notable element of project finance is that lenders’ assessments of risk rely entirely on the future cash flow that a project is expected to generate throughout its entire operational lifetime (Turley & Semple, 2013, p. 2). A private sector party typically generally raises project funds both in equity and debt finance for a PPP. The concessionaire is usually owned by one or more equity investors. Some of these shareholders may be contractors in the consortium, carrying out construction, design or facilities management work on the project (Jang, 2010, p.19; Molokwane, 2015, p. 44). Access to this private sector finance allows increased investment in public infrastructure, as compared to raising or budgeting additional funds. For this reason, governments worldwide have involved the private sector in provisioning infrastructure for energy generation and distribution, transport, telecommunications and water (Turley & Semple, 2013, p. 1).

Contract Term

PPPs give access to additional sources of long-term investment finance, private sector analysis, innovation, incentives and project life-cycle management (Mmolainyane, 2020, p.75). Long-term PPP contracts usually range from 25 to 50 years (Asian Development Bank, 2008, p. 36). A PPP contract's length typically extends the entire economic life of the asset, including the operation stage. This ensures that the private sector partner evaluates asset development in a whole life-cycle context. The contractor (the private partner) will then manipulate the asset in innovative and cost-effective ways over its entire economic life. In this way, both the cost of the project and VFM are maximised (Jang, 2010, p.18; Molokwane, 2015, p. 43). As these types of PPPs have long-term implications for future generations, their selection requires especially robust analysis and justification (European Court of Auditors, 2018, p.35). It must be noted however that literature on PPPs has a serious deficit on short-term PPPs. These types of PPPs exist to serve the public sector in comparatively short-term as compared to long-term PPPs. These may constitute projects or services ranging typically between 1 to 10 years. Some of the PPP arrangements available for implementation by government include: affermage or lease contracts; management contracts; service contracts; and some of the BOT arrangements (Molokwane, 2019, p. 162).

BOTSWANA'S REGULATORY AND INSTITUTIONAL FRAMEWORK FOR DEVELOPMENT

Botswana has a politically stable environment, underpinned by prudent economic management and strong institutions. As a result of rigorous economic management and strong political institutions, the country has managed to transform itself from one of the poorest countries at independence into an upper-middle-income country, characterised by good governance and macroeconomic management (Africa Development Bank, 2022, p. 1). Since independence, the government of Botswana committed itself to building a strong regulatory and institutional framework for development. Regulatory and institutional frameworks usually shape the scope and efficacy of interventions. Institutions, and the laws, regulations and policies they produce, define the 'rules of the game' that influence the actions and behaviour of economic actors and policymakers (Williamson, 2000). The quality of the regulatory framework is correlated to the investments in infrastructure in Africa (African Development Bank, 2018).

In all sectors of Botswana's national economy, laws, public policies and institutions were established. For purpose of scope, this chapter does not explore frameworks from all sectors. The discussion below describes the trajectory of the country's regulatory and institutional frameworks. Transitional Plan for Social and Economic Development was the first development plan in Botswana designed to guide the economic and social development of the country during a two-year period following independence (Lekgowe, 2016). The first National Development Plan followed between 1968 and 1973 and it was set out to foster local participation in commerce.

The government then established the Arable Land Development Programme with the aim of assisting small subsistence farmers to expand the production of basic food grains, legumes and sunflower in order to achieve self-sufficiency at both household and national levels and most importantly to raise rural revenues and improve income distribution (Lekgowe, 2016). In 1998 the policy on Small, Medium and Micro Enterprise was adopted in recognition of the numerous problems SMMEs faced in Botswana. The Local Enterprise Agency was established in 2007 to provide support services to SMMEs. This regulatory framework supported and emphasised the creation of an enabling environment, which in turn promotes the ability of Botswana to exercise greater ownership, management and participation in the economy.

Still on the SMME front, the government of Botswana relentlessly searched for, and introduced, business development interventions during the 1980s in an attempt to resuscitate the almost dead SMME sector. These included the 1984 Industrial Development Policy, an import substitution strategy that encouraged local firms to produce for the domestic market, and the FAP in 1982 whose objective was to provide direct government financial assistance to small-scale manufacturers, and to promote production and employment creation. Whilst the Selebi Phikwe Regional Development Programme was established to stimulate economic development in Selebi Phikwe and surrounding areas, the Integrated Field Services (IFS) was established to provide a training programme for SMMEs in recordkeeping, costing, business planning, marketing, buying, and stock control skills (Monyake, Setibi, Ditshweu & Mmereki, 2019; Monyake, Mmereki, Boy, & Kuruba, 2017). Other strategies and programmes included the:

- Small Business Promotion Agency (World Bank and BIDBPA Report, 2012);

- Industrial Development Policy and the Citizen Construction Industry Fund (Monyake, Setibi, Ditshweu & Mmereki, 2019; (Monyake, Mmereki, Boy, & Kuruba, 2017);
- Botswana Excellence Strategy;
- Sustainable Development Goals of the United Nations;
- Agenda 2063 of the African Union;
- Vienna Programme of Action.

Some of the policies introduced towards economic development include the Financial Assistance Policy (FAP) and the Localization Policy. The FAP was launched under the management of the NDB in 1982, with the intention of financing citizen-owned projects (Botswana, 2012). The Economic Empowerment and Privatization policy was established to reduce competition for citizen entrepreneurs in areas of the economy that the Botswana government considered to be easy investment areas (Republic of Botswana, 2012). In March 2010, the Economic Diversification Drive (EDD) was introduced. The policy relied on local procurement, the use of preference margins and citizen economic empowerment strategies, to promote local production and consumption (UNCTAD, 2016).

Public procurement in Botswana is the responsibility of the Ministry of Finance. Initially, procurement was done through the Central Tender Board. This board was replaced with the Public Procurement Disposal Board established in July 2002 (Molokwane, Bhata & Botlhale, 2019, p. 135). Its main function was to adjudicate and award tenders. The board ensured that public procurement entities enforced the preferences and reservation schemes when making procurement decisions (PPADB, 2003). Public procurement in Botswana was decentralised under the regulation of a new Procurement Act that was put into effect in April 2022. Procurement is now done at the Ministry level with the new procuring authority, Public Procurement Regulatory Authority (International Trade Administration U.S. Department of Commerce, 2023).

Economic diversification has always been a major policy objective of the Government of Botswana and has been a key determinant of both macro- and micro-economic policy. It is so important that the Ninth National Development Plan (NDP 9) covering the period from April 2003 to March 2009, adopted as its theme 'international competitive sustainable economic diversification' (Nkwe, 2012, p. 30). Following the 2008 global economic downturn, the government of Botswana introduced the Economic Stimulus Programme (ESP). The objective of the ESP was for the government to use its expenditure to expand the economy through accelerated economic diversification, while creating employment opportunities in the country including growth in the private sector. The programme was to involve increased public spending on short-, medium- and longer-term initiatives (Republic of Botswana, 2015).

PPPs became of interest to the government of Botswana as has been the case elsewhere in the region and beyond. PPPs are a recent phenomenon in Botswana, having been first mentioned in the Privatisation Policy of Botswana of 2000 and later in the country's Privatisation Master Plan of 2005. The government announced through the 2002/2003 budget speech and NDP 9 that PPPs would be used extensively as a form of procuring and financing infrastructure projects in the public sector (Molokwane, 2015, p. 27). In June 2005, the Public Enterprises Evaluation and Privatization Agency carried out a 'study to review the existing institutional and legal framework for PPP in Botswana' (Republic of Botswana, 2005, p. 45) in which the establishment of a clear policy on the implementation of PPPs, the establishment of a legal and regulatory framework that promotes commercial and innovative approaches to service delivery, and developing competitive bidding procedures and guidelines specific to PPPs were recommended (p. 45). PPPs are regulated through the Public Private Partnership Policy and Implementation Framework, which was introduced in 2009.

The current National Development Plan, that is, NDP 11 of Botswana, stipulates that the adoption of PPP will assist the government in project implementation by involving the private sector in the financing and implementation of various projects. This will augment the resources for undertaking projects in the country and minimise the risks to the government associated with the implementation of such projects. Despite the huge potential, uptake of PPPs has been slow due to a number of factors including: lack of experience in PPP implementation; weakness of the regulatory framework; and capacity constraints. The effectiveness of a government's PPP policy and delivery schedule is influenced by the effectiveness of its institutions, both formal and informal (Regan, 2014, p. 61).

In relation to doing business, the government of Botswana undertook a number of measures during NDP 10 in a bid to improve on the climate of doing business in the country. These included: the development of the Doing Business Roadmap; review and development of laws, policies and strategies; and strengthening structures for investment promotion. In this regard, the government reviewed the Industrial Development Policy, National Policy on Agricultural Development, National Trade Policy, and Co-operative Societies Act. In addition, the Special Economic Zones, National Quality Policy, Cooperative Transformation Strategy and the Entrepreneurial Policy were developed in order to improve the country's competitiveness, and promote economic growth, diversification, and sustainable job creation. Despite the efforts made to improve the country's rankings under the Doing Business and

Global Competiveness reports, some indicators for these rankings continued to drop, which had the potential to discourage potential investors (Republic of Botswana, 2016, p. 44).

POTENTIAL FOR ECONOMIC DEVELOPMENT THROUGH PPPs

Being a mineral-endowed continent, African countries have the potential to develop their economies through the implementation of diverse economic strategies. Challenges, however, seem to hold back the chances for economic development over realisation of opportunities. Two of these challenges are uncertainty and a lack of political will that act as barriers to successful PPPs. In addition, many public institutions lack capacity, which stokes fears of financial risk for private investors (Africa Renewal, 2018, p. 5). Factors working against successful PPPs include: inadequate legal and regulatory framework for PPPs; lack of technical skills to manage PPP programmes and projects; unfavourable investor perception of country risk; Africa's limited role in global trade and investment; small market size; limited infrastructure; and limited financial markets (p. 3). Regrettably, there aforesaid challenges are true in the case of Botswana.

Not much has changed in the country in relation to the implementation of PPP projects since the adoption of the PPP implementation and policy framework in 2009. The process has been providing public infrastructure and services through PPP at a snail's pace. The implementation body, the PPP Unit in the ministry of Finance, is still moderately staffed perhaps due to the size of the PPP sector in the country's economy. The Unit primarily offers technical assistance to line ministries intending to procure infrastructure through PPPs. The PPP activity in the country remains low with a few projects under implementation and some in the pipeline. Botswana is a country renowned not only for its stunning 8.7% average economic growth rate achieved between its independence in 1966 and 2008 but also for its remarkable record for good governance and prudent macroeconomic and natural resource management.

Minerals, and particularly diamond exports, have fuelled this astronomical growth and the government has sought to redistribute wealth equitably to the citizenry through investments in health, education and infrastructure development (Sikazwe and Hasan 2016; Tsie, 1998). Botswana is especially big on infrastructure development. Over the last 10 years, the Government of Botswana (GoB) has consistently invested between 24% and 31% of its total budget in infrastructure through its aptly named 'Development Budget'. This investment translates into some US$1.3 billion in 2008, growing to just over US$2 billion in 2018.

Annually, not more than 12% of these amounts are from development partners or foreign sources—the government has put its Pula where its heart is: in infrastructure (Sikazwe and Hasan, 2016). Notwithstanding, Botswana has huge infrastructure needs. The government faces challenges in the delivery of public services due to an infrastructure funding gap, including new investments, their maintenance, and operational obligations. Existing infrastructure requires constant upgrading to deliver public services more efficiently and effectively, and to a greater number of the population. Under the National Development Plan 11, for example, development expenditure of over P100 billion (USD 8.36 billion) was budgeted for the plan period 2017/18–2023/24. The bulk of this was to fund infrastructure projects in areas such as water, energy, tourism, agriculture, education and health, priority being given to the maintenance of existing infrastructure (African Development Bank, 2022, p. 2).

Hence, the few PPP transactions procured so far were done under the repealed Public Procurement and Asset Disposal (PPAD) Act. One of the successful examples is in the energy sector—Orapa and Mmashoro IPP that was developed by Karoo Sustainable Energy as a 90MW Simple Cycle Gas Turbine Power Plant. The project's CAPEX was US$104 million and financial closure was reached in 2011. The PPAD Act has now been replaced by the Public Procurement Act 2021. The new Act has taken on board some aspects of PPP. Sixteen projects are presently in the PPP project pipeline and these are at different levels of readiness. The pipeline includes a wastewater project, water transfer scheme, SEZ common facilities, fuel storage facility, prisoners' rehabilitation facility and an agro-commercial development project. There is huge potential for PPP in Botswana as the government has made a commitment to extensively use this as a means of procuring and financing infrastructure projects in the public sector to ensure sustainable investment in infrastructure. It is also a means of sustaining sound public financial management and reducing the pressure on the national budget (African Development Bank, 2022, p. 2).

Botswana's economic base remains narrow. Consequently, the benefits of growth have not sufficiently trickled down. There is a high level of multidimensional poverty at 20.8% (2020), high inequality at 53.3% [Gini Index 2015] and high unemployment at 26.0% (2021). In the absence of a robust and strong private sector, the government continues to provide some public services that ordinarily would be left in the hands of the private sector. In order to respond to growing unemployment and prepare for the post-diamond era, the country will need to implement a number of structural reforms aimed at shifting away from a public sector-led economy, and intensifying efforts to diversify the sources of growth, thereby curbing unemployment and income inequalities (African Development Bank, 2022, p. 1).

Infrastructure Demand

Having long ago realised the need to diversify the economy away from traditional mineral exports, infrastructure development has been identified as a key enabler of the government's EDD (Sikazwe & Hasan, 201). Infrastructure made a net contribution of just over 2 percentage points to Botswana's improved per capita growth performance in recent years. Raising the country's infrastructure endowment to that of the region's middle-income countries could boost annual growth by about 1.2 percentage points. Botswana has made significant infrastructure progress in recent years, spanning the transport, water and sanitation, power, and mobile telephony sectors.

But the country still faces a number of important infrastructure challenges. The most pressing is in the power sector, where the country is economically and financially exposed to a lack of generation capacity and insufficient power supply, leaving the economy vulnerable to power price shocks and load shedding. Botswana's international transport connections and Internet connectivity also lag behind those of comparable countries. Botswana's overall resource envelope of $800 million per year surpasses its $785 million needs estimate. Nevertheless, it loses $68 million a year to inefficiencies and faces a funding gap of $305 million per year, entirely in the power sector, traceable to the quality of spending decisions. Botswana will be in a good position to meet its infrastructure goals if it can reduce inefficiencies, increase public sector receipts, and attract more public funding (World Bank, 2021).

Domestic Capital and Debt Funding

There is substantial capital to finance PPPs in Botswana. Notably, the capital markets in Botswana are mature but small. Botswana market capitalisation accounted for US$3.216 billion in December 2022 (CEIC Data, 2023). Further to this, there are eight domestic banks operating in a small but well-regulated market; in terms of investment funds, the Non-Bank Financial Institutions Regulatory Authority currently supervises six locally incorporated and authorised investment funds, which consist of 23 unit portfolios of which 7 are dormant. Of the 16 unit portfolios operational, 4 are money market funds, 5 are equity funds, 4 are asset allocation/balanced funds and 3 invest predominantly in fixed income instruments (bonds) (NBRIRA, 2023).

PPP Projects in the Pipeline in Botswana

Of the 16 projects in the pipeline in Botswana, three are at the procurement of private party stage. The three include: Reclamation and Treatment of Gaborone Wastewater for Potable Use; the Ikaegeng XTL Project, which entails converting coal to liquids in order to guarantee oil products security for Botswana; and the Tshele Hills Project which entails construction of bulk petroleum products storage tank farm and ancillary installations near the Tshele Hills in Rasesa, Kgatleng District. The first project is in the water sector whilst the latter two are in the energy sector. Seven projects of the 16 in the pipeline are at the feasibility study stage.

These include the construction and maintenance of Magistrate Court in Serowe village; construction and maintenance of student residences at Botswana International University of Science and Technology in the town of Palapye; the Chobe-Zambezi Water Transfer Scheme which entails construction and operation of water supply pipeline from Kazungula to Moralane village; construction and maintenance of head office accommodation and staff housing for Botswana Prison Service in Gaborone; construction and maintenance of a prisoner rehabilitation centre in Lobatse; construction of a railway line from Mmamabula to Lephalale-SA for transportation of coal; and construction of a railway line from Mosetse village to Kazungula (Republic of Botswana, 2023b).

Three of the above-mentioned seven projects are in the sector of building infrastructure (office accommodation) while two are in the transport, and one in the water sector. The remaining nine projects are at the procurement of consultant stage and these include: the construction of housing units for secondary school teachers across the country; the Zambezi Agro-Commercial Development project which entails construction and operation of irrigation infrastructure in Pandamatenga; the construction of Security Wing, Farm and Staff Houses at Sepopa project which entails the construction and maintenance of a prison farm and staff houses in Sepopa village; construction and maintenance of the Francistown-Nata road; construction and maintenance of the Maun-Mohembo road; construction of a State Theatre facility for performing arts; construction/expansion of the Botswana Police Headquarters at the Government Enclave in Gaborone; construction of offices, a laboratory, confiscation warehouse, and a drug incineration facility; and the development of an Electronic National Identification System (e-NIS) project (Republic of Botswana, 2023b). The aforementioned projects are in the sectors of: education; agriculture; building infrastructure (farm and office accommodation), creative industry and information and communications technology. There is currently no PPP project that is at the project initiation stage in Botswana.

WAY FORWARD AND CONCLUSION

For PPPs to become an effective instrument through improvements in service delivery, efficiency and development impact over and above those attainable through public procurement, it is important that the public sector is able to: i) correctly identify and select projects where PPPs would be viable, ii) structure contracts to ensure an appropriate pricing and transfer of risks to private partners, iii) establish a comprehensive and transparent fiscal accounting and reporting standard for PPPs, and iv) establish legal, regulatory and monitoring frameworks that ensure appropriate pricing and quality of service. In other words, it is necessary that countries have in place the institutional capacity to create, manage, evaluate and monitor PPPs for conceptualisation (Jomo, Chowdhury, Sharma & Platz, 2016, p. 16).

Training of public servants both at the Ministry of Finance and line Ministries on PPPs is still requisite. The country has a great economic development track record; however, notable deceleration on this front has been discernible. Multiple factors known and unknown contributed to this. Amongst the most conspicuous, were the 2008 economic recession and the Covid-19 pandemic whose impact was and is being felt globally from the year 2020 to date. The government of Botswana has over the years expressed its interest to diversity its economy. It is critical as such for the government of Botswana to continue exploring alternative—innovative—ways of financing public infrastructure and services.

That most of the infrastructure that government provides is social is age-old factor. The country must note that PPP projects in sectors considered social such as education and health have been undertaken across the globe. Benchmarking against countries that have provided such projects, successfully for that matter, is imperative. For Botswana to realise substantial progress in its infrastructure development, the country must make a deliberate decision to upscale its PPP projects. What must be prioritised in this decision nonetheless is among others, enhancing VfM and sustainable financing.

REFERENCES

Africa Renewal. (2017). Partnerships giving Africa a new look: Private sector invests in mega projects. United Nations Department of Information, pp. 3–5, 7.

African Development Bank.2022. Project: Public Private Partnership Capacity Strengthening Project (PPP-CSP) Country: Republic of Botswana, Appraisal Report, p. 1.

African Development Bank. (2018). Thematic discussion I: Public-private partnerships for infrastructure development in Africa, African Development Bank. Available from https://idev.afdb.org/sites/default/files/Evaluations/2020-03/PPP%20for%20Infrastructure%20development%20in%20Africa.pdf.

Asian Development Bank. 2008. Public Private Partnerships Handbook, pp. 27, 29, 36, 38. Available at: https://www.ADB.org/sites/default/files/institutional-document/31484/ public-private-partnership.pdf.

Asian Development Bank. (2012). Public–Private Partnership Operational Plan 2012–2020 Realizing the Vision for Strategy 2020: The Transformational Role of Public–Private Partnerships in Asian Development Bank Operations, Philippines, p. 2.

Bavier, J. 2018. Ten African nations face $1 trillion infrastructure funding gap. Reuters, [online]. Available at: https://www.reuters.com/article/ us-africa-infra structure/ten-african-nationsface-1-trillion-infrastructure-funding-gapidUSKBN1J T2AZ.

CEIC Data. (2023). Botswana Market Capitalisation. Available from: https://www .ceicdata.com/en/indicator/botswana/market-capitalization.

Delmon, J. (2010). Understanding Options for Public-Private Partnerships in Infrastructure: Sorting out the Forest from the Trees: Bot, Dbfo, Dcmf, and Concession, Lease . . . Policy Research Working Paper 5173, The World Bank.

European Court of Auditors. 2018. Public Private Partnerships in the EU: Widespread shortcomings and limited benefit, Special Report No. 09, p. 35.

Glemarec, Y & Puppim De Oliveira, J. A. 2012. The Role of the Visible Hand of Public Institutions in Creating a Sustainable Future, *Public Administration and Development*, 32, pp. 201, 202.

Hayford, O & Utz, C. 2006. Successfully allocating and negotiating a PPP Contract, 6th Annual Private Public Partnerships Summit 16–17 May 2006,1- 4, 11,Sydney, Australia, pp. 3, 4.

International Trade Administration U.S. Department of Commerce. (2023). Botswana - Country Commercial Guide. Available from: https://www.trade.gov/country-commercial-guides/botswana-selling-public-sector#:~:text=Public%20procurement%20in%20Botswana%20is,Procurement%20Regulatory%20Authority%20(PPRA).

Jang, G.W. (2010). *The Bids-Evaluation Decision Model Development and Application for Public Private Partnerships transport Projects: A Project Risks Modelling Framework*, Colorado State University, pp. 43.

Jomo, K. S., Chowdhury, A., Sharma, K & Platz, D, 2016.Public-Private Partnerships and the 2030 Agenda for Sustainable Development: Fit for purpose? Department of Economic & Social Affairs, DESA Working Paper No. 148 ST/ESA/2016/DWP/148, p. 16.

Lekgowe, G. R. (2016). The Trajectory of Citizen Economic Empowerment in Botswana After Fifty Years: An Endless Road of Hapless Policies. *University of Botswana Law Journal,* Vol.22, pp. 138–171.

Maryoui, L. (2013). A Comparative Analysis of PPP Financing Mechanisms for Infrastructure Projects. PPP International Conference 2013 Body of Knowledge Public Private Partnerships University of Central Lancashire, Preston, UK 18–20 March 2013 ISBN: 9781901922912.

Mmolainyane, L. (2020). Financing Public Private Partnerships (PPPs) in Botswana through the Capital Market, BIDPA Working Paper 75. Botswana Institute for Development Policy Analysis, Gaborone, p.75.

Molokwane, T. (2019). Short Term Public-Private Partnerships—A starting point for Botswana in Sebola, M. P & Molokwane, T. (eds.). *4th Annual Conference of*

International Conference on Public Administration and Development Alternatives (IPADA), Southern Sun, OR Tambo International Airport, South Africa from 3rd to 5th July, 2019, pp. 159–167.

Molokwane, T., Bhata, T & Botlhale, E. K. (2019). Reforming Public Procurement Though Public Private Partnerships in Botswana, in Sebola, M.P., Molokwane, T & Kayuni, H (eds.), *Governance, Reforms and Public Affairs,* Batalea Publishers, South Africa, pp. 131–145.

Molokwane, T. (2015). *The Impact of Public Private Partnerships on the Delivery of Water Service in Botswana: The Case of Lobatse Management Centre*, Published Ph.D. Thesis, NorthWest University. South Africa, pp. 27, 40.

Monyake, J. M., Setibi, G., Ditshweu, T and Mmereki, R. (2019). Entrepreneurship Development As A Strategic Tool For Poverty Alleviation: Lessons for Botswana, *The 5th International Conference on Business Innovation and Growth (2019),* Gaborone, Botswana, pp.584–604.

Monyake, S.M.G., Mmereki, R.N. Boy, R.L. and Kuruba, G. (2017). Tourism Product Diversification: The Future Economic Stimulant for Botswana. *International Journal of Applied Services Marketing Perspectives*. Pezzottaite Journals, Vol.6(4), pp. 3200–3212.

NBRIRA. (2023). Investment Institutions, Non-Bank Financial Institutions Regulatory Authority. Available from: https://www.nbfira.org.bw/investment-institutions.

Nkwe, N. (2012). Role of SMES in Botswana, *American International Journal of Contemporary Research*, Vol. 2(8), p. 30.

Osei-Kyei, R., Tam, T and Ma, M. (2020). Effective Strategies for Developing Retirement Village Public—Private Partnership, *International Journal of Housing Markets and Analysis*, Emerald Publishing Limited.

Osei-Kyei, R., Chan, A.P.C. and Trinh, M.T. (2019). Retirement Village Development for the Elderly: Applying the Concept of Public-Private Partnership. *Global Encyclopedia of Public Administration, Public Policy, and Governance*, Springer Nature Switzerland AG 2019.

Partnerships Kosovo. (2009). *Public Private Partnerships,* Ministry of Finance and Economy, USAID, p. 8.

PPADB. (2023). About PPADB. Available from: http://www.ppadb.co.bw/Pages/AboutPPADB.aspx#:~:text=The%20Public%20Procurement%20and%20Asset,award%20tenders%20for%20Central%20Government.

Regan, M. (2014). Value for Money in Project Procurement. *Faculty of Society and Design Publications.* Paper 120. http://epublications.bond.edu.au/fsd_papers/120.

Quick, R. (2003). *Long Term Ties: Managing PPP Contracts*, Public Infrastructure Bulletin, Vol.1 (2), Article 5, p. 2.

Republic of Botswana. (2023a). 2023 Budget Speech, delivered to the National Assembly on 6 the February 2023. Available from: www.finance.gov.bw.

Republic of Botswana. (2023b). List of Potential Public Private Partnership (PPP) Projects, Ministry of finance, Government of Botswana.

Republic of Botswana. (2016). National Development Plan 11, Vol. 1, Republic of Botswana, Government Printing and Publishing Services, pp. 44, 83.

Republic of Botswana. (2015). A Summary of the Economic Stimulus Programme (ESP): A Strategy for Employment and Growth, BWGovernment. Available from: https://www.facebook.com/BotswanaGovernment/posts/a-summary-of-the-economic-stimulus-programme-esp-a-strategy-for-employment-and-g/905619826187343/.

Republic of Botswana. (2012). *Government Paper no 1: The Citizen Economic Empowerment Policy,* Gaborone: Government of Botswana.

Republic of Botswana. (2005). Privatisation Master Plan, Gaborone, Ministry of Finance and Development Planning, Government of Botswana, Government Printer, p.158.

Robinson, D. O., Gaertner, M & Papageorgiou, C. (2011), Tanzania: Growth Acceleration and Increased Public Spending with Macroeconomic Stability in, Chuhan-Pole, C and Angwafo, M. (Eds.). *Yes Africa Can: Success Stories from a Dynamic Continent*, The World Bank, Washington, DC. p. 21.

Sikazwe, C. J and Hasan, S. M. Q. (2016). Ensuring Value for Money in Infrastructure Projects—The Botswana way, The World Procurement Framework, The World Bank.

Soomro, A. A and Zhang, X. (2011). An Analytical Review on Transportation Public Private Partnerships Failures, *International Journal of Sustainable Construction Engineering & Technology*, Vol 2(2), pp. 62, 63, 64.

The Economist Intelligence Unit. (2014). Evaluating the Environment for Public Private Partnerships in Asia-Pacific, The 2014 Infrascope, The Economist Intelligence Unit Ltd., and Asian Development Bank, pp. 56, 26.

Tsie, B. (1998). State and Development Policy in Botswana, in Hope Snr, K, R & Somolekae, G. (eds.) *Public Administration and Policy in Botswana*, Juta & Co. ltd.

Tshombe, L. M & Molokwane, T. (2016). An analysis of Public Private Partnership in Sub-Saharan Africa, *African Journal of Public Affairs* (AJPA), African Consortium of Public Administration, Vol. 9(2), June 2016, pp. 72–86.

Turley, L and Semple, A. (2013). Financing Sustainable Public Private Partnerships, Institute for Sustainable Development.

UNCTAD, 2016. *Trade Policy Framework - Botswana,* New York: United Nations.

Williamson, O. (2000). The New Institutional Economics: Taking Stock, Looking Ahead. *Journal of Economic Literature*, Vol. 38/3, pp. 595–613. Available from https://doi.org/10.1257/jel.38.3.595. Date of access: 18th December, 2022.

World Bank. (2021).Botswana's Infrastructure: A Continental Perspective, World Bank Open Knowledge Depository. Available from: https://openknowledge.worldbank.org/handle/10986/3655?show=full&locale-attribute=fr.

Chapter 7

The Drivers and Impediments of Public-Private Partnerships in Kenya

Joseph O. Obosi

The inability of the public sector to independently meet the increasing demand for infrastructure and services has prompted many governments to adopt public-private partnership (PPP) as an alternative strategy. In world-wide practices, however, there are mixed results and controversy in the application of PPP model (Hodge & Greve, 2017). Public-private partnership (PPP) can be defined as a 'more or less sustainable cooperation between public and private actors in which joint products and/or services are developed and in which risks, costs and profits are shared' (Klijn & Teisman, 2003). Fiscal constraints and growth in public project size and complexity have led governments to seek alternative policy tools to finance and deliver public services.

These include mechanisms such as privatisation and contracting out or intergovernmental agreements (Brown, Potoski & Van Slyke, 2006). The public-private partnership (PPP) model has been used to finance major infrastructure and urban renewal projects as well as provide professionalised services such as healthcare and education (Hodge & Greve, 2017). The PPP arrangement enables the public and private sectors to establish long-term cooperative relationships for producing goods and services. While there are different hybrid forms that render a single definition of PPP difficult, two common features include the participation of private organisations in the decision-making process and the existence of a contractual agreement between the two sectors to share risk (Hodge, Greve & Boardman, 2017).

Since the 1990s, PPPs have been widely adopted by governments around the world. In particular, developing countries in regions such as Latin America, Africa and Asia have begun to rely on PPPs to finance and develop local infrastructure projects (Turner, 2014). On the one hand, the lack of legal and regulatory systems, the lack of economic stability and the lack of governance institutions may act as significant impediments. However, tighter budgets and limited government capacity to build infrastructures and deliver public services may serve as incentives for public officials to look towards adopting PPP arrangements (Ismail & Harris, 2014). Moreover, international institutions such as the World Bank and the International Monetary Fund have directed financial assistance towards developing countries that is contingent upon the adoption of principles such as market liberalisation and the development of effective governance institutions (Jutting, 1999).

Despite increasing private sector participation in developing countries, there is a need for more systematic assessment of the factors that influence the adoption and implementation of PPPs in the context of such regions (Osei-Kyei & Chan, 2017). PPPs became popular due to the increasing demand by citizens of different countries for quality and affordable services in sectors such as transport, water and sewerage, telecommunications, power, and social services. These demands could not be fully met by the public sector alone, hence the adoption of the arrangements.

There are different types of PPP arrangements which include: Build-Operate-Transfer (BOT): the private sector institution finances, builds, maintains and operates a facility for a given period of time and recoups its investment by collecting tolls during the concession period; Build-Own-Operate (BOO): the private entity will finance, build and operate the project but there will be no transfer back to the government; Build-Own-Operate-Transfer (BOOT): the private sector builds, owns, operates and eventually transfers the PPP project to the public sector after an agreed period of time; Build-Transfer-Operate (BTO): the private organisation finances, builds and upon completion, transfers the ownership to the public sector agency. The public sector agency then leases the facility back to the private developer under a long-term lease. During the lease, the private developer operates the facility and earns a return from user charges; and Design-Build-Finance-Operate (DBFO): the private sector is responsible for financing, designing, construction and operation of the project and is compensated by service payments from the government during the life of the project.

There is no doubt that public-private partnerships have been a dominant issue in both governmental rhetoric and practice. In many countries governments have turned to the idea of public-private partnerships, or partnerships in general, as a vehicle to realise better policy outcomes, or to enhance investments in fields like infrastructure health or even social policy. According to World Bank, PPPs are presented not only as a way of bringing needed additional investment to public infrastructure but also as a mechanism for improving infrastructure planning and project selection (Leigland, 2018). It is also a mechanism for enhancing project management and guaranteeing adequate maintenance, avoiding cycles of construction followed by persistent neglect and then high-cost reconstruction.

The International Finance Corporation as part of the World Bank Group advises governments implementing PPPs on technical, legal, and regulatory requirements; building capacity; addressing social and sustainability issues; and devising the strategies necessary to deliver successful PPPs, and this has helped governments leverage the expertise and efficiency of the private sector, raise capital, and spur development. PPPs therefore do not imply 'less government' but a different governmental role, occasioned by a stronger position of the private partner in such partnerships , more active government participation is often needed (Yang, Hou & Wang, 2013).

PPP has found itself in Public Policy in Africa both as a process and an outcome of public sector reforms. In either case, it has gained a lot of currency in Public Policy Practice across different sectors in various countries across Africa (Obosi, 2021). The sectors have ranged from water, health, infrastructure, energy, natural resources, and environment to the service industry to mention but a few in Africa. In whichever case, it has mainly been used as a means to either reverse the poor performance or jumpstart a non-performing sector in Africa with mixed results. In some sectors privatisation has been used synonymously with PPP. This has prompted the question why some countries have preferred some forms of PPPs to others in particular sectors with different results by looking at PPPs in transport, water and health sectors in Kenya. The chapter argues that PPPs in Africa have no one-size-fits-all implementation strategy but rather are sector specific even within the same country. Whereas PPPs are driven by need for good service delivery, the implementation is impeded by requisite resource needs.

PUBLIC PRIVATE PARTNERSHIPS (PPPs) FRAMEWORK IN KENYA

The Water Act, 2002 and later revised to Water Act, 2016 was the first effort to embrace public-private partnership (PPP) in public service under the water sector reforms. It opened up space for private involvement in various proportions in the hitherto public sector-dominated water service delivery (Obosi 2015). It was not until 2011, when a formal framework for PPPs in Kenya was established under PPP Policy Statement 2011, and later revised in Act 15 of 2013 titled 'Public Private Partnership Act'. The Act stipulated that: i) the government retains total strategic control on the service, ii) the government is mandated to secure new infrastructure which will become the government's asset at the end of the contract period, and iii) allocation of project and performance risks is to the party best able to manage or mitigate. Before then, the PPP arrangements occurred without formal government policy on the same. With the enactment of the PPP Act of 2021, Kenya established a comprehensive legislative framework, which was intended to address the shortcomings of the PPP Act 2013 by including a framework for streamlined project processes with clear timelines, expanded procurement options and robust processes for Privately Initiated Investment Proposals (PIIP).

The Act: i. established the Directorate of Public Private Partnerships to replace the PPP Unit under 2013 legislation, and conferred broad but separate functions from those of a PPP aimed at establishing open, efficient and equitable processes for the implementation, management and monitoring of projects; capped concession period for investors involved in State-owned Build-Operate-Transfer (BOT) projects at 30 years to enable investors to recoup their major initial investments with the contracting authorities taking into account the lifespan of the technology used, investment standards required, economic and financial viability, and the consideration for maintaining delivery standards; expanded the role of the private sector in PPP initiatives beyond financing to include construction, operation and maintenance of the projects to include public-private joint ventures and strategic partnerships, hence broadening the scope of what is classified as a PPP, funnelling more contracting arrangements between the public and private sectors; streamlined and rationalised the regulatory, implementation and monitoring mandates of the relevant agencies; and allowed the county governments to enter into PPP agreements with a private party and be responsible for the administration of the entire project after conducting a feasibility study (Republic Of Kenya, 2021).

The government, based on the PPP framework, has therefore made an effort to create enabling environment to boost trend towards PPP-prioritised project implementation in the following sectors: Transport and Infrastructure; Health Solutions including Telemedicine; Green and Blue Solutions including, Forestry, Fish Processing and Wildlife Conservation; Water and Sanitation; Housing including Student Hostels; Industrial Parks and Manufacturing; and ICT including Intelligent Traffic Management System. This exercise has been facilitated by certain drivers such as need for effectiveness, public interest, value for money and benefits while more often than not the pace of success has been hampered basically by resources, both human and capital.

PPPs IN TRANSPORT SECTOR

PPP initiative in the transport sector has included the construction of roads, ports, and railways. Government initiatives to improve the transport sector has been complemented by the efforts of the private sector through PPPs and PIIPs, which have catapulted numerous development projects including: the 27.1 km Nairobi Expressway, a PPP road project between the national government through the Kenya National Highways Authority (KENHA) and the China Road and Bridge Corporation (CRBC) on a build-operate-transfer (BOT) model. Other roads include Thika Super highway, Southern, Northern, Eastern, and Western Bypasses completed to improve the transport infrastructure. The bypasses were touted to and have indeed significantly cut the time motorists spend on unending traffic snarl-ups as the vehicles avoid transit through the CBD to their destinations.

The multi-billion-shilling projects were aimed at easing the growing traffic on the key road that link motorists from the Jomo Kenyatta International Airport and Mombasa-Nairobi Highway to Thika Superhighway, bypassing the congested central business district. Nairobi traffic jams are estimated to cost the Kenyan economy Sh100 billion every year, or about Sh11 million per hour. The completion of the roads has therefore boosted service delivery which was a big driver in the government partnering with the Chinese construction companies. Due to the high costs associated with budgetary constraints, the government of Kenya partnered with Chinese companies which had the financial muscle accompanied with technical capacity. The following table shows a sample of the roads financed through PPP in Kenya in the last eight years.

Table 7.1 shows that the Chinese companies have dominated construction of major roads in Kenya to the extent of doing 14 road projects worth Sh25.5 billion while Kenyan companies controlled 22 road projects worth Sh13.3 billion. Due to their financial capacity, all the projects awarded have been completed on time so as to enable the Chinese companies secure other

Table 7.1 A Sample of Roads Constructed through PPPs in Kenya from 2012 to 2022

Road	*Partners*
Nairobi Expresswas	Government of Kenya (GOK) and the China Road and Bridge Construction Corporation (CRBC)
Waiyakiwas	China Wu-Yi Construction company and Government of Kenya (GOK)
Nairobi-Western Bypass	Government of Kenya (GOK) and China Exim Bank
Thika Road	Africa Development Bank (AfDB), Government of Kenya (GoK), Chinese Government
Southern Bypass	Government of Kenya (GOK) and the China Road and Bridge Construction Corporation (CRBC)
Northern Bypass	Government of Kenya (GOK) and the China Road and Bridge Construction Corporation (CRBC)
Eastern Bypass	Government of Kenya (GOK) and the China Communication Construction Company (CCCC)

Source: Developed by the Author

projects, while their competitors could still struggle to complete their respective assignments. China's influence on Kenya's mega projects development started gathering steam with the construction of the Thika Superhighway between January 2009 and November 2012 at a cost of nearly Sh32 billion. These were followed in quick succession by other projects awarded. CRBC and CCCC bagged the lion's share of Kenya's mega projects, at least two railways, two ports and 23 road projects. The projects include the $3.5 billion (KSh393.82 billion) standard gauge railway (SGR), a $398 million (Sh44.78 billion approx. US$3.7 billion) oil terminal at the Mombasa port and road projects such as Southern and Eastern Bypass in Nairobi.

Table 7.2 shows different PPP forms and characteristics defining each model as it were applied for the different road projects. It is observed that tariff regulation is undertaken by the pubic partner for all the five roads, while utility management is undertaken by private partner. The government of Kenya considered concessions, joint ventures, and build-operate-transfer (BOT) scheme. The Mombasa-Nairobi Highway constructed through Design, Build, Finance, Maintain, Operate, Transfer (DBFOMT) depicts a concession contract involving various partners including African Development Bank (AfDB), World Bank, European Development Bank (EDB) and Government of Kenya (GoK). Working capital investment, utility management and commercial risk were provided by the private partner while tariff regulation was undertaken by the government. Nairobi-Nakuru-Mau Summit Highway was done through a DBFOMT and O&M PPP model, with capital investment from the World Bank. Capital investment, commercial risks and utility management were delegated to the private partner while tariff regulation was undertaken by the public partner. The table also shows that the Nairobi-Thika Superhighway (DBFOMT) was a special joint investment PPP arrangement between the Government of Kenya, Chinese government and the African Development Bank. Capital investment was by all the parties, commercial risk was by both public and private, tariff regulation was undertaken by government while utility management was by the private partner. The construction of Nairobi Southern Bypass was through a joint venture between the government of Kenya and Chinese government, both providing the working capital. Commercial risk was by both public and private while utility management was by the private partner.

The government retained tariff regulation for the project. Regarding the Ngong-Kiserian-Isinya-Kajiado to Imaroro road, a special PPP vehicle under the Annuity Programme was idealised. The concession contract involved partners including National Treasury (public), participating commercial banks (KCB Group) and contractor. The government used different forms of PPPs for different roads. For instance, Mombasa-Nairobi Highway, Nairobi-Nakuru-Mau Summit highway and Ngong-Kiserian-Isinya and Kajiado to

Table 7.2 Roads Constructed through PPPs by Forms of PPPs

	Road	*Form of PPP*	*PPP Model*	*Contract partners*	*Working Capital Investment*	*Commercial risk*	*Tariff regulation*	*Utility management*
1	Mombasa-Nairobi Highway	BOT/Concession contract	DBFMOT	AfDB; World Bank, European Development Bank(EDB), Government of Kenya(GoK)	Private	Private	Public	Private
2	Nairobi-Nakuru- Mau Summit Highway	Concession contract	DBFMOT O&M	World Bank	Private	Private	Public	Private
3	Nairobi-Thika Highway	Joint Venture	DBFOMT Currently under O&M	AfDB, GoK, Chinese Government	Public /Private	Public /Private	Public	Private
4	Southern Bypass	Joint Venture	DBFOMT Proposed for O&M	Gok Chinese Government	Public/Private	Public/Private	Public	Private
5	Ngong-Kiserian-Isinya-Kajiado to Imaroro	Concession contract(Road Annuity Programme)	DBFOMT	N.Treasury, commercial banks-KCB Group), Private contractor	Private	Private	Public	Private

Source: Developed by the Author

Imaroro were done through concession contracts while Nairobi-Thika Superhighway and Southern Bypass adopted the joint venture contracts. The drive for particular PPP arrangements was associated with elements including financing, operational efficiency and risk management for either the public or private entity. For example, the table highlights commercial risk for both public and private partners for joint venture projects (Nairobi-Thika Highway and Southern Bypass) while the construction of the remaining three roads that was implemented using BOT/concession contracts indicates commercial risk for the private partner only.

The government of Kenya has considered joint venture, BOT and concession contracts with preference for DBFOMT and O&M. This shows that the governments' choice would by and large be influenced by the prevailing economic situation of the country. This has seen a trend in which more developing countries are shifting to DBFOMT. However, the nature of PPPs alone is not a sufficient driver since governments sometimes go for hybrid PPP models provided they are appropriate for ensuring efficiency and quality of road projects. Overall, it can be concluded that PPP road projects in Kenya show a growing preference for DBFOMT model, even where different PPP arrangements (concessions or joint venture) exist—a further indicator of cost implications as an impediment to choice of the alternatives.

PPP IN THE HEALTH SECTOR

In recent years the use of PPPs has become increasingly popular and governments around the world are looking for ways of coping with simultaneously increasing healthcare costs and decreasing governmental budgets (Blanken and Dewulf, 2010). The problems in contemporary healthcare are wicked problems that are too complicated for governments to solve individually (Torchia, Calabrò, and Morner, 2015), hence the need for a strategic partner. Both the public and the private sectors recognise their individual inabilities to address the emerging public health issues that persist both at both the international and national policy agendas (Nishtar 2004). Traditional public health groups are confronted by limited financial resources, complex social and behavioural problems, and rapid disease transmission across national boundaries, and reduced state capabilities (Nishtar, 2004).

At the same time, private for-profit organisations have come to recognise the importance of public health goals for their immediate and long-term objectives, and to accept a broader view of social responsibility as part of the corporate mandate (Nishtar, 2004). Thus, many governments deal with such problems now by establishing PPPs between healthcare providers (public sector), building and management companies, and financers (private sector). PPPs in the healthcare sector therefore seem to be both unavoidable and imperative (Torchia, Calabrò, and Morner, 2015). In this context, partnerships between the public and the private sector have a contribution to make in improving the health of the poor by combining the different skills and resources of various organisations (public and private) in innovative ways. Regulation provides assurance to the private sector (protection from expropriation, respect of contract agreements, etc.) and to the public sector as well, by ensuring that essential partnerships operate efficiently and optimise the resources available to them in line with broader policy objectives (Jamali, 2004).

Moreover, the rapid change in the provision of healthcare meant that governments around the world are dealing with problems such as booming healthcare costs and decreasing governmental budgets. For many governments, PPPs between healthcare providers and the private sector represented a way of coping with problems such as ageing populations, medical-technological developments, and policy changes (Torchia, Calabrò, and Morner 2015). PPPs in the health sector can take a variety of forms depending on the degrees of public and private sector responsibility and risk.

They are characterised by the sharing of common objectives, risks, and rewards, as might be defined in a contract or manifested through a different arrangement (Nikolic and Maikisch 2006). PPPs, when appropriately structured and implemented, help address specific cost and investment challenges, deliver improvements in service efficiency, and enhance service quality. Knowledge and expertise combined with competent management of the contractual arrangements are critical for the awarding health authority's effective control of theft of PPPs' outputs and for making its own contribution to outcomes. Any of these could be either a driver or an impediment towards the choice of a particular PPP form by a government.

In 2015, the Kenyan government selected GE Healthcare as one of its main partners to deliver a seven-year Managed Equipment Services (MES) Partnership to provide Kenya's 46 million strong population with access to teleradiology services across 98 Ministry of Health hospitals in Kenya's 47 counties. An MES is a form of PPP that enables customers to adopt a 'pay for service' expenditure plan and affords a number of financial benefits including funding to cover equipment, maintenance and other project costs such as training (J. O. Obosi 2019). The main driver in this instant was the need for service delivery which was under stress, benefits to an increased number of citizens, public interests, and value for money. However cost of the equipment was indeed an impediment due to serious budgetary constraints, hence, the need for a strategic partner to bridge the gap.

The model allowed the Kenyan government to budget healthcare expenditure over several years by deferring upfront capital outlay. The Ministry of Health could then assign critical funds to address the country's most pressing healthcare challenges while also addressing the bigger picture and improving the wider healthcare system. The project represented one of the government's flagship programmes to deliver tangible benefit to people locally by decentralising specialised healthcare services from national referral hospitals to a county level. The aim of this partnership was to increase access to affordable healthcare for all and enable earlier diagnosis and treatment of various diseases. The programme covers radiology infrastructure modernisation in 94 county hospitals across 47 counties and 4 national referral hospitals.

The radiology modernisation lot awarded to GE Healthcare represents the largest of seven tranches of Kenya's progressive Kshs 38 billion (USD 420 million) health development plan. Through the programme, GE Healthcare brought a comprehensive package, including its advanced technologies and capabilities in design and software, covering: 1. The deployment of over 585 units of diagnostic imaging equipment including X-ray and ultrasound systems supported by a long-term servicing contract; 2. Training and education programmes in line with GE Healthcare's focus on skills development and capacity building; 3. Scope for the assessment and potential establishment of a GE Healthcare Training Centre to be run jointly with an accredited local partner. In a precedence setting move, Kisumu County has partnered with Oasis Doctors Plaza, a private entity in a five-year renewable contract to manage Victoria Sub-County Hospital, a peri-urban health facility.

The reported deal involved Oasis injecting a 236 million shillings capital investment with an initial infrastructural improvement costing 50 million shillings. The expected outcomes of the project include improvement of clinical services quality and increasing access to specialised services. In the health sector, construction of a 300-bed private hospital at the Kenyatta National Hospital had been tendered. The project involves contracting with a private operator to build, operate and transfer a new private facility that provides specialty healthcare at competitive and affordable rates. The private party would finance, construct, operate and maintain, and then transfer the facility to Kenyatta National Hospital at the end of a specified term that shall not exceed 30 years. In addition, preparations for procurement of transaction advisor are underway for the Pwani University Teaching and Referral Hospital, Amenity Wing at Kisii Teaching and Referral Hospital, Cancer Centre at Meru Teaching and Referral Hospital, and upgrading of Nyamira Level 5 Hospital.

The major PPPs in the health sector in Kenya target service delivery, whether in the enhanced provision of healthcare or in the infrastructure. The main drivers in provision of health-care are the enhanced services in which a strategic partner, GE with the 47 county governments or Oasis Doctors Plaza with the case of Kisumu county, were to provide the missing link to health service provision. The built-operate-transfer system being mooted was also a result of the need to provide service facilities. Due to the key impediment of cost, the government in each case sought partnership with both GE to provide the facilities and particular private partners to construct hospital amenities and training facilities to accommodate more people. The Government of Kenya partnered with GE through a service contract.

PPP IN THE WATER SECTOR

In Kenya, several strategies were implemented in the water sector. These included provision of water by the state through both Water and Local Government ministries up to 2002. This, despite the realization that increased access to clean water was inimical. After 2002, the government and the private sectors went into partnership in an effort to improve water service delivery to households. The main drive for the PPPs in Kenya was both mitigation against budgetary constraints and implementation of water sector reforms towards improving public service delivery (J. Obosi 2018).

The implementation of Water Act of 2002 in Kenya was therefore a realisation that neither the government nor the private entities alone could succeed in delivering water in the desired quality and quantity to the citizens. The government therefore acknowledged four types of water service providers as the Public Limited companies, Community Water Projects, National Water Conservation and Pipeline Corporation, and Private Individuals through the commercialisation principle (K'Akumu 2007). Whether as public enterprises, joint ventures, management contracts or built-operate-Transfer (BOT), public-private partnerships (PPPs) became part and parcel of water service provision in Kenya.

The World Bank and UN Habitat's approaches have each facilitated the integration of small-scale water service providers into the formal water sector so that they could expand their services and help improve the services to the poor and those in the peri-urban settlement through legal recognition of the informal providers, development of cooperation of utilities, informal providers and government authorities, regulatory measures for pricing and quality, encouragement of the formation of vendor associations and consideration of microfinance initiatives to facilitate their investments. The government agencies partnered with various private actors in the provision of water. Alternatively, private actors in the form of local communities, individuals, corporates and non-governmental organisations invited government facilitation in various manner and extent in water service delivery (Obosi 2018).

The spontaneity and random manner in which water service providers sprung and interacted with other stakeholders prompted proliferation of PPP arrangements in Kenya. In the context of water service provision in Kenya, at face value, there are public water companies, private water entities and community water projects, water service regulators and water service financiers. Public water companies are under private management contracts to provide water to both public and private consumers. The community water projects are indeed a conglomeration of private individuals in the same locality who then invite support from the government and continue to operate as private entities in delivering public good. Table 7.3 shows the nature and scope of PPPs in water sector service provision in Kenya.

Table 7.3 shows that all WSPs partner with the government in one way or another to provide water services. Whereas public limited companies formed by the respective local authorities engage private management through management contracts under a service provision agreement (5) years, the private/community water service providers are subjected to government regulation including pricing, water abstraction permits and quality control. The PLCs continue to use the water infrastructure (lines) owned by the respective governments. The government of Kenya through its respective agencies is instrumental in infrastructure development for the WSPs through underwriting of the loans and grants from bilateral donors. It owns the assets for the public water companies of KIWASCO, Chemosit, SNWSCO and MIKUTRA. It also facilitated operations, and negotiated and underwrote loans for infrastructure development of the WSPs. For example, LVSWB guaranteed loans from SANA in support of Boya community water project. In Migori, LVSWB supplied chemicals, water meters and facilitated trainings for Nyasare Water Supply Association.

The PPP in water is also manifested in financing. The methods used vary and for purposes of our analysis, we classify them as peoples organisations, non-governmental organisations, governmental institutions and development partners. Whereas peoples organisations are the most dominant partners in all the community water projects, development partners are more dominant in management contracts through Water Service Boards. The other important financial partners for community water projects included non-governmental organisations and governmental organisations like National Government-Constituency Development Fund (NG-CDF), Water Service Trust Fund (WSTF) and county governments to help in boosting storage and network distribution.

This could be illustrated by the following cases. Kisumu East Constituency had through its CDF funded sinking of boreholes in Manyatta area. Likewise, Nyando CDF funded the purchase of a 24,000-litre capacity storage tank for Boya community water project. In the same manner,

Table 7.3 The Nature and Scope of Water Service Provision in Kenya

Water Service Provider (WSP)	*Form*	*Nature*	*Partners*	*Scope of PPP*
Kiwasco	Management Contract	Public Limited company	GOK/County Governments/ Water Company(WSP)	Service Provision Agreement to citizens
Chemosit	Management Contract	Public Limited company	GOK/County Governments/ Private Managers/Staff	Service Provision Agreement to citizens
Boya	Private	Community water Project	GOK/County Governments/ Private Water Service Provider (WSP)	Service Provision Agreement/Issue water abstraction permits/ Quality Control/ Price Regulation
SNWSCO	Management Contract	Public Limited company	GOK/County Governments/ Water Company (WSP)	Service Provision Agreement to citizens
Nyasare	Private	Community water Project	GOK/County Governments/ Private Water Service Provider (WSP)	Service Provision Agreement/Issue water abstraction permits/ Quality Control/ Price Regulation
Mikutra	Management Contract	Public Limited company	GOK/County Governments/ Water Company (WSP)	Service Provision Agreement to citizens
Mogombet	Private	Community water Project	GOK/County Governments/ Private Water Service Provider (WSP	Service Provision Agreement/Issue water abstraction permits/ Quality Control/ Price Regulation

Source: Author

Karachuonyo CDF provided Kshs 1 million and Kshs 700,000.00 (USD 7,000) for the rehabilitation of lines from Omindi to Wagwe areas and water lines in Kanam B to set a power transformer at Miti Mbili. There were also cases where the government's Water Services Trust Fund (WSTF) channelled funds to community-based Organisations and WRUAs through Water Service Boards. For example, In SNWSCO, WSTF provided over Kshs 7 million each to Koguta and Rabuor community water projects in West Karachuonyo scheme to set up water storage tanks. The development partners were key partners to state-driven utilities, Public water companies, through the water boards in the form of either international financial institutions offered development assistance through state undertakings or bilateral state negotiations for loans/grants.

In Bomet, the major donors included the European Union (EU) which donated personal computers to Litein Water Supply Scheme, German Development Agency (KFW), and Nile Basin Initiative which facilitated expansion of the water pipeline from Nyangores River to the tune of Kshs 12 million. In Kisumu city, the Danish International Development Agency (DANIDA) and French Agency for Development (AFD) also facilitated expansion and development of KIWASCO water network and treatment. United Nations Children's Fund (UNICEF) provided 400 pipes and two 5,000 litres water storage tanks for Boya community water project. DANIDA facilitated the expansion of Homa Bay (Asego) supply while AFD provided 5 million shillings for repairs of water lines in West Karachuonyo community water supply scheme in 2003.

In MIKUTRA, ADB financed rehabilitation of water pipeline network in Migori town, and Rongo, while Korean International Cooperation Agency (KOICA) supported a similar initiative in Awendo town. Austrian Development Cooperation (ADC) on two occasions, 1997–2003 and 2003–2008, through HORIZON3000 financed the expansion of programme for Nyasare Water Supply Association (J. O. Obosi 2017). Again, through collaboration with the Water Sector Trust Fund (WTSF), the implementing agency of the World Bank-backed Output- Based Aid (OBA) programme, the WASH-FIN programme assisted Mathira Water and Sewerage Company (MAWASCO) to access finance to rehabilitate and expand urban water supply in Karatina town. MAWASCO raised Ksh 108 million ($1.08 million) in commercial financing, which has seen water network rehabilitation of 45.3 km across the town. Through the same collaboration, the WASH-FIN programme also assisted Nyeri Water and Sanitation Company (NYEWASCO) to undertake a debt capacity assessment, which enabled the company to increase an existing OBA loan by $800,000. The financing enabled NYEWASCO to provide new sewer connections to about 2,600 households, resulting in over 22,000 people benefiting from improved sanitation (TetraTech, 2017).

CONCLUSION

This chapter concludes that the implementation of PPPs in Kenya is driven by the need for enhanced service delivery, value for money, public interest and the potential benefits arising from whereas the major impediment is the cost factor. Whereas the need for enhanced service delivery drives implementation of PPPs across all the sectors, transport, Health and Water, the value for money is more prominent in the Health and water sectors. Partnerships between the public and the private sectors are often seen as offering innovative methods with a good chance of producing the desired outcomes. One primary benefit is that each sector contributes what it can best offer, and the combination of these skills, abilities, and powers has the potential for producing the best results. Yet neither the public nor the private sector is capable by itself of solving the numerous problems in the sectors in which strategic partnerships have been invited. This has been more pronounced in health sector, where the benefits to all the citizens across the acquisition of medical equipment which the government of Kenya could not buy on its own, hence the drive for the government to enter into a seven-year partnership with GE to lease the same.

The second drive was the need for a critical policy reflection. The interactions between public and private sectors are likely to both positively and negatively impact on the achievement of the expected outcomes. In the roads sector, there was need for a proven policy paradigm in which public-private relationships are seen as potentially problematic interactions between two separate spheres where could not put the interest of the public at risk. The use of BOT which was adopted for the Nairobi Express Highway by the CRBC completed the construction of road in time so that it could start recouping the funds invested without putting at risk the tax payers' money so that the road can be transferred back to the government after 27 years.

The third drive for efficiency and Value for Money influenced the government to adopt the cheapest and fastest mode of the PPPs at the expense of traditional methods. The private sector generally achieves higher operational efficiency in asset procurement and service delivery by applying its expertise, experience, and innovative ideas/technology. Despite the involvement of the private sector in PPP projects, the government needs to continue playing the role of regulator, especially in all the sectors where accountability is critical and the public interest is at stake. In particular, the public sector should continue to set standards and monitor product safety, efficacy, and quality, and ensure that citizens have adequate access to the products and services they need.

Finally, there is more flexibility in the implementation of PPPs in the water sector more than any of the other two sectors especially in water service provision. However due to the heavy budget involved in the infrastructure development, the cost is an impediment, hence the need for a partner with a heavy financial muscle usually involving either underwriting by the government or bilateral governmental negotiations.

REFERENCES

Blanken, A and G. Dewulf. 2010. "Ppps in Health: Static or Dynamic?" *Australian Journal of Public Administration* 69(SUPPL. 1).

Brown, T. L., Potoski, M and D. M. Van Slyke. 2006. "Managing Public Service Contracts: Aligning Values, Institutions, and Markets." *Public Administration Review* 66(3): 323–31.

Business Daily. Available from: https://www.businessdailyafrica.com/bd/economy/chinese-firms-now-capture-bulk-of-kura-roads-3692838. Date of Access: 23rd January, 2023.

Cyntonn. (2022). Public Private Partnerships in Kenya. Available from: https://www.cytonn.com/topicals/public-private-partnerships-2. Date of Access: 23rdJanuary, 2023.

Hodge, G. A and C. Greve. 2007. "Public-Private Partnerships: An International Performance Review." *Public Administration Review* 67(3): 545–58.

———. 2017. "On Public–Private Partnership Performance: A Contemporary Review." *Public Works Management and Policy* 22(1).

Hodge, G., C. Greve and A. Boardman. 2017. "Public-Private Partnerships: The Way They Were and What They Can Become." *Australian Journal of Public Administration* 76(3).

Ismail, S and F. A. Harris. 2014. "Challenges in Implementing Public Private Partnership (PPP) in Malaysia." Procedia - Social and Behavioral Sciences 164(August).

Jamali, D. 2004. "Success and Failure Mechanisms of Public Private Partnerships (PPPs) in Developing Countries. Insights from the Lebanese Context." *International Journal of Public Sector Management* 17(5): 414–30.

Jutting, J. 1999. "Public-Private-Partnership and Social Protection in Developing Countries : The Case of the Health Sector." *The Extension of Social Protection* (January 1999): 1–14.

K'Akumu, O. A. 2007. "Toward Effective Governance of Water Services in Kenya." *Water Policy* 9(5): 529–43.

Leigland, J. 2018. "Public-Private Partnerships in Developing Countries: The Emerging Evidence-Based Critique." *World Bank Research Observer* 33(1).

Nikolic, I. A and H. Maikisch. 2006. The World Bank Public-Private Partnerships and Collaboration in the Health Sector : An Overview with Case Studies from Recent European Experience.

Nishtar, S. 2004. "Public-Private 'partnerships' in Health - A Global Call to Action." *Health Research Policy and Systems*, pp. 1–7.

Obosi J. 2021. "Public-Private Partnership and Public Policy in Africa." In *Routledge Handbook of Public Policy in Africa*, pp. 213–23.

Obosi, J. 2018. "Nature and Scope of Public Private Partnerships in the Water Sector in Kenya." *Open Journal of Political Science* 8: 12–34. http://www.scirp.org/journal/ojps.

Obosi, J. O. 2015. "The Public Service Delivery Challenge: A Public Private Partnership in Water Service Provision in Kenya." Book: 1–237. www.omniscriptum.com.

———. 2017. "Public-Private Partnerships in Kenya's Water Sector Management." Global Encyclopedia of Public Administration, Public Policy, and Governance: 1–8. https://link.springer.com/referenceworkentry/10.1007/978-3-319-31816-5_3356-1.

———. 2019. "Decentralized Governance in the Management of Urban Health Care Systems in Developing Countries." *Open Journal of Political Science*.

Osei-Kyei, R and Chan, A. P. C. (2017). "Implementing Public–Private Partnership (PPP) Policy for Public Construction Projects in Ghana: Critical Success Factors and Policy Implications." *International Journal of Construction Management* 17(2).

Republic of Kenya. (2021). *The Public Private Partnerships Bill*. Nairobi.

TetraTech. (2017). "Expanding Finance for Water Service Providers in Kenya." (April).

Torchia, M., A. Calabrò and M. Morner. 2015. "Public–Private Partnerships in the Health Care Sector: A Systematic Review of the Literature." *Public Management Review* 17(2): 236–61.

Turner, B. 2014. *The Statesman's Yearbook,* Asian Development Bank Institute, pp. 75.

Yang, Y, Yilin, H and Y. Wang. 2013. "On the Development of Public-Private Partnerships in Transitional Economies: An Explanatory Framework." Public Administration Review 73(2): 301–10.

Chapter 8

Public-Private Partnerships in Nigeria

Socio-Economic and National Security Impact and Challenges

Richard Obinna Iroanya, Gabriella Nguluwe
and Salomo Ndapulamo

The increasing popularity of public-private partnerships to infrastructure development is better appreciated in light of dwindling foreign development aid due to: donor fatigue; increasing budgetary constraints as a result of poor economic performance; and diminishing interests and opportunities (PricewaterhouseCoopers, 2019). PPPs are thus projected as a veritable alternative to budgetary allocation and deficit financing. Notwithstanding, PPPs do not seem to have achieved a high level of success in Nigeria in terms of stimulating economic growth and development as well as enhancement of the national security of the country as will be demonstrated in subsequent sections of this chapter.

The chapter is structured into five sections including the introduction. The second section contextualises the adoption of PPP in Nigeria. This entails a discussion of Nigeria's socio-economic development with specific focus on infrastructural situation justifying urgent call for the adoption of the PPP approach. The third section discusses the impact of PPP on the Nigerian economy, society and national security. This entails among other things the discussion of selected PPP projects in Nigeria with the view of showing their socio-economic and national security impacts. The fourth examines the inherent challenges of the PPP approach within the Nigerian context while the fifth section concludes the discussion.

CONTEXUALISING PUBLIC-PRIVATE PARTNERSHIP IN NIGERIA

Nigerian economy has come to be characterised by infrastructure deficit or gap due to neglect over the years. Successive governments in Nigeria either insufficiently invested in physical infrastructure or completely neglected this critical sector of its economy and society. Infrastructure gap entails among other things the lack of good roads and a railway transportation network; inadequate airport and seaport facilities capable of driving economic development; and dilapidated energy infrastructure resulting in poor power generation, transmission and distribution across the country (Ebuh, Ezike, Shitile, Smith & Haruna, 2019). Infrastructure deficit further entails poor communication, education, and healthcare service delivery systems (Ebuh *et al.,* 2019). The absence of these or their deplorable conditions mean that individuals, communities and businesses cannot use them as inputs in the production of further goods and services in Nigeria (Chan, Lam, Chan, Cheung & Ke, 2009).

The State of Roads in Nigeria

In this regard, the deplorable conditions of Nigerian roads are well documented (Babalola, 2021; Ojo, 2021; Nigeria Bureau of Statistics, 2022). Although there have been efforts in recent years to revive Nigeria's rail transport system, road transport system remains the most common means of transportation for low- and medium-income Nigerians. According to Nigeria Bureau of Statistics (2022), road transport contributes about N826 billion (approximately US$1.8 billion) or 1.75% to Nigeria's gross domestic product (GDP). The country's extensive network of roads is categorised into three according to authorities responsible for their design, construction, operation and maintenance.

In this regard, Trunk 'A' roads are federal government roads which link various states and geopolitical zones of the Nigerian federation. Trunk 'B' roads refer to roads constructed and maintained by federating units (states) and they link cities within each state. The third category of Nigerian roads is the Trunk 'C' roads which are roads owned by municipal (local government) authorities. These roads link various local towns and villages (Dam, Alaci, Udoo, Jacob, Atser, Ujoh & Gyuse, 2021). In total Nigeria's road network is estimated at 193,2000km (Infrastructure Concession Regulatory Commission, 2023).

Share of ownership of the roads in terms of construction and maintenance is broken down as follows: the central government owns an estimated 36,000km; state governments (federating units) own about 17,000km; and local governments own about 140,000km of the roads. Interestingly, only about 60,000km of this road network is paved; others are either in deplorable conditions due to poor maintenance or completely unpaved (Infrastructure Concession Regulatory Commission, 2023).

This situation according to the World Bank contributes to about '40% of Nigerian population or 83 million people living below the poverty line' (Otaru, 2022). Similarly, 25% of Nigerians or 53 million people remain in vulnerable conditions, especially rural dwellers without accessible roads to markets where farm products can be sold. High rates of inflation witnessed between 2020 and 2022 as a result of a global pandemic (COVID-19) further pushed about 8 million Nigerians into poverty (Otaru, 2022).

Infrastructure

Infrastructure deficit in Nigeria appears more pronounced in the country's housing sector. The Nigerian economy and society suffer from poor quality housing due to negligence over the years by successive national and state governments. Quality of housing in a country provides a good indication of the quality of life of its citizens and economic viability of a country. Housing also makes significant contribution to the overall socio-economic well-being of any country. However, as Ekpo (2019) notes, the importance of housing in Nigerian appears less recognised as a result of gross negligence over the years.

The housing problem in the country continues to worsen since the dawn of Nigeria's independence. In 1991, for example, it was estimated that Nigeria had a housing deficit of 7 million. However, this increased to 14 million in 2010 and 17 million in 2018 (International Bank for Reconstruction and Development, 2016; World Bank, 2018). To overcome Nigeria's housing deficit, the World Bank further estimates that the country will need to construct at least 700,000 housing units per year over the next 20 years to accommodate Nigeria's rapidly growing population (Akinpelu, 2019).

With Nigerian population growth outpacing its housing and economic growths, Ekpo (2019) observes that overcoming the housing deficit in Nigeria will be 'highly unattainable'. With this situation, it is obvious that Nigeria's housing crisis needs addressing to accommodate a rapidly growing population estimated at about 219 million people (Ekpo, 2019). The urgency of closing housing and other infrastructure deficits is increased by rapid rural-urban migration which stresses inadequate infrastructure in major cities of Nigeria.

Energy

Apart from deplorable road conditions, Nigeria's electricity supply remains in a state of quagmire because of extremely weak power generation capacity.

The country has been unable to generate up to 6,000MW of electricity since its political independence in 1960. The highest ever generated was 5,802MW in 2021. Since then power generation has dropped down to 4,000MW. Accordingly, it is estimated that about 70% of the Nigerian population does not have access to electricity (Oyedepo, 2012). Thus, a huge deficit exists in the power production and delivery sector. There are only 28 power generating companies comprising three hydro-powered stations and 25 thermal stations which presently function below installed capacity. Together these companies generate an average of about 4,000MW (Association of Nigerian Electricity Distributors, 2022). This is hardly enough for industrial and domestic usage.

Estimating from international standards of 1,000MW per a million population, Nigeria requires about 200,000MW of power production to meet the growing electricity need of its teeming population of about 200 million people. Currently, only about 4,000MW of electricity produced from an installed production capacity of about 13,000MW from 28 power generating plants are available for distribution directly to homes and businesses in the country (Association of Nigerian Electricity Distributors, 2022). Still available electricity hardly gets to Nigerians due to challenges in connecting and transporting produced electricity from gas and hydro sources to the national grid. This persistent challenge caused by technical faults and leakages as well as poor repair and maintenance culture characterise the Nigerian society.

The extent of infrastructure deficit facing the country can be inferred from various estimates by international institutions and experts. The World Bank, for example, warned that it might take 300 years for Nigeria to close its infrastructure gap, if current rate of expenditure allocations is not revised (Faminu, 2022). Similarly, at the 26th UN Climate Change Conference of the Parties (COP 26) in Glasgow, Nigerian President Muhammadu Buhari informed world leaders that Nigeria would require about US$1.5 trillion in 10 years to close its infrastructure gap (Ukpe, 2021). Later in 2021 the country's Vice President Yemi Osinbajo stated that Nigeria would require about $3 trillion in the next 30 years to reduce its infrastructural deficit. Some experts further estimate that the country requires an investment of approximately between US$100 and US$150 billion annually over the next 10 years to reduce its infrastructural deficit (Ukpe, 2021).

The State of the Economy in Nigeria

Consequently, the Nigeria's economic growth remains stagnant as well as susceptible to global market volatility due to its monolithic nature. The country operates in a global economic system where forces of demand and supply cause commodity shocks and trade imbalances resulting in devaluation of national currencies of developing countries. Furthermore, trade controls, deficit financing, rising inflation, and debt burden combine to stagnate economic growth. The country ranks 158 in the World Bank's Human Capital Index (TheGlobalEconomy.com, 2021; Ujah, 2018). This ranking is better appreciated when examined against the backdrop of high poverty rate as a result of gross inequality in terms of income and access to resources; lopsided development across the six geopolitical zones of the country; terrorism as evidenced by Boko Haram and ISWAP (Islamic State West African Province) attacks; banditry; and separatist agitations.

Economic stagnation implies that the Nigerian economy is not growing at a rate that can resolve endemic poverty, underemployment and unemployment especially among its restive youth. Currently, the country's population is growing at a rate of 2.4% annually. At this rate, it is projected that the population will increase by 7.7 million by 2024 while the economy is projected to grow by 3.2% subject to stability in international oil prices and improved production rate as well as stable security situation (World Bank, 2021). At the current growth rate, the economy cannot absorb the teeming population of unemployed Nigerians currently at 9.79% (World Bank, 2021). For the Nigerian economy to resolve its endemic socio-economic problems, it needs to grow by 6%–8% annually (PricewaterhouseCoopers, 2019). The country's economic stagnation is complicated by decline in oil production and export, increase in importation of refined petroleum products and government's fiscal policies which have resulted in scarcity of foreign exchange that stagnates growth and development of non-oil sectors of the economy.

Despite profiting so much from oil boom in the past, Nigeria has not succeeded in diversifying its economy away from oil dependency through efficient management of surplus revenue and massive investment in infrastructural development. Thus, overreliance on oil engenders unhealthy competition for scarce resources among Nigeria's diverse ethnic groups, and facilitates corruption in government, criminality and insecurity in the country. Consequently, illegal oil bunkering, vandalisation of oil pipelines, and social unrest and separatist agitations have forced a historic low oil production in Nigeria. The country remains among the members of Organization of Petroleum Exporting Countries (OPEC) not meeting their production quotas despite being the sixth largest oil producer in the world. Low productivity in the oil sector means that Nigeria is not benefitting substantially from surging oil prices caused by the ongoing Russia-Ukraine War which has disrupted global oil supply. Furthermore, the collapse of oil refineries in Nigeria and consequent perennial problem of petrol subsidy continue to gulp a larger share of the country's gross oil revenue preventing the country from fulfilling other obligations such as the provision of adequate funding for education and maintenance of hospital facilities and roads (Ahon, 2022; Aduloju, 2022; Edeh, 2022).

Socio-Economic and National Security Link/Context

With respect to national security profile of Nigeria, it is evident that lack of efficient infrastructure is blamed for inconsequential contribution of the manufacturing, agricultural and tourism sectors to the economy as well as increase in illegal mining of non-oil resources such as gold. In the same manner, massive housing gap contributes to the rise in criminal activities, as well as widespread communicable diseases, exorbitant house prices, poor living standards and high mortgage costs (Ekpo, 2019). Furthermore, deplorable condition of roads equally contributes to insecurity in Nigeria. Reported cases of robberies, kidnappings and attacks by terrorists and other criminal elements occur on poorly maintained roads as depressions on road surfaces force motorists to drive carefully at snail speed thereby rendering them vulnerable to attacks by criminal elements (Babalola, 2021).

Poor state of road coupled with poor communication system and porous borders contributes directly and indirectly to violence orchestrated by international terrorist organisations such as Boko Haram and the incursion of others into Nigeria from neighbouring states. Among notable terrorist organisations whose operations impact Nigeria's national security are Movement for Oneness and Jihad (West Africa) and Ansa Dine (Mali); Al-Qaeda in the Islamic Maghreb (AQIM); al-Shaabaab in Somalia; Islamic State in the West African Province (ISWAP), Ansar al-Jihad (Maghreb); and Ansar al-Sharia (Tunisia). Besides these, deplorable road conditions cause several road accidents in Nigeria. According to Road Transport Report by National Bureau of Statistics and the Federal Road Safety Corps (FRSC), around 2,080 accidents involving 3,334 vehicles occurred in the 2nd quarter of 2020 alone, resulting in the deaths of 855 people and the injuring of 5,353 others (National Bureau of Statistics, 2021).

Specifically, the lack of infrastructure in rural and semi-urban areas and deplorable conditions of existing ones in major cities in the north-east of Nigeria have contributed to persistent violence perpetrated by Boko Haram. The consequences of infrastructure gap in Nigeria's development trajectory are huge warranting the country's various descriptions as 'sleeping giant', 'fantastically corrupt', 'unproductive', and 'hopeless, by various commentators. Among these unfortunate consequences are the absence of peace and security; endemic poverty; low literacy rate; unemployment; high prevalence of communicable diseases; gross human rights abuses; and wanton destruction of fragile ecosystem. These factors trigger a deep sense of social injustice, religiosity, anger and willingness to resort to violence as a means of dispute resolution among Nigerians.

The urgent need to reduce poverty, stimulate economic growth and create jobs requires substantial investment in physical infrastructure because infrastructure is the catalyst for development across all sectors of a country's economy. However, poor economic performance, dwindling foreign development aids due to donor fatigue and increasing budgetary constraints mean it will be difficult for Nigeria to close its infrastructure gap through budgetary allocation or financing through government revenue. It will also be difficult to rely solely on deficit financing or loans provided by foreign and domestic financial institutions and governments to close the infrastructure deficit. These two approaches previously used for capital project funding in the country have proven grossly inadequate to close the country's infrastructure gap as they are heavily dependent on stable commodity prices, and interest and willingness of lending institutions.

IMPACT OF PUBLIC-PRIVATE PARTNERSHIP PROJECTS IN NIGERIA

Huge capital investment on infrastructure is justified on the ground that infrastructure promotes development of other sectors of the economy. Succinctly put, all aspects of the Nigerian economy depend on physical infrastructure such as road, railway, air, and sea transportation as well as buildings. A good road network, for example, enables smooth travelling and timely arrival at destinations and smooth movement of goods and services across the country. Poor road network and underdeveloped rail lines among others obstruct transportation of goods around the country.

As Nedozi, Obasanmi, Ighata (2014) put it, excellent infrastructure contributes towards better quality of life for all citizens by creating and facilitating transport, energy distribution, communication services and macroeconomic stability. Conversely, poor or inadequate infrastructure such as incessant electricity supply and poor telecommunication services in strategic cities result in low productivity and macroeconomic instability.

Furthermore, good infrastructure provides social comfort to citizens while infrastructure deficit results in colossal disruption of the entire economic system and the lowering of people's quality of life both physically and mentally or otherwise (Aworinde & Akintoye, 2019). Poor power supply, for example, mostly affect small and medium enterprises (SMEs) which help to enlarge a country's middle class and directly contribute to its social stability and economic growth by increasing access to economic resources and employment opportunities.

Studies have shown that PPP enhances economic growth or increases national and per capita income of a country (Lee, Han, Gaspar & Alano, 2018; Deep, Kim & Lee, 2019; Fabre & Straub, 2021). Economic growth in turn leads to economic development or observable structural changes in various dimensions of an economy over a sustainable period of time. These structural changes lead to improvement in the material well-being of the state, society and people; hence, the resort by the Nigerian government to the PPP approach. The Nigerian government listed several federal assets for concession in order to make them more productive and profitable and as part of its efforts to revamp the physical infrastructure in the country.

Among candidate assets were the National Arts Theatre in Iganmu, Lagos; Tafawa Balewa Square in Lagos; and the River Basin Development Authorities at the cost of N836 million (approximately US$1.8 million). Other assets include the National Stadium, Lagos; the Moshood Abiola Stadium, Abuja; and two others at N100 million (approximately US$218 thousand). These listed projects will take various forms of PPPs such as service contracts; management and operating contracts; lease contracts; concessions; and joint ventures. Each PPP form has its own specific levels of participation and amount of risks acceptable to the private sector.

Accordingly, the Bureau for Public Enterprises is ready to privatise the Afam Power and Yola Distribution Company. Terminal B of the Warri old Port is also slated for concession while the government seeks to restructure and commercialise the Bank of Agriculture, and partially commercialise the Nigeria Postal Services, the River Basin Development Authorities, national parks and the power sector. The initiative to privatise and concession these assets is against the background that doing so will enable the government to sufficiently fund its budgets as well as enable the enterprises to perform well (Iroanusi, 2021). Since 1999 the private sector has engaged more strategically with the Nigerian government in developing, rehabilitating and maintaining socio-economic infrastructure of the country.

The operation of PPP in Nigeria is legally guided by the Public-Private Partnership and Road Infrastructure Development Order No. 007 of 2019; the Public Procurement Act 2007; and the Infrastructure Concession Regulatory Commission Act of 2005. Other legal bases include the Debt Management Office Act of 2003; the Public Enterprises through the Privatization and Commercialization Act of 1999; and the National Planning Commission Act of 1993, among others. Since coming into existence in the 1990s, the Infrastructure Concession Regulatory Commission of Nigeria has directed investment in national infrastructure through various forms of PPPs such as leasing, franchising, concessions, equity and joint venture participation. Both the federal and state governments of Nigeria have constructed roads; built bridges, rail lines, and housing estates; and rehabilitated airports in order to improve transportation and movement of people, goods and services across the country.

Among projects completed through PPPs are the expansion of Lagos-Ibadan Expressway into five lanes; the construction of Victoria Island- Epe

Express road; Dolphin Estate; Nigeria Port Authority Terminal; and the Lagos State Bus Rapid Transit. Scholars have noted that partnership between the public and private sectors in Nigeria, especially in the housing sector, has immensely contributed to the up scaling of housing provision in states such as Lagos. Similarly, PPP model of Design-Build-Finance-Own (DBFO) entered into by the Federal Capital Authority and Salini Construction Company Limited resulted in the development of the Millennium Park, Maitama Abuja. This project does not only beautify Abuja landscape but also contributes to the city's social interaction and economic development.

The quality of services provided by the Nigerian Port Authority has also improved in terms of efficiency and turnaround time in the handling of cargoes, easing of international trade, and clearing and forwarding businesses. It should be recalled that in 2004 about 16 terminals belonging to the Nigerian Ports Authority were acquired through concession by some private firms. In places such as Lagos State, there has also been remarkable improvement in public transportation. The operation of Bus Rapid Transit (BRT) has lessened the difficulty of the movement of people in Lagos in terms of time taken to move around the state using BRT routes. Previously, owing to congestion due to overcrowding and traffic gridlock, moving around Lagos city was difficult. With BRT however, the ever-busy roads of Lagos have become decongested to a reasonable extent as they carry an estimated 5 million or more people per year (Afolabi & Fashola, 2016).

Partnership with the private sector in Nigeria has contributed significantly to the development of capital projects. Several public agencies have embarked on capital projects they could not undertake in the past due to budgetary constraints and limited access to loan and credit facilities offered by commercial banks in Nigeria. In cases where public agencies are unable to embark of capital projects of their own they have been able to operate from state-of-the-art leased premises and facilities that are designed, constructed and operated by private investors in major Nigerian cities. From cost-benefit analysis, public agencies and ministries operating from leased facilities save the government from financial risks of engaging in capital projects and abandoning them halfway due to insufficient funds and endemic corruption. Again, by operating from leased premises and facilities, they equally save the government the cost of maintaining such office spaces and information technology facilities.

Despite the popularity of PPP and its advocacy as the way forward to solving Nigeria's infrastructure deficit, the application of the framework in the country has exhibited serious limitations. For example, the impact of privatisation as an aspect of PPP on the Nigerian economy has to a large extent been minimal. Since 2004 about 142 public enterprises have been privatised by the Bureau for Public Enterprises. Contrary to expectations however, about 37%

of privatised enterprises (52 companies) are categorised as non-performing or performing poorly (Olawoyin, 2018).

Problem of non-performing privatised public assets in recent years has led to serious protests by trade unions. Incessant labour unrest against privatisation come from the fact that privatisation has so far favoured mainly the political class and their cronies. Thus, it is characterised as an elite's enrichment programme. This characterisation has made privatisation unattractive to both the federal and state governments as a model for infrastructure development, maintenance and service provision. Specifically, massive protests by Nigerians against the privatisation of downstream sector of the Nigerian oil industry and energy sector cautioned the Nigerian government against further privatisation of national assets.

The irony of privatisation programme in Nigeria is that contrary to expectations that it would result in improved productivity and efficient public service delivery, the opposite has largely been the case. The partially privatised energy sector, for example, remains unstable, grossly mismanaged and unable to produce beyond 4,000MW of electricity. Total energy generation in Nigeria remains stagnant at 4,000MW despite huge financial investments in the sector through privatisation (Nnaji, 2011). It is noted that prior to privatisation the country had targeted to generate about 11,879MW of electricity by 2012 and had a post-privatisation target of 14,218MW and 40,000 MW by 2013 and 2020, respectively (Nnaji, 2011). This projection did not materialise for a number of reasons including corruption.

With respect to the Murtala Muhammed International Airport Terminal 2 (MMIAT2), for example, the Nigerian government awarded concession to Bi-Courtney Limited in 2003 to develop, finance, manage and operate the MMIAT2 under a Design-Build-Operate-Transfer (DBOT) arrangement (MMA2 & Bi-Courtney Aviation Services Limited, 2020). The contractual arrangement required Bi-Courtney to design the new airport terminal, raise the required fund, construct, equip and operate the facility for 36 years. The visible impact of this project is measured by improved capacity of the MMA2 to around 75% of the domestic flights in Nigeria (MMA2 & Bi-Courtney Aviation Limited Services, 2020).

The new terminal provides efficient air transport services through the use of state-of-the-art technologies such as the Common Users Passenger Processing System (CUPPS), Self-service Check-in kiosks; and Automated Access Gates, among others. The completion of the MMA2 project has resulted in increased customer satisfaction and the number of both local and international travellers has increased (MMA2 & Bi-Courtney Aviation Limited Services, 2020). Unlike in the past, PPP has contributed to increased productive collaboration between state governments and the central government in recent times. This is evidenced by collaboration between Lagos State and the federal government. Furthermore, several PPP projects are contributing to institutional and technological transformation in Nigeria and have led to job creation in the country. This invariably has resulted in the increase of people's real income, savings and investment. By contributing to the increase in peoples' income, PPP projects invariably contribute to the growth of Nigeria's GDP.

Ekpo (2019) stressed that housing makes both economic and social contributions to the Nigerian society. Therefore, PPP investment in the housing sector has been contributing to the building of fixed capital assets in the country in some states such as Lagos. Besides helping to create fixed capital assets in Nigeria, PPP investments are also creating employment and business opportunities for the Nigerian populace. For example, the estate agency business in the country is dominated by youth entrepreneurs. People of other professions such as lawyers have also entered into the estate business as an additional or integral part of their legal practice in recent times. Although still inadequate, PPP investment in the housing sector in Nigeria is helping the growth and development of other sectors in what has been described as organic backward and forward linkage within the economy.

Socially, investment in housing is helping to create good quality housing for Nigerians who can afford to rent or buy housing units from the developers. Private partnership investments in public hospitals are also contributing to the upgrading of health facilities as well as creating access to healthcare services in Nigeria. This is also true of the Nigerian educational sector where investment in private universities is promoting good quality education services. In the public education sector where infrastructure is in deplorable condition, PPP investments help to improve educational facilities as individuals and corporate entities are constructing and donating buildings to schools. These developments that are happening against the backdrop that enhanced access to health and education services as well as employment opportunities in the country will eventually result in higher productivity and increased income for low socio-economic groups in Nigeria (Ekpo, 2019).

The effects of PPP approach on development are also being felt in the security sector, especially in the fight against terrorism in the north eastern part of the country. The privatisation of the communication sector has resulted in improvement in satellite communication system in Nigeria. This has helped the Nigerian army in different ways to register significant successes in the fight against Boko Haram. Firstly, improved communication system is helping to track down terrorists, intercept communications and locate the exact hideout of criminals in the forests. Secondly, improved communication and technology is equally helping to push terrorists to the fringes of Nigerian territories where the presence of government is not well felt.

Despite the noticeable positive impacts of PPP projects on different sectors of the Nigerian economy, the framework is still saddled with a lot of challenges.

CHALLENGES OF THE PPP FRAMEWORK IN NIGERIA

The precarious socio-economic profile of Nigeria and expert prognoses show that it would be almost impossible for Nigeria to overcome infrastructure deficit through budgetary allocation and deficit financing. Donor fatigue, increasing budgetary constraints and poor economic performance support this conclusion and a recourse to PPP approach. As Rana and Izuwah (2018) argue, the private sector can source funding from national and international sources. Triveno and Hamilton (2017) add that government may not be able to access funding from several of the sources open to the private sector.

The recourse to PPP is also predicated on the robustness of the PPP framework as an approach that combines the advantage of competitive contract tendering process, flexible negotiations and risk distribution across contracting partners on agreed basis. These factual attributes of PPP approach notwithstanding, its operation in Nigeria is fraught with several challenges. The PPP framework is supposedly a contractual arrangement between the public and private entities whereby the private sector entity has requisite expertise, access to technologies, and financial capability to complement those of government in developing the infrastructure of a country. However, experience has shown that PPP works efficiently well where the private sector is well developed and capacitated. In this regard, the challenges confronting PPP operations in Nigeria take various forms.

Poor performances of enterprises that run through PPP models in Nigeria are attributed to two structural factors. The first is the lack of enabling business environment in Nigeria. For example, unstable power supply and dilapidated infrastructure affect the cost of operating a business in the country. This in turn affects productivity and profitability of privatised enterprises. This fact accounts for why many private and public enterprises close down or move to neighbouring countries but still target the Nigerian market (Anekwe, Ndubusi-Okolo & Enemuo-Uzoezie, 2019). The second factor relates to endemic corruption in the country. Scholars have shown that corruption is a key challenge to PPP operations in Nigeria (Arimoro, 2019).

Thus, the poor performance of enterprises that run through PPP models has been partially linked to allegations of complicity between those in government and private investors during the bidding processes to acquire and manage public enterprises through PPP models. In many cases concessions were awarded to investors who lacked capacity in terms of access to funds, managerial competence, and requisite technology to revamp acquired enterprises and make them profitable. Thus, despite government mantra of making these enterprises become efficient and profitable through modernisation of operations and technologies and increased productivity, these enterprises have become non-performing.

National policies and PPP legislation provide the basis on which contractual agreements are made for effective operation. Thus, contract documents clearly provide for risk distribution between public entities and private investors in a PPP operation as well as functions to be performed by each partner to the agreement. Thus, success or failure of any PPP project is then dependent on the extent to which various stakeholders carry out assigned functions. It is therefore of critical importance that PPP contracts are written in unambiguous language to avoid differential interpretation and understanding of their contents.

In some sectors of the Nigerian economy where PPP is recognised as a means of closing infrastructure gap, there exists no national policy framework to guide stakeholders. The absence of national policy framework to guide stakeholders' operations in most cases disadvantages low socio-economic groups in Nigeria. In this regard, Aduwo, Ibem and Onyemaechi (2017) note that despite the recognition of the housing sector as one sector in which the Nigerian government requires partnership with the private sector to close a huge gap, there is no national policy framework or legislation to guide PPP stakeholders. As a result, developers carry out PPP housing projects based on guidelines which tend to promote housing for the rich and wealthy in the country.

In sectors of the Nigerian economy where national policy framework exists to guide stakeholders in PPP operations, it has been observed that contractual agreements are often characterised by inconsistencies in the interpretation of provisions and definition of roles of partners. Disagreements therefore negatively impact on smooth operations of PPP projects in Nigeria. Some empirical examples will suffice to illustrate this challenge. The Nigerian government granted concession to the Bi-Courtney Highway Services Limited (BCHSL) to repair and expand the Lagos-Ibadan Expressway in 2006. The concession agreement suggested that BCHSL was to serve as manager of the project but not as a contractor (Oluwaseun & Odun, 2014).

This role entailed arranging for and coordinating project funds as well as engaging the services of contractors to develop the road. In the end, BCHSL was unable to find investors for the project, and assumed the role of a contractor. This affected the project as it could not take off until 2016, 10 years after concession agreement was signed. Considering the strategic importance of the expressway, the Nigerian government had to abandon the PPP arrangement and reverted to the former contracting system by engaging the services of

Messrs. Julius Berger Construction and RCC Limited through funds provided by the Presidential Infrastructure Development Fund established to accelerate the development of strategic infrastructure projects critical to the growth and transformation of the Nigerian economy (Oluwaseun & Odun, 2014).

Governance or administration in general is supposed to operate as a continuum towards socio-economic development of a country. This implies, in large part, stability of macro-economic policies and continuation of projects of previous governments which lead to development among others. This major attribute of governance and administration is largely absent in Nigeria and in particular among its federating units (states). In this regard, many privatised public enterprises face the challenge of discontinuity of PPP projects by incoming administrations or governments. Present administrations have tended to withdraw from PPP arrangements made by previous administrations especially if such projects are deemed not to have immediate impact on or benefits to those in authority. The case of Ogun State with respect to cargo airport project and the Gateway Hotels project are often cited as evidence of the challenge of discontinuity of PPP programmes by successor governments.

The Ogun State government embarked upon the development of a cargo airport as a PPP project in 2004 in a strategic location that would enable the state to leverage on its close proximity to Lagos to advance its own development. Under the PPP arrangement, the state government kick-started the project by finding suitable contractors and entering into agreement with them and private investors interested in carrying out the project. The project was however abandoned in 2009, a year after the tenure of the government that started it ended (Oluwaseun & Odun, 2014). The succeeding government abandoned the project because it became marred in controversies and allegations of corruption during the contract awarding processes. Similarly, the Gateway Hotels, owned by Ogun State, was also abandoned due to disagreements over its concession. The two cited cases are not unique to Ogun State. Allegations of corruption are rift in the concessions of many public enterprises across Nigeria which in many cases had prompted competent private partners to back off from bidding to acquire and manage public enterprises. In other cases, private entities which lack adequate resources to run acquired public assets have ended up shutting them down completely (Oluwaseun & Odun, 2014).

As previous alluded to, the private sector in Nigeria has limited access to adequate financial resources, expertise, and technical and managerial capabilities necessary for the efficient operation of PPP framework. These weaknesses are seen from the development of projects such as the Lagos-Ibadan Expressway and the Second Niger Bridge, which were conceived as PPP projects in 2006 and 2010, respectively. However, they could not take off until 2016 because the private partners involved lacked access to required funds to repair and expand the Lagos-Ibadan Expressway and to construct the Second Niger Bridge. This reality forced the Nigerian government to abandon the PPP agreements and to revert to former system of contracting through budgetary allocation (Majeed, 2021).

The second Niger Bridge was estimated to cost N206 billion (approximately US$450 million) but the private partners were unable to raise the fund due to limited capacity of Nigerian banks to lend up to N200 billion (approximately US$437 million) or more to any individual without sovereign guarantee. Even where capacity to do so exists, the banks always ask for a sovereign guarantee. What this means is that the federal government will end up paying for the projects (Afolabi & Fashola, 2016, Majeed, 2021). Another demonstration of the weakness or lack of sufficient capacity of the Nigerian private sector to provide effective partnership with the Nigerian government is the Lekki-Epe Expressway. The concession agreement was signed in 2005 but private investors could not raise the needed funds to execute the project until the Lagos State government stepped in by taking loan to kick start the project. Project was dormant for five years (Afolabi & Fashola, 2016). The poor state of the road hindered economic development of the area during those dormant five years.

The banking institutions in Nigeria are more risk averse in funding capital projects. Perhaps, this is as a result of the difficulties associated with loan recovery in Nigeria as well as unstable interest rates. High interest rates cause borrowers to default on loan recovery. Similarly, poor securities offered as collaterals by entities requesting for loans to fund capital projects are in many cases inadequate. Sometimes when loans are due, beneficiaries are unable to pay back and the securities offered to lending institutions are inadequate to recoup their losses; hence, the reason for seeking a sovereign guarantee. Foreign investors are also scared to invest in the Nigeria's infrastructure sector because of insecurity in the country. As noted previously international terrorism, separatist agitations, banditry and other criminal activities continue to happen in Nigeria. Sourcing funds internationally has also become difficult due to unstable macroeconomic policies (Mobuogwu, 2019).

The issue of limited access to resources is not peculiar to road project investors alone. Even in the housing sector a serious challenge of sustainable sources of funding exists. Private partners in the housing sector act as owners or operators as well as leaseholders and financiers. In this regard, they take substantial risk in developing commercial, industrial, residential, recreation and tourism projects in Nigeria. However, obtaining and repaying loans from financial institutions in Nigeria to implement PPP projects remains difficult. This difficulty emanates from restrictive lending and borrowing which financial institutions in Nigeria practice and the time given for loan repayment at high interest rates.

Given that PPP developers are required to pay back loans at high interest rate and earn profit from their investment as quickly as possible, they resort to investing time and money on housing projects that tend to target the rich and wealthy in Nigeria. The resort is based on economic analysis which shows that such moves guarantee quick returns on investment. The gross effect of restrictive lending and borrowing practice and high interest rate is that in the absence of government subsidy, PPP developers are unable to construct houses that are affordable to low- and middle-income groups where the bulk of housing deficit in the country exist.

Besides the experience of investors in property development, private partnership with the public sector in providing adequate housing services to the Nigerian populace is equally confronted with challenges. Low-income earners experience difficulty with accessing mortgage services to buy and own houses because the financial institutions require the provision of strong collaterals in addition to meeting other limiting conditions governing loans and credit services.

The setting of restrictive conditions for accessing mortgage services is not only done by commercial banks but also by the Federal Mortgage Bank of Nigeria which administers the National Housing Fund (NHF) scheme in which civil servants contribute at least 2.5% of their income monthly towards buying and owning a house (Aduwo *et al.,* 2017). The Federal Mortgage Bank of Nigeria provides that for contributors to NHF to access loans towards buying and owning their own houses, they have to apply through a registered and duly accredited primary mortgage institution (PMI). The service costs of PMI registration are high. Thus, only few low-income earners afford such services. These severe gatekeeping conditions prevent many low-income contributors to the NHF scheme from accessing loan and credit facilities to buy and own their own houses.

CONCLUSION

This discourse departed from the premise that a mutually interlinked and reinforcing relationship exists between infrastructural development and the national security of a country. Therefore, the reliability of infrastructure such as reliable power supply; good road network; airport and seaport transportation; telecommunication; good water supply and proper sanitation; educational institutions and health services are essential prerequisites for rapid socio-economic development and national security enhancement.

The chapter also affirmed that it will be extremely difficult for Nigeria to close its huge infrastructural deficit if it relies on budgetary allocation and deficit financing. This conclusion agrees with the World Bank estimation that it would take the country about 300 years to close its infrastructure gap at the current rate of investment in the sector. In support of this conclusion the chapter presented and discussed the unenviable infrastructure profile of Nigeria which informed the sustained call for the adoption of PPP approach to infrastructure development. The chapter agrees that PPP has the potential to close Nigeria's infrastructure deficit which in turn will enhance its economic growth and development or the continuous and directional expansion of the various dimensions of its economy.

Noticeable improvement in service delivery in some privatised sectors of the economy attest to the fact that PPP is indeed a veritable alternative means of infrastructure development in Nigeria if rightly implemented. Conversely, the failure of several privatised public enterprises shows that if PPP is wrongly implemented it can result in the destruction of the economy. Thus, overcoming several challenges which currently impact the PPP implementation in Nigeria is necessary if the country is to close its infrastructure gap. These challenges include but not limited to the issue of corruption which results in the engagement of private sector partners without adequate technical, managerial, financial and marketing resources in PPP operations. It is also necessary for governments at national and state levels to secure sufficient political will in terms of continuity of PPP projects embarked on by previous administrations.

REFERENCES

Aduloju, B. (2022). Nigeria misses OPEC quota as oil production shortfall hits 6.9m bpd in 11 months. Available from: https://www.thecable.ng/nigeria-misses-opec-quota-as-oil-production-shortfall-hits-6-9m-bpd-in-11-months. Date of access: February 08, 2023.

Aduwo, E. B., Ibem, E. O and Onyemaechi, P. (2017). *Challenges and Opportunities in Public-Private Partnerships (PPPs) for Housing Low-Income Earners in Nigeria.* The World Bank: Public-Private Partnership Legal Resource Center.

Afolabi, O.J and Fashola, O.K. (2016). Assessment of bus rapid transit in efficient movement of commuters in Lagos State, *European Journal of Humanities and Social Sciences.* Vol. 35, (1), pp.1951–1963.

Ahon, F. (2022). OPEC: Nigeria not meeting her oil production quota, FG cries out. *Vanguard.* Available from: https://www.vanguardngr.com/2022/08/opec-nigeria-not-meeting-her-oil-production-quota-fg-cries-out/. Date of access: February 08, 2023.

Akinpelu, Y. (2019). Nigeria needs 700,000 homes yearly — but govt plans to build only 2,383. *Premium Times.* Available from: https://www.premiumtimesng.com/news/headlines/359274-nigeria-needs-700000-homes-yearly-but-govt-plans-to-build-only-2383.html. Date of access: February 08, 2023.

Anekwe, R. I., Ndubusi-Okolo, P and Enemuo-Uzoezie, C. (2019). Sustainability in the Nigerian business environment: Problems and prospects. *International Journal of Academic Management Science Research*, Vol. 3(3), pp.72–80.

Arimoro, A. (2019). Corruption and public-private partnerships in Nigeria: Good governance and ethical considerations. In A. Agada (Ed). *Combating the menace of corruption in Nigeria: A multi-disciplinary conversation.* Black Tower Publishers.

Association of Nigerian Electricity Distributors. (2022). ANED Analytics Reports. Available from: http://www.anedng.com/resources/analytics-reports/. Date of access: February 08, 2023.

Aworinde, O. B and Akintoye, I. R. (2019). Institutions, infrastructure and economic growth in Nigeria, Acta. *Universitatis Danubius. Œconomica*, Vol. 15 (3), pp.205–216.

Babalola, A. A. (2021). The deplorable condition of the Nigerian road: A bane to economic sustainability. *Vanguard.* Available from: https://www.vanguardngr.com/2021/10/the-deplorable-condition-of-the-nigerian-road-a-bane-to-economic-sustainability/. Date of access: December 15, 2022.

Chan, A. P. C., Lam, P.T., Chan, D.W., Cheung, E., and Ke, Y. (2009). Drivers for adopting public-private partnerships—Empirical comparison between China and Hong Kong special administrative region, *Journal of Construction Engineering and Management,* Vol. 135 (11). Doi: 10.1061/ (ASCE) CO.1943-7862.0000088.

Dam, D.P., Alaci, D., Udoo, V., Jacob Atser, J., Ujoh, F., and Gyuse, T. P. (2021). Structure of road network connectivity in the Benue basin of Nigeria. *International Journal of Geography and Regional Planning Research,* Vol. 6 (1), pp.62–75.

Deep, A., Kim, J., Lee, M. (Eds). (2019). *Realizing the Potential of Public–Private Partnerships to Advance Asia's Infrastructure Development.* Metro Manila, Philippines: Korea Development Institute.

Ebuh, G. U., Ezike, I. B., Shitile, T. S., Smith, E.S and Haruna, T. M. (2019). The infrastructure–growth nexus in Nigeria: A reassessment, *Journal of Infrastructure Development*, Vol. 11(1–2), pp. 41–58.

Edeh, H. (2022). Again, Nigeria fails to meet OPEC oil production quota, with 927,000 bpd August output. *International Centre for Investigative Reporting.* Available from: https://www.icirnigeria.org/again-nigeria-fails-to-meet-opec-oil-production-quota-with-927000-bpd-august-output/. Date of access: February 08, 2023.

Ekpo, A. (2019). Housing deficit in Nigeria: Issues, challenges and prospects. *Economic and Financial Review*, Vol. 7 (4). pp. 177–188.

Fabre, A and Straub, S. (2021). *The Impact of Public-Private Partnerships (PPPs) in Infrastructure, Health and Education.* Working Papers No.986. Toulouse School of Economics.

Faminu, G. (2022). Nigeria's infrastructure gap may close in 300 years-WorldBank. *Africa Business.* Available from: https://businessday.ng/news/article/nigerias-infrastructure-gap-may-close-in-300-years-worldbank/. Date of access: February 08, 2023.

Infrastructure Concession Regulatory Commission. (2023). *135,000km road network in Nigeria un-tarred- ICRC.* Available from: https://www.icrc.gov.ng/135000km-road-network-nigeria-un-tarred-icrc/. Date of access: February 01, 2023.

International Bank for Reconstruction and Development. (2016). Nigeria developing housing finance. Available from: https://documents1.worldbank.org/curated

/en/102491481528326920/pdf/110897-WP-P131973-PUBLIC-HousingFinanceNigeriaweb.pdf. Date of access: February 08, 2023.

Iroanusi, Q. E. (2021). Nigeria confirms plans to sell govt properties to fund 2021 budget. *Premium Times*. Available from: https://www.premiumtimesng.com/business/business-news/436687-nigeria-confirms-plans-to-sell-govt-properties-to-fund-2021-budget.html?tztc=1. Date of access: February 01, 2023).

Lee, M., Han, X., Gaspar, R., & Alano, E. (2018). Deriving macroeconomic benefits from public–private partnerships in developing Asia. *ADB Economics Working Paper Series*. Available from: https://www.adb.org/sites/default/files/publication/438786/ewp-551-macroeconomic-benefits-ppps-asia.pdf. Date of access: November 13, 2022.

Majeed. B. (2021). Why FG abandoned PPP arrangements on Second Niger Bridge, Lagos-Ibandan Expressway-Fashola. *Premium Times*. October 25. Available from: https://www.premiumtimesng.com/news/top-news/491717-why-fg-abandoned-ppp-arrangements-on-second-niger-bridge-lagos-ibadan-expressway-fashola.html. Date of access: February 02, 2023.

MMA2 & Bi-Courtney Aviation Limited Services. (2020). Our history. Available from: https://www.mma2.com.ng/corporate-information/our-history/. Date of access: December 02, 2022.

Mobuogwu, M. (2019). Rural land and credit access in Nigeria. Focus on Land in Africa. Available from: file:///C:/Users/riroanya/Downloads/gatesopenres-184555.pdf. Date of access: January 20, 2023.

National Bureau of Statistics. (2012). Annual Abstract of Statistics, 2012. Federal Republic of Nigeria. Available from:
https://www.nigerianstat.gov.ng/pdfuploads/annual_abstract_2012.pdf. Date of access: January 06, 2023.

Nedozi, F.O., Obasanmi, J.O., Ighata, J.A. (2014). Infrastructural development and economic growth in Nigeria: Using simultaneous equation. *Journal of Economics*, Vol. 5 (3), pp. 325–332.

Nigeria Bureau of Statistics. (2022). Nigerian gross domestic product report (Q2 2022). Available from: https://nigerianstat.gov.ng/elibrary/read/1241219. Date of access: February 02, 2023.

Nnaji. B. (2011). Power Sector Outlook in Nigeria: Governments Renewed Priorities. Abuja: Securities and Exchange Commission. Available from: https://sec.gov.ng/files/Prof%20Nnaji%20Presentation.pdf. Date of access: February 02, 2023.

Ojo, A.E. (2021. Sustainable infrastructure for Nigeria's sustainable economic development: whither transportation or electric power supply. *Journal of Mega Infrastructure and Sustainable Development*, Vol. 2 (3), pp.248–261.

Olawoyin, O. (2018). 37 per cent of privatised Nigerian firms are failing—BPE. *Premium Times*. Available from: https://www.premiumtimesng.com/news/headlines/259286-37-per-cent-of-privatised-nigerian-firms-are-failing-bpe.html?tztc=1. Date of access: February 08, 2023.

Oluwaseun. O & Odun. O. (2014). Public private partnership and Nigerian economic growth: Problems and prospects. *International Journal of Business and Social Science*. Vol. 5(4), pp.132–139.

Otaru, A. (2022). 40% of Nigerian population live below poverty line, says report. *The Guardian*. Available from: https://guardian.ng/business-services/40-of-nigerian-population-live-below-poverty-line-says-report/. Date of access: February 02, 2023.

Oyedepo, S. O. (2012). Energy and sustainable development in Nigeria: The way forward, *Energy, Sustainability and Society*, Vol. 2, (15). pp. 1–17.

PricewaterhouseCoopers. (2019). Solving the liquidity crunch in the Nigerian power sector. White Paper Presented at Power Sector Roundtable Conference hosted by Mainstream Energy Solution Limited on September 24, 2019 at Kainji Dam Hydropwer Plant, Niger State. Available from: https://www.pwc.com/ng/en/assets/pdf/solving-liquidity-crunch-nigerian-power.pdf. Date of access: February 08, 2023.

Rana, F and Izuwah, C. (2018). *Infrastructure and Africa's Development—The PPP Imperative*. World Bank's Infrastructure and Public Private Partnership Publication.

TheGlobalEconomy.com. (2021). Human development - Country rankings. Available from: https://www.theglobaleconomy.com/rankings/human_development/. Date of access: January 21, 2023.

Triveno, L and Hamilton, E. (2017). *Three Misconceptions in the Way of Better Housing Policies*. World Bank's Building Sustainable Communities Research Publication.

Ujah, W. (2018). Human dev't index: W/Bank ranks Nigeria 152nd out of 157 countries. *Vanguardng*. Available from: https://www.vanguardngr.com/2018/10/human-devt-index-w-bank-ranks-nigeria-152nd-out-of-157-countries/. Date of access: January 07, 2023.

Ukpe, W. (2021). Nigeria needs $1.5 trillion to close Infrastructure deficit in ten years—Buhari. *Business News*. Available from: https://nairametrics.com/2021/11/03/nigeria-needs-1-5-trillion-to-close-infrastructure-deficit-in-ten-years-buhari/. Date of access: February 08, 2023.

World Bank. (2021). *The Word Bank in Nigeria*. Available from: https://www.worldbank.org/en/country/nigeria/overview. Date of access: February 02, 2023.

World Bank. (2018). *Nigeria Affordable Housing Project (P165296)*. Available from: https://documents.worldbank.org/curated/en/278041531299329812/pdf/Concept-Project-Information-Document-Integrated-Safeguards-Data-Sheet-Nigeria-Affordable-Housing-Project-P165296.pdf. Date of access: February 02, 2023.

Chapter 9

Public-Private Partnerships and Toll Road Concessions in South Africa

Thabo Daniel Borole

The current economic meltdown coupled with misappropriation of funds affects the government's balance sheet adversely. The abovementioned challenges contribute hugely on the financial distress that the South African (SA) government finds itself into, and to make matters worse the same government is faced with the ballooning financial responsibility towards social welfare (i.e., social grants, social relief of distress, etc.). On the other hand, global warming effects such as Kwazulu-Natal and Eastern Cape floods, and dwindling water levels in dams across the country force the government to redirect funds from pre-planned infrastructure projects. Energy crisis experienced by the country, inability of government to deliver infrastructure projects and other services compound the deterioration of government's capacity and financial ability.

All aforementioned competing priorities placed on SA government dictate that the public sector considers contractual partnerships with the private sector in order to address its mandate of delivering public infrastructure projects to citizens. The private sector has few options to intervene in order to assist the government, and one of those options is that of entering into public-private partnership (PPP) arrangements with government. And as things are standing in SA, there are three PPP arrangements in the road subsector (namely, N3, N4 (East Toll Road), N1N4 (West Toll Road)), and the Gauteng Freeway Improvement Plan Toll Road (GFIP) had just been recently scrapped as the toll concession. Since the introduction of public-private partnerships in South Africa's toll road subsector in the late 1990s, the government has had some degree of relief in the financing, designing, constructing, operating and maintenance of the infrastructure on the toll road concessions mentioned above. In ensuring that the forms of risks mentioned above are transferred to the concessionaires, the government adopted the design, construct, finance, operate and maintain (DCFOM) model, since this model protects the government against risk exposure.

The agency that entered into contractual agreement with private sector on behalf of government is South African National Roads Agency (SOC) Limited (SANRAL). Ninety-four of South Africa's 22,253-kilometre national road network is managed, improved, and maintained by SANRAL, with remaining 6% being administered through PPPs and allocated 30-year concession period (SANRAL, 2018:24).

LITERATURE REVIEW

In contributing to the improvement of the toll road concessions as a form of PPPs, the literature review for this study consisted of relevant secondary information. Bordens and Abbott (2008:63) describe the method of finding, gathering, reviewing, and evaluating research material in a particular area of interest as a literature review. The following SA government documents were obtained for this study:

- National Treasury PPP Unit 2007, Introducing public-private partnerships in South Africa;
- National Treasury PPP Unit Date 2007, Municipal Service Delivery and PPP Guidelines;
- National Treasury PPP Unit 2004, PPP Practice Note;
- National Treasury PPP Unit 2004, Standardized PPP Provisions;
- National Treasury, Public Finance Management Act, 1999: Treasury Regulation 16;
- South African National Roads Agency Limited South African. 2018. Integrated Report Volume 1;
- South African National Roads Agency Limited South African. 2018. Integrated Report Volume 2: Corporate Governance and Financial Statements; and
- South Africa (SA). 2012. National Development Plan 2030.

The textbooks relevant to the study were obtained from the North-West University libraries (Potchefstroom (Ferdinand Postma Library) and Vaal Triangle campuses), and where necessary, the inter-library facility was used. The EBSCO host (i.e., EconLit, Academic Search Premier, etc.) was used to avert plagiarism, and other databases such as Nexus, Index of South African Periodicals, Google Search and the catalogues of theses of South African Universities formed part of the resources and materials used for this study. The international perspective needed for the scope of this study was located and obtained using international agencies such as the International Monetary Fund, United Nations, World Bank, among others, for publications, reports, journals and articles. The literature review provided insight into how the researcher could restrict the scope of the study to a required area of investigation or inquiry (Creswell, 2009:23).

METHODOLOGY

Research methodology is the branch of knowledge concerned with methods (Punch, 2016:65). To determine how SANRAL can effectively perform its institutional function with regard to the toll road concessions investigated, the research methodology was used as the roadmap to guide this study. To achieve this, the qualitative research method was used. The most fundamental definition of qualitative research is that words are used as data, gathered and then analysed in many ways (Braun & Clarke, 2013:3). This is achieved by interviewing the participants (primary data) and the documentary (secondary data) analysis data collection in the case of this study. Various documents were used at the start of this study to generate ideas for the semi-structured interviews. Data collection procedures require interviews and document analysis in qualitative research (Creswell, 2014:190).

Research Design

According to Creswell (2009:5), a research design is a plan or proposal for the research that incorporates philosophy, investigation or inquiry using particular methods. The plan to conduct this research involved analysing documents to generate new ideas and to better understand the challenges of the phenomenon and this assisted to formulate the relevant questions later asked in the study. These questions took the form of semi-structured interviews and the organisations that participated in the study are given in Table 9.1.

Exploratory Research Design

Exploratory research design aims to gain new insights, find new ideas and increase knowledge of the phenomena being studied (Burns & Grove, 2001, p.374). Exploratory research design was used in this inquiry to investigate an issue that is not clearly defined and to highlight the core of the problem. Importantly, exploratory research design explains and identifies the nature of the challenge; it does not offer definitive evidence; it promotes more investigation; it is not rigorous; it encourages the utilisation of small sample sizes; and the findings may shape your future study (Swanson, 2015, p.16).

Table 9.1 Organisations Participating in the Study

Section	*Organisation*	*Type*
Section A	• Department of Transport (DoT) • National Treasury (Infrastructure Finance) • National Treasury (Transaction Advisory and PPP Unit in GTAC)	• National Government Departments
Section B	• South African National Roads Agency (SANRAL) • N3 Toll Concession (N3TC) • Bakwena Platinum Corridor Concessionaire (BPCC) • Trans African Concessions (TRAC)	• State-Owned Enterprise • Concessionaires
Section C	• Road Freight Association (RFA) • Organisation Undoing Tax Abuse (OUTA) • South African Federation of Trade Unions (SAFTU)	• Business • Civil Society Group • Trade Union
Section D	• African National Congress (ANC) • Economic Freedom Fighters (EFF)	• Political Parties

Source: Developed by the Author

According to the above, exploratory research design clarifies the nature of the problem by collecting either primary or secondary data and interpreting it. This research design accommodates the use of a small sample size, as was used in this study, and the results are expected to trigger further research. Most importantly, these results should be based on the conditions of interest and explore the challenges. The primary priority of exploratory research is to determine the limitations of the setting or environment in which the challenges, possibilities or conditions of concern are most likely to exist, as well as the significant factors or variables that may be uncovered and are pertinent to the studies (Van Wyk, 2019; online).

Punch (2016, p.81) denotes that qualitative data improves and explains results by delving deeper into exploring the views of the participants. Therefore, the results of this study are useful to delve deeper to have an in-depth understanding of the research problem.

PPP DEFINITIONS—GLOBAL AND SOUTH AFRICAN PERSPECTIVES

There is no definitive definition for PPPs since every nation, country or region will have its own definition depending on its developmental, political, social and economic needs, goals or objectives. The Organisation for Economic

Co-operation and Development (OECD) (2014, p.19) alludes that PPPs are a concept that, despite the lack of a definite definition, is frequently used, and Roman (2015, p.1) further posits that not only is there no consensus on a single definition for a PPP, there is also much discussion about what constitutes a 'true' PPP and what does not, with some adamantly supporting the view that only a PPP in service of infrastructure is a 'true' PPP. Therefore, it is widely accepted globally that there is no definitive definition for PPPs and as demonstrated above, nations grounded their individual definitions on developmental, political, social and economic policies, and on their laws and regulation objectives. The definitions below illustrate these differences.

> *A PPP is defined as an agreement between a public agency and a private entity in which the private entity carries out a task that is typically performed by the public sector and/or makes use of state property in accordance with the conditions of the PPP agreement. (South African National Treasury, 2017, p. 159)*
>
> *PPP is the overarching term for partnerships that include a wide range of activities, including operating infrastructure and offering services on behalf of the general public as well as creative ways to finance for these services. (United Kingdom Trade and Investment Ministry, 2013, pp.2–3)*
>
> *The goal of a PPP is to provide both better services and value for money, largely through transferring risk appropriately, stimulating innovation, maximizing the use of assets, and implementing integrated whole-of-life management, all of which are supported by private finance. (Australian Government, 2015, p.3)*
>
> *PPPs are long-term partnerships between the public and private sectors for the delivery of services. (Singapore Ministry of Finance, 2012, p. 4)*

By comparing PPP definitions helps to close the gaps that usually occur when one definition is being used. All of the definitions above negate the most important element of PPPs, re-negotiation. It is in the nature of PPP contracts to have amendments due to disputes arising from other partners or stakeholders. Because they are long-term contracts, re-negotiations are bound to take place on matters relating to financial model, user fees, subcontracting, project overruns, scope, performance report, risk insurance, late payments, and others.

Since PPPs are intended to benefit the civil society, non-governmental involvement is crucial from the beginning to the end of the PPP process. The definitions underscore and emphasise the partnership between the public and private sector although they do not mention different components of a typical PPP project. Nwangwu (2016, p.2) argues that the breakdown of various PPP project components, such as the design, financing, construction, and operation, should be included in PPP definitions. The next section deals with the theoretical exposition of PPPs in toll road concessions.

THE REVIEW OF PPPs

The PPPs formalise and professionalise the relationship between the public authorities and private entities in that the functions, roles and responsibilities amongst both partners are clearly outlined in the contractual agreement. Interestingly, PPPs are predominately adopted when the government decides to contract the private sector to build or renovate the infrastructure because of a financial constraint and in some instances reduces the government borrowing restrictions. This approach assists in bringing in the efficiency and effectiveness to the infrastructural project being constructed and minimises the project overruns due to the expertise brought in by private sector. The return on investment is achieved by means of user fees and the other portion of tariffs accumulated by private sector is used to service the debt. As a result, the private sector's involvement or role in PPPs might vary depending on the instrument employed, whether through a direct equity, challenge fund, mezzanine loan, loan, venture fund, syndicated loan, frontloaded or innovative fund (Byiers, Große-Puppendahl, Huyse, Rosengren & Vaes, 2016, p.3).

The Advantages and Disadvantages of PPPs

PPPs are guided by three principles: (1) the government has the ability to provide public infrastructure to the general public; (2) in terms of profitability, the private sector can gain significantly; and (3) it is possible to obtain reasonable community pricing for infrastructure services (Berawi, 2019, p.1). These three principles give rise to advantages that PPPs have over traditional procurement. The key advantages of PPPs are that private partners ensure that the projects are completed within a set schedule, and this is critical in the sense that cost overruns are avoided because all the activities are completed within budget. It is therefore necessary to mention that if project activities are completed within budget, therefore, PPPs have an edge over traditional procurement. For the reason that the private partner possesses the necessary expertise and experience, the efficiency and effectiveness levels become higher. It is in the nature of PPPs to be more responsive comparatively to traditional procurement in the sense that maintenance is routinely done; also, PPPs are responsive because toll fees become affordable to users in the long term. Transfer of skills and knowledge from the private to the public sector takes place, the quality and standard of infrastructure is improved or well maintained. At the end of the concession period, the asset returns to the public sector becoming public property once again but with improved quality.

On the other hand, PPPs have disadvantages, and Nwangwu (2019, p.36) alludes that due to the transfer of public ownership and management of public assets to a private entity, PPPs are inherently political and contentious.

As a consequence, a lack of political will can derail the success of a PPP in the sense that some sector of society might not appreciate the divesting or transferring of public control and assets to a private company which in the long term could have been beneficial to them and the government. The PPP legislations, laws and policies are ambiguous and cumbersome, and usually derail the completion of the PPPs due to confusion faced by the partners in interpreting the legislations, laws and policies.

As a consequence, PPPs must be based on a long-term political commitment, a strong policy base, and an environment with solid and stable regulatory and legal frameworks (Farquharson, de Mästle, Yescombe & Encinas, 2011, p.5). Lack of experience and expertise in matters surrounding PPPs can jeopardise their progress. Also, a lack of experience and expertise creates uneasiness due to a deficit of trust amongst the partners and these issues increase the likelihood for unhealthy relations and rivalry.

Providing Value for Money (VFM)

It is important for every PPP to have a VFM component. The life-cycle cost and product or service quality combination is known as VFM, and is intended to meet the user's needs (U.S. Department of Transport, 2012, p.p. 1–2). Erlendsson (2002) defines VFM as an assessment of whether a given entity has gotten the most out of its use of the products and services, given the resources at its disposal. In reference to these two definitions, VFM is not about accepting the lowest initial pricing but rather about the quality of service or goods. Again the decision to select PPP over traditional procurement should be based on cost, affordability, quality, risk factor and most importantly service to the public. This decision is taken on the basis of satisfying the concept of VFM.

The VFM is considered standard when a significant risk component of the project is transferred to the private partner. Another requirement for VFM is achieved when the performance of a private partner can be measured, and if the performance is satisfactory, the appropriate incentive can be handed out. The management skills brought into the project by the private partner are considered beneficial when the project's specification is achieved in time and the project cost is kept within budget.

More accountability and efficiency are expected in the realisation of VFM by means of PPPs. In achieving the accountability and efficiency for better VFM, the process should include credible cost, optimum risk allocation, transparency on fiscal implications and safeguarding citizens' welfare. Most importantly, this question should be asked: Does the project as a whole offer good value for money when compared to a traditional procurement?

Distribution and Transfer of Risk

A PPP model enables the transfer of risks from the government to a private party, freeing it of the burden of managing risks including cost overruns, long-term asset maintenance, and construction delays (Hovy, 2015, p.1). In this type of PPP arrangement where a significant amount of risk is being transferred to private partner, there should be a clearly articulated position from the beginning. Outlining the risks and deciding who is most qualified to take responsibility for them in the partnership should be the starting point of the partners' discussions (Hovy, 2015, p.2; Forrer, Kee, Newcomer, and Boyer, 2010, p. 479; Goldsmith & Eggers 2004, 141). However, the risk transfer process during the contract review stage is typically subjective and exaggerated due to the challenges associated with assigning, defining and valuing risks (Froud & Shaoul, 2001).

In order to eliminate this tendency, a thorough due diligence by both partners is necessary. There is also a possibility to share the risk between the government and the private sector since this will also assist in the elimination of subjectivity and exaggeration because both partners will be compelled to do a thorough homework. For this reason, it is necessary to clearly define and justify risk in order to avoid misleading (i.e., overpricing and overcompensate the risk component) the other partner. This will depend on the level of negotiation between the two parties to share the risk. It is critical for both the public and private sectors to clarify their expectations from the start in order to make it clear to the other partner which level of risk the other partner is willing to take.

On the same note, the government should outline from the beginning that its interest in the PPP project is to maximise public benefit and the private partner must explain that it is in the project for profit. This disclosure should aid both partners to identify risk before committing. Again, this disclosure will also give an indication to both partners which knowledge, skills and resources are required in the execution of the project. However, in South Africa, the Public Finance Management Act (PFMA), of 2004, demands that a substantial portion of the risk be placed on the private sector.

Transferring a significant amount of the risk to the private partner does not eliminate the public entity's risk entirely. For example, if anything like force majeure situation (i.e., natural disaster, riots, etc.) occurs and badly inflicts damage on the toll road infrastructure, the government has to stand in as a guarantor. During this period the private partner does not have the ability to generate any income through toll fees because the infrastructure is damaged, and the implication of this is that the government has to service the loan from its coffers. However, both partners can circumvent this challenge by taking insurance and any unforeseen circumstances can be covered.

Another risk factor for the government is that it has to provide a partial guarantee to the private sector in order to access funding from lenders. Therefore, funding for PPP project can only be unlocked when the government commits itself to stand in as the guarantor, and this should prompt the government to make a proper background check with regard to the private partner's capacity, expertise, skills and finances. This process will assist the government in ensuring that the private partner will complete and manage the PPP project appropriately without committing many unnecessary mistakes because public funds are at stake.

TOLL ROAD CONCESSIONS AS THE FORM OF PPPs

South Africa is no exception to the rest of the world in adopting the toll road concessions as the form of PPPs. In 1999, South Africa followed the global trend for the popularity of PPPs by establishing a formal PPP structure within the National Treasury, and the first form of PPPs were toll road concessions. The concessions are the widely used form of PPP in the delivery of public infrastructure and its maintenance thereafter. There is an acknowledgement that concessions as a form of PPPs are not a new concept but of note is the contractual and exclusivity details of each and every concession. According to Mouraviev and Kakabadse (2016, p.74) and Nikolic and Maikisch (2006, p.3), a concession involves the construction or renovation of a road by a private party (concessionaire) utilising private funding, and in some cases, the transfer of an asset from a public entity to a private sector partner.

Whether a road as an existing asset is being transferred to a private party or the private party initiates the construction of the road from the beginning to the end (Greenfield project), both instances require private funding and the private partner takes the market risk for it. It should be remembered that there are instances where the government provides guarantee in order to protect the concessionaire from anticipated lower earnings and other financial exposures. However, it is worth mentioning that in some instances during the negotiation with the host government, there is a possibility to transfer all of the project risk to the private sector. Alternatively, the private investor can accept the risk-sharing arrangement between the two parties. This is not the definitive process because there are instances where private partners can refuse to take on any of the risk for the project.

In circumstances where the host government transfers all of the project risk to the private sector, the private partner bears significant investment risk. In support of this, Munya (2010, p.1) argues that when a private partner assumes control of a state-owned road for a predetermined length of time while also accepting substantial investment risk, this is known as a concession. For taking on all these risks, an agent (private sector partner or concessionaire) is compensated in numerous ways depending on the contractual agreement. The first method of reimbursement is for a private business to recover its investment and operating costs by charging user fees (Mouraviev *et al.*, 2017, p.74). The second form of compensation is for the principal to use a shadow toll as a form of payment. Shadow tolls are fees based on traffic volumes that are paid at predetermined locations along the road by the principal to the agent on behalf of the ultimate user (Williams, 2003, p.9).

It is the responsibility of the private partner to operate and maintain the toll road and this is made possible by the collection of toll fees, therefore the selected private partner must be up to the task since the private partner selection process is rigorous. Although the private partner is selected through a competitive procedure, the most important consideration is the amount of the concession fee that the private party submits (Cui, Sharma, Farajian, Perez & Lindly, 2010, p.19). Therefore, the competitiveness of the company is not the only criterion that qualifies it but its capacity to raise the needed funding is also crucial.

Unlike in the past, governments now have options for determining implementation strategies using appropriate management and funding models to suit the toll road context in terms of cost effectiveness, reliability and socioeconomic sustainability. However, this does not mean the decision taken by government is unilateral; concessionaires are allowed to express their viewpoint and their primary goal is to make as much profit. And the government objective is to ensure the value for money aspect is achieved.

CONSIDERABLE ISSUES FACING TOLL ROAD CONCESSIONS IN SA

SA has challenges as far as toll road concessions are concerned and this section will focus on issues facing all four toll road concessions (N3, N1N4, N4 and Gauteng Freeway Improvement Project (GFIP)). The discussions around the GFIP will be separated from that of the other three because there were uncertainty around its future. Before the scrapping of GFIP, its concession contract was intended to run for 20 years using the design, construct, finance, operate and maintain (DCFOM) model.

Dissolution of the Gauteng Freeway Improvement Project (GFIP)

The uncertainty around the GFIP (also known as e-tolls) saw the SANRAL's balance sheet being adversely impacted. In 2021, SANRAL has lost two main project funding opportunities (estimated at R14 billion) due to this scheme. According to former SANRAL CEO, Macozoma (2021), the entity was denied R7 billion funding opportunity by Multilateral Investment Guarantee Agency (MIGA), and was unsuccessful to secure another R7 billion from New Development Bank (NDB). He further stated that due to SANRAL's unsatisfactory balance sheet, since 2016, the entity has not participated in the bond market; however, the entity has completed some profitable private placements with investors who are familiar with its track record and trust its brand. Since 2014 to March 2022, the government has spent R45, 936 billion to assist SANRAL to service its ballooning e-toll debt. In July 2022, R3, 74 billion was allocated to the e-toll scheme and additionally, R1.8 billion more was anticipated to be granted by the end of 2022.

As a result, the GFIP scheme is the major contributor towards SANRAL's debt. Lesufi (2022), the newly installed Premier of Gauteng Province, alluded that due to GFIP, SANRAL has the debt of R47 billion (initially was R45, 936 billion till March 2022), and R26 billion has already been paid in interest. However, Duvenage (2022), the CEO of Organisation Undoing Tax Abuse, disputes this figure by pointing out that while SANRAL may have a total debt of R45, 936 billion (which is currently amounting to R47 billion), they cannot accept that R43, 031 billion of this is attributed to GFIP. Despite the competing views (in terms of figures) expressed above, all stakeholders including OUTA agree that the GFIP scheme is the major contributor towards SANRAL's debt.

Naturally, in terms of e-toll pricing, one would expect that SANRAL together with concessionaire involved in the project have subjected their pricing method to their process of internal auditing and legal probity checks at the beginning prior to the implementation phase. However, due to user fee boycott one would also expect debt to escalate, and then the fundamental issue will shift to whether the stakeholders are unison to the figure presented as the debt amount. The anti-e-toll sentiment was started by what the public deemed or perceived as imposition because they felt that the government never consulted them during thc planning phase of this road network, which resulted in motorists and lobby groups refusing to register into the e-toll scheme. Another sentiment registered was that the government and SANRAL were unable to provide evidence to support claims that the planning and implementation of the road network depended on a designated fund which is sustainable and sufficient enough over the long term (Matsiliza, 2016, p.5).

Howcver, on the 26 October 2022 during the Medium-Term Budget Policy Statement (MTBPS), the Minister of Finance, Godongwana (2022(a)) announced that the national and Gauteng governments will inherit SANRAL's R23,7 billion debt in order to settle the GFIP. Th national government will take on 70% of debt while Gauteng government will only take on 30%.

Going forward, the Gauteng Provincial Government will take over the GFIP and should decide on the best method of maintaining the infrastructure of this project. According to Godongwana (2022a, p. 14) Gauteng Provincial Government will pay for any further road improvements that are supported by either the new toll plazas or the current electronic toll system, or by any other income stream within its purview. It is worth mentioning that by 31 December 2022, a consensus on how each party should proceed in terms of their commitments was anticipated.

Nonetheless, by January 2023 the scheme was still in existence not deactivated and the delay was placed on outstanding issues related to Memorandum of Understanding (MoU), and this could include ironing out issues that lead to acceptable terms by all parties involved. The sticky issue is that toll road concessions in SA are a competency of national government together with concessionaires, and the transition to hand them over to a provincial government appears to be a tedious and complex process which requires more time than previously allocated. The repurposing of gantries such as their usage in fighting crime, monitoring traffic transgressions and other purposes demand a multi-prone approach by various government departments and stakeholders, and all of these require more time and consultations.

While the Gauteng Provincial Government is still busy exploring hybrid models of servicing the e-toll debt and raising funds for its road maintenance, the traditional toll road method is being considered as one of many methods to raise funding. The fundamental question to rise from the above statement is whether the public and lobby groups will be receptive to the idea of using the existing electronic toll infrastructure or new toll plazas to raise additional investment. According to Duvenage (2021), it would be fascinating to watch what other finance mechanisms or models the Gauteng Provincial Government adopts. However, Godongwana (2022(b)) contends that road user fees continue to be the most efficient and fair method of funding road construction as well as a tool for controlling transportation demand, which has an influence on mode preference and spatial inequality. Another method being considered to raise additional funding towards the servicing of e-tolling debt is the renewal of license disc. All other forms of technology and infrastructure found along the e-toll road network can also be repurposed in order to meet other objectives.

One of the fundamental issues that needs to be answered and addressed urgently is the question of motorists who have been complying with the payment of e-tolls. Gauteng government made an undertaking to refund those motorists who had been complying with the e-toll payments. According to Mhaga-Spokesperson for Gauteng Premier (2023), government entities were debating when and how to reimburse payments. The amount to be refunded to motorists is estimated to be just below R7 billion.

Creation of Alternative Free Roads to Toll Roads Concessions in SA

The principle of alternative free roads (alternatively known as 'shunpiking') to toll roads is a globally accepted basic standard, and almost every country in the world practises it. SA as a country does have alternative roads to toll road concessions under discussion. However, the state of these roads is undesirable in terms of infrastructure. These roads are plagued with potholes—after every rainy season the number of potholes multiplies on the alternative roads. This presents a serious challenge for motorists in terms of accidents and condition of their vehicles.

The abovementioned challenges are due to lack of proper maintenance (i.e., routine, periodic and emergency). It is disconcerting to observe that, despite the fact that the government should be the driving force behind constructing and maintaining road infrastructure on alternative free roads, construction and maintenance are frequently neglected because there is a lack of coordinated planning and financing (Bratland, 2010, p. 40). For this reason, the motorists in most cases are left with no option but to revert to toll road concessions whether they can afford or not. Another reason compelling motorists to toll road concessions is the crime factor. In SA it is much safer to travel on toll road concession than on shunpiking.

SA is a circular country with highly opinionated population which is not shy to voice out its opinions and dissatisfaction through demonstration and protests. Therefore, provision of alternative free roads in SA is being viewed as a trade-off between the government and its citizens despite it being a globally accepted basic standard. According to Ragas (2018, p. 22), offering an alternative free road seems to be a compensatory strategy to overcome opposition to toll roads that do not take all of the implications and effects into account. The inability to counteract resistance by government was clearly demonstrated in the case of GFIP.

Maintenance of Toll Roads Concessions in SA

In the context of toll road concessions, the principals and agents must ensure that the maintenance investment is available and well spent in order to save significant future costs. Due to ever-increasing traffic volumes and ageing toll road infrastructure there is a need for maintenance. The consequences of a lack of maintenance should serve as a trigger to force SANRAL and concessionaires to implement preventive maintenance since it is cost effective and more reliable than corrective maintenance. Moghaddam and Usher (2010, p. 271) revealed that preventive maintenance involves maintenance tasks such as monitoring, inspection, lubrication, cleaning, adjustment, alignment, replacement, repair and maintenance of toll road infrastructure before failures occur.

In terms of cost, Moghaddam (2010, p.1) alludes that preventive maintenance entails a fundamental trade-off between the costs of performing maintenance activities and the cost savings realised by lowering the overall rate of occurrence of infrastructure defects. This implies that the long-term benefits are enormous and outweigh the financial cost of maintenance. This is clearly evident when one travels along the toll road concessions in SA. The road conditions are in a good state, and this simply confirms that concessionaires do spend enough money on maintenance which in turn ensures that the road infrastructure lasts for long.

Therefore, it is necessary for SA government to reduce its political interference in the selection process of capable private partner to SANRAL. As a result, SANRAL should have more discretion in appointing the right partner to oversee maintenance contracts and collect toll fees to fund maintenance costs (Burningham & Stankevich, 2005, p.2). For example, the SA government gave SANRAL legal powers to work hand-in-glove with the concessionaires to mitigate the cost of maintenance for the toll roads.

FINDINGS

This study revealed that amongst the three concessionaires, only one has a full maintenance department, and that the other two concessionaires prefer to outsource their maintenance. The primary goals of outsourcing are to reduce costs, save time, and increase the quality of outputs, and concessionaires may find competent professionals to complete the task for less amount, more quickly, and more effectively (Dogerlioglu, 2012, p. 22). The study established that the toll road concessions examined for this study are embroiled in secrecy due to a lack of transparency which other stakeholders perceive as the real obstacle to accountability. Although the Public Finance Management Act emphasises the need for transparency and accountability in public procurement, there is no comprehensive regulatory framework that addresses the many transparency and accountability issues that occur in PPPs in South Africa (Fombad, 2014, p.84).

In terms of the DCFOM model, the data collected for this study revealed that the concessionaires took on all the risk for the design, construction, finance, operation and maintenance of the concessions awarded to them. The three toll road concessions examined for this study are nearing the end of their contracts, and going forward, SANRAL must reconsider the model, especially regarding the risk-sharing for design. In future concessions, SANRAL can also consider a differentiated or individualised model for each concession and repackage the risk-sharing factor according to the needs, requirements and circumstances of individual toll road concessions.

The data also revealed that politics can either positively or negatively influence the adoption of the PPP model. The data indicates that there are cases were political tampering was used to push for the selection of a PPP model with no regard for the country's institutional quality, preparedness, circumstances, requirements and needs. The study also revealed that one of the reasons for adopting the DCFOM model was that the government was running short on funds and the only way out was to invite the private sector to participate in the rollout for toll road infrastructure.

According to the data, the strength of the DCFOM model is that the demand risk is not the burden of the government in toll road concessions, and if some big event leads to a revenue shortfall, then the government will come out unscathed because the model transfers the demand risk to the concessionaires. However, according to the data, the weakness of the model is that the toll road concessions accommodate both trucks and cars indiscriminately, and trucks inflict damage on the toll road infrastructure without serious consequences due to the fact that this model is based on traffic volumes. This study discovered that the SANRAL and National Roads Act, No. 7 of 1998, empowers SANRAL but consequently has given SANRAL too much power. It was discovered that SANRAL plays two roles in the toll road concession space, first as a player and second as a referee, and the SANRAL and National Roads Act, No. 7 of 1998, aids in enabling SANRAL to play both these roles.

SUITABLE MODEL FOR THE TOLL ROAD CONCESSIONS STUDIED

The DCFOM model is in use for all three of the toll road concessions examined, not the design, finance, build, operate and transfer (DFBOT), therefore, the private partner assumes the design, construction/build, financial, operational, maintenance and demand risks under this model. As a result, the government is immune to the major risks associated with toll road concessions, although not completely immune under this model. For example, if something major happens to the toll road concessions where the private partners are unable to service their debt to lenders, then the government will have to step in due to the fact that it has already committed itself through a partial credit guarantee. The durations still left on the toll road concessions under investigation range from 5 to 8 years, and they were all allocated 30-year period.

The decision regarding the extension of the three toll road concessions once their current contracts have ended has not been made yet. At the end of the current toll road concession contracts, the other option available to the government is to absorb the toll road concessions. As a result, the decision to extend the current toll road concessions or enter into new concessions with new private partners will involve the SANRAL's board of members internally and the Minister of Transport and the National Treasury externally. If the relevant decision-makers decide on the extension of the toll road concessions examined going forward, then this process must be informed by the feasibility studies. The feasibility studies must demonstrate whether the PPP model of choice is affordable, transfers appropriate technical and operational risk to the private party and gives value for money (National Treasury Module 4, 2004, p. 3).

Furthermore, according to Section 16.4.1 of the PFMA, Regulation 16 of 1999, to determine whether the proposed PPP is in the best interests of an institution (SANRAL in this case), the accounting officer must undertake a feasibility study that explains the strategic and operational benefits of the proposed PPP for the institution in terms of its strategic objectives and government policy. For these reasons, the chief executive officer of SANRAL is compelled to oversee the feasibility study process to ensure it satisfies the conditions of the PFMA. A PPP model is proposed in the next section.

THE PROPOSED MODEL AND ITS JUSTIFICATION

This study proposes the Improve, Finance, Maintain, Operate and Transfer (IFMOT) model. This proposed model will be relevant if the SA government (N3 & N1N4), along with the Mozambican government (N4), decides to extend the current toll road concession contracts or enter into completely new toll road concession contracts with new private partners at the end of the current toll road concession periods. The study proposes that the N3, N4 and N1N4 toll road concessions adopt the IFMOT model because these infrastructures already exist and constantly require improvements. In terms of the financial and design risks associated with this model, the SA government, through SANRAL, can share these risks with the private sector on an equal basis (50/50). It is important to mention that some improvements will still require designs despite the road construction being completed. Therefore, the design risk will fall under improvement in this model (IFMOT).

The financial and design risk-sharing will improve the government's benefits gained from these PPP arrangements since the more risk one takes the more one benefits from the project, and this will ensure rewards are evenly shared amongst partners. Most of disputes arise between partners due to the private partners assuming most or all of the financial and design risks and profiting more than the government due to the increased risk taken. The government is currently sourcing for other means of improving its public funds and taking more calculated risks, such as increasing its shareholding in the special purpose vehicles (SPVs) of these toll road concessions.

By assuming more financial and design risks the government can improve its reserves significantly. Therefore, by sharing the design and financial risks with the private sector on an equal basis, it will enable the government to increase its struggling public funds in the long term. It should be noted that under this type of PPP arrangement (namely sharing of financial and design risks) the public sector is still going to benefit from the private sector. The goal of the PPP is for the public sector to profit from the financial resources, industry knowledge, and technical skills of the private sector (Khahro, Ali, Hassan, Zainun, Javed & Memon, 2021, p.2).

The aforementioned premise lends weight to the PPP's risk allocation concept, which advocates for assigning risks to the party most qualified to manage them (Hovy, 2015, p.1). In the current PPP arrangement, the three concessionaires are allocated all the design, financial, construction, operation, and maintenance risks. Based on the number of years these three toll concessions have been in operation, the government should have gained the necessary expertise and capacity to handle the financial and design risks hand-in-glove with the private partners.

It should be noted that the current concession contracts have a skills transfer clause, in which the concessionaires are expected to share new skill sets and technology with SANRAL because road technology, like other types of technologies, is constantly evolving. However, it is also worth noting that SANRAL has been independently running and operating traditional toll roads on behalf of the government for decades (i.e., N1, N2 South, etc.), and it has been bearing all of the associated risks regarding these toll roads. As a result, SANRAL is already in possession of the requisite skills, technology, expertise and experience to successfully assume the financial and design risks on a 50/50 basis with the concessionaires of the toll road concessions.

Below is the risk-sharing structure for the proposed model:

From the above risk-sharing structure, the government and private sector will be allocated design and financial risks on a 50/50 basis and this means that all three of the toll road concessions will be financed by a mixture of equity and debt if their current contracts are extended or new partners are brought in at the end of the contracts. It is important to note that changes in exchange rates, interest rates, ownership, and other factors might affect the returns or profits from a debt and equity combination (Shen, Platten & Deng, 2006, p.593).

The above proposed risk-sharing structure can bolster the SPV's funding to lenders because the credit viability or credit score of the SPV will be made up

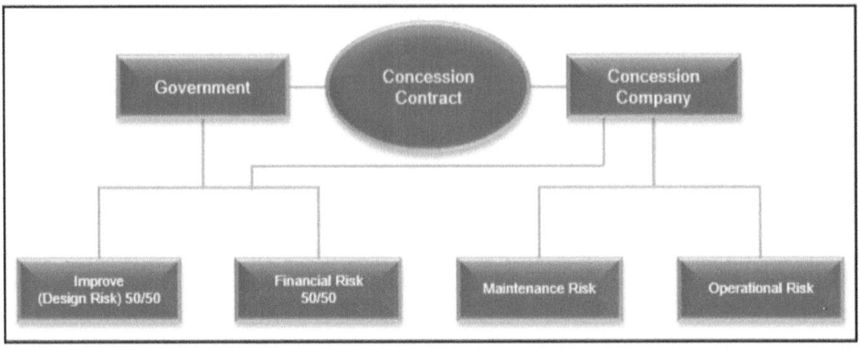

Figure 9.1 Risk-Sharing Structure for the Proposed Model. *Source*: Created by the author.

by the concessionaires and the government equally. The lenders' decisions to provide debt financing are based on the SPV's financial and credibility capabilities (Ehlers, 2014, p.10). As a result, the credibility and financial capacity of both partners are critical to unlock debt financing. This study recommends that the user fee payment be used to enable both partners to earn returns on their investment under the risk-sharing structure shown in figure 9.1 above. As a consequence, both partners bear the demand risk.

This risk-sharing structure places the operation and maintenance in the hands of the concessionaires. For operation and maintenance, the IMFOT model provides a single-party risk allocation (National Academies of Sciences, Engineering and Medicine, 2009, p. D–10). As a result, the details of a new contract management should exclude the construction risk. It is appropriate to leave the operation and maintenance in the hands of a private partner because they are able to implement operation and maintenance activities quicker than the public sector. The reason for this, in the context of SA, is that the private partner is not limited by the PFMA in executing operation and maintenance activities, particularly in PPP arrangements.

From the above risk-sharing structure, it is worth noting that the design risk falls under improvement. Therefore, to improve the existing toll road infrastructure everything starts with design. The contributor also proposes 20-year long-term contracts between SANRAL and the concessionaires if the existing concession contracts are extended or new private partners are brought in at the end of the current concession period for the toll road concessions. The proposal for a 20-year duration is informed by the fact that a return on investment will be reached sooner for both SANRAL and the concessionaires because the road infrastructure for the proposed toll road concessions is already in place and in good condition.

CONCLUSION

Research Objective 1: To examine the nature of the contractual agreement that regulates the partnership between SANRAL and the concessionaires for the toll road concessions examined for this study.

It was assumed that SANRAL conducted a feasibility study to ensure that the concession agreements satisfied all the VfM requirements and that SANRAL could afford to enter into these agreements before they signed any of the contractual agreements for the toll road concessions investigated for this study. SANRAL is empowered by legislation to conduct feasibility studies and is deemed capable to produce such a study. Based on the contractual agreement, the DoT and the National Treasury can support SANRAL by playing an oversight role. SANRAL is empowered by legislation to monitor the performance of the concessionaires for the toll road concessions. Therefore, it is worth mentioning that SANRAL, as a government agency, is the only organisation permitted to conduct monitoring as a means of satisfying these contractual agreements.

Under the conditions and terms of the current PPP model in use, which forms part of the contractual agreement, the concessionaires are expected to design, construct, finance, operate and maintain the toll road concessions. Any disputes arising from non-compliance of the aforementioned activities should follow a specific dispute resolution process which is clearly defined and outlined in the contractual agreement.

Research Objective 2: To propose a suitable model for toll road concessions going forward.

The reason for selecting the DCFOM PPP model currently in use is because the government did not have enough funds to rollout the toll road infrastructure on its own, hence the invitation to the private sector. Therefore, the government transferred all of the risks and the costs for the overall toll road infrastructure onto the concessionaires. However, this study proposes the adoption of the IFMOT model for these PPPs when at the end of their concession contracts. This can only happen if the existing concession contracts are extended, or new private partners are found. The decision to extend or find new private partners lies with the National Treasury, DoT and SANRAL. The IFMOT model will enable SANRAL and the concessionaires to share the design and financial risks for the toll road concessions.

REFERENCES

Australian Government. 2015. National Public Private Partnership Policy Framework. Available from: https://www.infrastructure.gov.au/sites/default/files/migrated/infrastructure/ngpd/files/National-PPP-Policy-Framework-Oct-2015.pdf. Date of access: 01 February 2023.

Berawi, M.A. 2019. Public–Private Partnership: Generating Mutual Benefits for Stakeholders. *International Journal of Technology*, Vol. 10(1), pp. 1–4.

Bordens, K.S., & Abbott, B.B. 2008. *Research Design and Methods: A Process Approach*. 7th ed. Boston, MA: McGraw-Hill.

Bratland, J, 2010. Capital Concepts as Insights into the Maintenance and Neglect of Infrastructure. *The Independent Review,* Vol.15, pp. 35–51.

Braun, V., & Clarke, V. 2013. Successful Qualitative Research: A Practical Guide for Beginners. Thousand Oaks, CA: Sage.

Burningham, S., & Stankevich, N. 2005. *Why Road Maintenance is Important and How to Get It Done*. Washington, DC: World Bank.

Burns, N & Grove, SK. 2001. *The Practice of Nursing Research: Conduct, Critique & Utilisation*. 4th edition. Philadelphia: WB Saunders.

Byiers, B., Große-Puppendahl, S., Huyse, H., Rosengren, A & Vaes, S. 2016. Principles for Public-Private Partnerships—Towards Sustainability? Lessons from SAGCOT, Healthcare in Lesotho, and Better Factories Cambodia. European Centre for Development Policy Management.

Creswell, J. W. 2009. *Research Design: Qualitative, Quantitative, and Methods Approaches*. London: Sage.

Creswell, J. W. 2014. *Research Design: International Student Edition, Qualitative, Quantitative, and Mixed Methods Approaches* (4th Ed.). London: Sage.

Cui, Q., Sharma, D., Farajian, M., Perez, M. & Lindly, J. 2010. Feasibility Study Guideline for Public-Private Partnership Projects. University Transportation Centre for Alabama: Alabama.

Delmon, J. 2011. *Public-Private Partnership in Infrastructure: An Essential Guide for Policy Makers*. Cambridge: Cambridge University Press.

Dogerlioglu, O. 2012. Outsourcing Versus In-House: A Modular Organisation Perspective. *The Journal of International Management Studies,* Vol. 7(1), pp. 22–30.

Duvenage, W. 2021. Sanral Loses R14 bn in Project Funding Opportunities. Available from: https://www.moneyweb.co.za/news/companies-and-deals/sanral-loses-r14bn-in-project-funding-opportunities/ Date of access: 21 August 2022.

Duvenage, W. 2022. Next Big e-tolls Storm Brewing in South Africa. Available from: https://businesstech.co.za/news/government/641041/next-big-e-tolls-storm-brewing-in-south-africa/ Date of access: 16 December 2022.

Ehlers, T. 2014. *Understanding the Challenges for Infrastructure Finance*. BIS Working Papers No 454. Basel, Switzerland: Bank for International Settlements.

Farquharson, E., De Mästle, C.T., & Yescombe, E. 2011. *How to Engage with the Private Sector in Public-Private Partnerships in Emerging Markets*. Washington, DC: The International Bank for Reconstruction and Development/The World Bank.

Fombad, M.C. 2014. Enhancing Accountability in Public–Private Partnerships in South Africa. *Southern African Business Review,* Vol. 18(3), pp. 66–92.

Forrer, J., Kee, J.E., Newcomer, K.E., & Boyer, E. 2010. Public–Private Partnerships and the Public Accountability Question. *Public Administration Review,* George Washington University. Vol. 70 (3), pp. 475–484.

Froud, J., & Shaoul, J. 2001. Appraising and Evaluating PFI for NHS Hospitals. *Financial Accountability and Management,* Vol. 17 (3), pp. 191–297.Godongwana, E. 2022(a). Medium-Term Budget Policy Statement (MTBPS). Government Gazette.

Godongwana, E. 2022(b). Government Clears Up What's Happening with e-tolls—and You're Not Going to Like It. Available from: https://businesstech.co.za/news/government/640707/government-clears-up-whats-happening-with-e-tolls-and-youre-not-going-to-like-it/ Date of access: 16 November 2022.

Hovy, P. 2015. Risk Allocation in Public-Private Partnerships: Maximizing Value for Money. International Institute for Sustainable Development, Discussion Paper. Available from: https://www.iisd.org/sites/default/files/publications/risk-allocation-ppp-maximizing-value-for-money-discussion-paper.pdf. Date of access: 15 August 2022.

Khahro, S.H.; Ali, T.H.; Hassan, S.; Zainun, N.Y.; Javed, Y.; Memon, S.A. 2021. Risk Severity Matrix for Sustainable Public-Private Partnership Projects in Developing Countries. *Sustainability.* MDPI.

Lesufi, P. 2022. E-tolls: Lesufi Says R47 Billion Debt a 'time bomb' Because Citizens Refused to Pay. Available from: https://www.citizen.co.za/news/e-tolls-sanral-debt-time-bomb-lesufi/. Date of access: 16, December 2022.

Macozoma, S. 2021. Sanral Loses R14 bn in Project Funding Opportunities. Available from: https://www.moneyweb.co.za/news/companies-and-deals/sanral-loses-r14bn-in-project-funding-opportunities/. Date of access: 21 August 2022.

Matsiliza, N.S. 2016. Critical Factors in Respect of Managing the E-Toll Road Project in Gauteng, South Africa. *African Journal of Hospitality, Tourism and Leisure,* 5(1): 1–10.

Mhaga, V. 2023. Gauteng Drivers Who Paid for E-Tolls Set to be Refunded Nearly R7bn. Available from: https://www.africannewsagency.com/news/gauteng-drivers-who-paid-for-e-tolls-set-to-be-refunded-nearly-r70bn-8a11ce35-2fd2-47b2-8959-13bf2ce36d72/ Date of access: 10 January 2023.

Moghaddam, K.S. 2010. Preventive Maintenance and Replacement Scheduling: Models and Algorithms. University of Louisville.

Moghaddam, K.S., & Usher, J.S. 2010. Optimal preventive maintenance and replacement schedules with variable improvement factor. *Journal of Quality in Maintenance Engineering,* Vol. 16 (3), pp. 271–287.

Mouraview, N., & Kakabadse, N.K. 2016. Public–Private Partnerships: Policy and Governance Challenges Facing Kazakhstan and Russia. London: Palgrave Macmillan.

Munya, A. 2010. The Advantages and Risks of Pursuing Public Private Partnerships Elements of Express Lane Networks in California, USA: Lessons for Developing Countries, 46th ISOCARP Congress 2010 Nairobi Kenya.

National Academies of Sciences, Engineering and Medicine. 2009. *A Guide for the Evaluation of Project Delivery Methods*. Washington, DC: The National Academies Press.

Nikolic, I.A., & Maikisch, H. 2006. *Public-Private Partnerships and Collaboration in the Health Sector: An Overview with Case Studies from Recent European Experience*. Washington, DC: The World Bank.

Nwangwu, N. 2016. *Public Private Partnerships in Nigeria: Managing Risks and Identifying Opportunities*. London: Palgrave Macmillan.

Nwangwu, G. 2019. Stakeholder Opposition Risk in Public-Private Partnerships. *International Journal of Economics and Financial Research,* Vol. 5(2), pp. 36–42.

Organisation for Economic Cooperation and Development. 2014. Public-Private Partnerships in the Middle East and North Africa: A Handbook for Policy Makers. https://www.oecd.org/mena/competitiveness/PPP%20Handbook_EN_with_covers.pdf. Date of access: 17 September 2022.

Punch, K. F. 2016. *Developing Effective Research Proposals*. 3rd Edition. London: Sage.

Ragas, I. 2018. *Decision Makers' Guide to Road Tolling in CAREC Countries*. Philippines: Asian Development Bank.

Republic of South Africa. 1998. *SANRAL and National Roads Act, 1998 (Act No. 7 of 1998).* Pretoria: Government Printers.

Republic of South Africa. 1999. *Public Finance Management Act, 1999 (Regulation 16 of 1999).* Pretoria: Government Printers.

Republic of South Africa. 2004. *National Treasury PPP Practice Note Number 04 of 2004.* Pretoria: Government Printers.

Republic of South Africa. 2017. Public-Private Partnerships. Available from: https://www.treasury.gov.za/documents/national%20budget/2017/review/annexure%20e.pdf. Date of access: 01 February 2023.

Roman, A.V. 2015. A Guide to Public-Private Partnerships (PPPs): What Public Procurement Specialists Need To Know. Herndon, Virginia: The NIGP Business Council.

Shen, L.Y., Platten, A., & Deng, X.P. 2006. Role of Public Private Partnerships to Manage Risks in Public Sector Projects in Hong Kong. *International Journal of Project Management,* Vol. 24, pp. 587–594.

Singapore Government. 2012. Public Private Partnerships Handbook Version 2. Available from: https://www.mof.gov.sg/docs/default-source/policies/procurementprocess/ppphandbook2012.pdf. Date of access: 02 February 2023.

South African National Roads Agency Limited. 2018. Integrated Report Volume 2: Corporate Governance & Financial Statements. Pretoria: SANRAL.

United Kingdom Government. 2013. Public Private Partnerships Available from: https://assets.publishing.service.gov.uk/government/uploads/system/uploads/attachment_data/file/266818/07_PPP_28.11.13.pdf. Date of access: 01 February 2023.

United States Department of Transportation. 2012. Value for Money Assessment for Public-Private Partnerships: A Primer. Available from: https://www.fhwa.dot

.gov/ipd/pdfs/p3/p3_value_for_money_primer_122612.pdf. Date of access: 20 September 2022.

Van Wyk, B. 2019. Research Design and Methods Part 1. Available from: https://www.uwc.ac.za/Students/Postgraduate/Documents/Research_and_Design_I.pdf. Date of access: 10 August 2022.

Williams, T. 2003. Moving to Public-Private Partnerships: Learning from Experience around the World. IBM Endowment for the Business of Government, 1–40. Available from: www.businessofgovernment.org. Date of access: 12 September 2022.

Chapter 10

Public-Private Partnerships in Uganda's Health Sector

John Paul Settumba and Alex Nduhura

Most developing nations experience heavy burdens of disease due to weak health systems and inadequate funding (Hanson, Gilson, Goodman, Mills, Smith, Feachem & Kinlaw, 2008). As such, access to the most crucial healthcare services is an important part of the development agenda. Both developed and developing nations are increasingly implementing PPPs as an approach to increase access to quality healthcare services by leveraging the investment, expertise, and managerial capacity of private sector entities to improve quality care, effectiveness, efficiency, responsiveness, and provision of healthcare services of governments (Basabih, Prasojo & Rahayu, 2022; Jomo, Chowdhury, Sharma, & Platz, 2016; Cheng, Wang, Xiong, Zhu & Cheng, 2021). Formerly founded on the traditional infrastructure industry, such as energy, water, and transport, PPPs are being implemented also in the social infrastructure sector such as the provision of health services to the population (World Bank Group, 2016).

The public focus has shifted from how the government can finance and deliver healthcare services to now include how the private sector entities can be included and managed to align their activities to help attain public health goals (Whyle & Olivier, 2016). As a critical component of strengthening health systems, PPPs enable the public sector to partner with the private sector in resource mobilisation, combining the technical and managerial skills to improve the overall health status of the population (Family Health International 360, 2012). PPPs are defined as an arrangement between the public agency and private sector entity, with the main aim of providing public projects, facilities, and services. These long-term collaborations are characterised by transferring or sharing risks, rewards, capital, and responsibilities for the shared benefits of both the government and private actors (Hellowell, 2012; Ondategui-Parra, 2022).

PPPs are changing how the public sector operates and collaborates with private entities. They are recognised and used in the management of public resources in most governments across the world. These are institutional tools being used to achieve many goals. For instance, providing quality healthcare services, finance, and human resource capital to the world's impoverished population is one of the social issues that needs urgent partnerships for better care. However, there has been insufficient information in Uganda's context about the importance of implementing PPPs to get relief from financial burden and low level of experts in the public sector (Tashobya, Musoba & Lochoro, 2007). This means that previous studies have not fully examined the importance of PPPs in the healthcare sector. As a result, this presents a gap between the previous pieces of literature and the current study. Based on the above background, the study examined the importance of PPPs in the health sector in Uganda.

LITERATURE REVIEW

Governments worldwide continue to face a broad range of multifaceted healthcare challenges fuelled by the ever-increasing demographics, rising healthcare costs, rapidly growing medical technologies, and an increasing burden of chronic and endemic diseases (Filip, Gheorghita Puscaselu, Anchidin-Norocel, Dimian, Savage, 2022). The healthcare systems across the world are increasingly struggling and strained with how to increase access to high-quality healthcare products and services, while delivering affordable care. These challenges need to be addressed if the governments and international development agencies, including World Health Organization, want to embrace Universal Health Care Coverage (UHCC) and realise Sustainable Development Goal 3 (SDG3—to promote well-being for all, at all ages) by 2030 (Abuzaineh, Brashers, Foong, Feachem, Da Rita, 2018; UNDP, 2020).

To successfully achieve the UN's SDG3, governments need at all levels to implement the concept of PPPs and identify the best models to attain Universal Health Coverage (UHC) to deliver affordable and high-quality healthcare services to the population (World Health Organization, 2022). PPP concept is implemented as a mutual agreement between the government and private sector actors, who join with the primary goal of providing public infrastructure, and community-based facilities, goods, and services. Though studies offer diverse definitions, PPP is defined as a long-term collaboration, which is characterised by sharing the responsibilities in terms of investments, risks allocation, and benefits for both actors involved (Abuzaineh *et al.,* 2018; Buse & Walt, 2000; Great Britain Treasury Taskforce, 1998).

The long-term partnership ensures project financing to improve the quality of services, which directly benefits the target population. PPPs involve strategic planning, implementation, and maintenance of public infrastructure at a cost-effective approach to delivering better and long-term public services to the citizens. Public and private sector entities can agree to mobilise necessary resources, and voluntarily bring in their resources such as human resources, materials, and finances. This enables both parties to have a bigger pool of necessary resources and share possible risks, which may not be managed by a single party (World Bank Institute, 2012). Therefore, PPP collaborations are implemented to ensure the long-term and sustainable provision of goods and services.

As such, previous studies show that PPP is increasingly being used by governments to deliver public projects and services (Mahoney, McGahan & Pitelis, 2009; Roehrich, Lewis & George, 2014). Studies indicate that promoting partnerships helps to deliver better quality infrastructure projects and services at an optimal fee and transfer risks (Anderson, 2012; Kwak, Chih & Ibbs, 2009). In 1993, the World Health Assembly urged the World Health Organization (WHO) to extensively mobilise and solicit the support of all development partners in the health sector, such as non-governmental organisations and entities in the private sector. As such, the PPP for health is referred to as a government programme that allows the participation of private sector actors (Buse & Waxman, 2001; Jensen, 2016)—this definition allows different types and scopes of PPPs.

PPPs is a long-term contract entered between a public or government agency and a private company to offer public goods or services, in which the private company accepts all the risks and management role, and finances associated with the performance (Alonazi, 2017; World Bank Group, 2018). This type of partnership entails a broad range of programmes based on the nature of engagement and the unfamiliar risks involved (Roehrich *et al.,* 2014). On the other hand, there are NGOs, private for-profit organisations, and/or large multi-stakeholder engagements such as The Vaccine Alliance (GAVI), Global Polio Eradication Initiative, Tuberculosis and Malaria, Roll Back Malaria, and The Global Fund (Jensen, 2016).

Most governments in sub-Saharan Africa are increasingly implementing PPPs for the provision of quality health projects and services to their community (Asasira & Ahimbisibwe, 2018); Hellowell, 2019; Nduhura, Nuwagaba, Settumba, Molokwane & Lukamba 2020; Joudyian *et al.,* 2021; Roehrich *et al.,* 2014). Whereas there is a large literature on PPPs in Africa, little is known about their importance in Uganda.

PPP TRENDS IN GLOBAL HEALTHCARE

The current data about PPPs, both internationally and across all sectors, focus on global financial support and infrastructure projects. For instance, the Project Finance and *Infrastructure Journal* offer an estimation of 600 healthcare infrastructure assets and projects internationally, and a majority of them are PPPs (United Nations Economic Commission for Europe, 2016). This data offers a remarkable understanding of the geographical scope and trends of PPPs in the healthcare sector, such as referral hospitals, and health centre PPPs, which are in operation, under development process, under construction, and in pre-development stages. More than 60% of the PPP infrastructure identified by Project Finance and *Infrastructure Journal Global* is in Europe; 15% from the United States, whereas by comparison, Sub-Saharan Africa, North, and Central Africa, all joined comprise less than 5% of PPP projects globally (Abuzaineh *et al.,* 2018).

However, the Global Health Group adds that in the present times, most PPP project-driven programmes globally have been adopted in non-healthcare sectors and wealthy countries, with transportation networks, making the transport subsector laden with a bulk of projects. Nevertheless, an increasing number of middle- and lower-income nations are embracing health PPP projects. Regardless of these trends in the health sector, it is still difficult to give the exact scope of the health PPP market for some critical reasons, such as the different levels of PPP development; for example, pipeline vs. signed vs. operational; limited information available on the health sector, Ministry of Health; the broad and varying range of PPP models; and the tendency of health PPPs to join together with other social sectors like PPPs in the education, transportation, water, and energy sector (Abuzaineh *et al.,* 2018).

BACKGROUND OF PPPs IN UGANDA'S HEALTH SECTOR

The PPP Health, known as (PPPH) in Uganda's health sector, was incepted in 1997 by the Ministry of Health (Ministry of Health, 1993)– the private sector is recognised as Private Not-for-Profit (PNFP) and Private-for Profit (PFP) entity. The recommendation for the integration of the private sector into the public health sector was done after the 1987 Health Policy Review Commission Report that highlighted the importance of PPPs in healthcare settings (Awor *et al.,* 2018). The report created the foundation for the 1993 Government White Paper on Health Policy that stressed the need for the private sub-sector in the healthcare system (Ministry of Health, 1993). However, it required that this issue be aligned squarely with the government health policy agenda. This has been widely due to a more sympathetic political leadership during the process and the economic crisis that had struck many of the PNFP institutions and NGOs led to various meetings between these institutions and the Ministry of Health (Tashobya, Musoba & Lochoro, 2007) stressing the need for a public-private partnership for health (PPPH) in Uganda.

The PPP Act, 2015 defines the partnership as a commercial transaction between the government as the contracting authority and private entities, where the private sector entities perform the role of the government over a given timeframe (Ministry of Finance, Planning & Economic Development, 2015; Ministry of Health, 2017). Since then, many reforms have been made in Uganda's health sector and one of the main reforms has been the public-private partnership for health (PPPH) (Tashobya, Musoba & Lochoro, 2007). The first official form of PPPH in Uganda is the mutual relationship between private actors and the Ministry of Health, which is traced back to the early 1960s, General Notice 245 of 1961, serving as a government tool used to offer possible support to PNFP. However, this initiative declined and ultimately stopped during the 1970s economic crisis (Bataringaya & Lochoro, 2002).

Public-Private Partnership Act, 2015

Uganda passed the PPP Act 2015 on 5 August 2015, which implements the partnership as a commercial approach for engagement and/or transaction, between the government agency and private sector entity (Ministry of Finance, Planning & Economic Development, 2015). Under the PPP arrangement, the private sector assumes the use of government property, assets, equipment, and other public resources (World Bank, 2015). The private sector entities take the role of providing finances, and technical and operational risks as per the functions, use, and performance of the public assets and equipment. Uganda's PPP Act 2015 acts as principal legislation that governs the PPPs and aspires to guide the relationship that exists between the government and private sector actors in the implementation of PPP arrangements. The structures of monitoring, procurement, and regulation of PPPs are established in this Act; it also lays out the roles and responsibilities of the various entities in the implementation of PPPs. It further sets out a PPP Unit and PPP Committee, and entails information about the procurement rules that PPPs have to abide by (Initiative for Social and Economic Rights, 2019).

The Auditor-General is required, as provided in the PPP Act, to audit every PPP project annually from its inception to the conclusion, and also to report to parliament in a period, not more than nine months from each audit. Even though the Act points out various commendable provisions, it does not substantially regulate the nature of PPPHs. To start with, the PPP definition provided by the document states that, the private actor approves the use of certain national assets, and in exchange assumes substantial risks and also receives benefits via the government or user fees. This language may not be fit enough for donor-funded PNFP projects in areas where the private entity does not necessarily acquire a national asset or does not necessarily assume financial risk, and might not get benefits from the government (Initiative for Social and Economic Rights, 2019).

In addition, the Act, particularly its application, focuses on the infrastructure projects instead of the implementation of social services, and as a result, does not lend substantial guidance on the implementation of PPPs in health service delivery. This is a shortcoming which in turn renders the Act's remedial mechanism redundant because this flow forms contractual obligations and yet PPPs in health are currently predominantly executed by way of MoU. Moreover, the Act still places forth that in the implementation of PPPs, ensuring value for money will be a guiding principle, thus attracting much emphasis on particularly the indicators that are mainly, quantity, quality, and substantial risk transfer (Ministry of Finance, Planning and Economic Development, 2015). It also discusses equity and guidance on the information which has to be submitted.

The Motivations for PPPs in Uganda's Healthcare

This section highlights the constraints that have anchored the motivation for private sector involvement through public-private partnerships. The advocates of PPPH have offered numerous reasons for embracing PPPs in Uganda's health systems. The USAID's private sector within health shows that health PPPs create an effective resource mobilisation of the private health sector (PHS) to enhance healthcare outcomes in Uganda. This partnership also complements the effort of the Ministry of Health towards achieving Universal Health Care (UHC), which required practical policy and a working environment that enabled public-private engagement, public-private dialogue, and public-private partnership (U.S. Agency for International Development, 2016). The most critical motivations for designing the policy documents are described below:

PPPH increases access by combining private sector efficiency and work ethic. The guidelines for the proper implementation of the National Policy on Public Private Partnerships in Health (NPPPPH) puts more emphasis on that, 'joint planning and management' between public and private subsectors will 'increase fair access to healthcare by optimizing the use of available resources in line with the standard of complementarity' (Ministry of Health, 2012). This partnership promotes harmony in reporting, procedures, standards, decision making, implementation processes, and efficiency in the utilisation of available resources (Initiative for Social and Economic Rights, 2019). The policy provides an in-depth understanding of how health PPP can help to achieve these goals. The Health Sector Development Plan (HSDP) in Uganda stipulates that the Ministry of Health should also increase access to health services, by utilising private sector efficiency, work ethic, geographical coverage, personal and financial mobilisation, and physical facilities (Ministry of Health, 2015).

Health PPPs are mainly implemented to provide health funding and bear risks. Uganda's Health Financing Strategy Policy (HFSP) indicates that the current input-based memorandum of understanding (MoU) system, where funds are provided to support infrastructure projects regardless of the services being offered, is not fully flexible, and thus might require revising and replacing with an output-based PPPH engagement. HFSP shows that within the public sector, procurement of healthcare services relies typically on the traditional input-based method, in which the government outsources health services from PNFP health centres through the provision of grants for certain health services based on the terms and conditions as stipulated by the Ministry of Health. As such, the traditional input-based method seems to be problematic due to the growing need for increased flexibility in the distribution of the available funds as needs increase (Ministry of Health, 2016).

The input-based approaches being used have a built-in inflexibility, which cannot allow the available funds to be redistributed based on the needs of the population. In other words, output-based engagement emphasises the practice of reimbursement for the health services offered, including fee-for-care services, voucher schemes, and/or results-based financing. In addition to supporting the health sector with more flexible funding modalities, the proponents have claimed that the private sector should bear the potential risk, or at least there should be risk-sharing with the government (Initiative for Social and Economic Rights, 2019). Health PPPs increase equity and improve health outcomes in Uganda. One of the key justifications for the PPPHs, with the PNFP in the form of financial subsidy, indicates that such engagements improve equitable access to healthcare by reducing or eliminating user fees for PNFP hospitals and health centres. In terms of subsidies, the Government of Uganda provides to the PNFPs, in the form of PHC grants, which offers the reasons to the effect that the Government of Uganda subsidies to the sub-sector are supposed to reduce economic obstacles to public health users, increasing affordability and access for the low-income earners to basic health services. These can be allocated based on agreed outputs that can comply with the priority of the Health Sector Strategic and Investment Plan (HSSIP) 2010/11–2014/15 (Government of Uganda, 2010).

That implies that the Government of Uganda subsidies will be utilised to implement any approach that can facilitate access to a healthcare facility. It may also result in a wide range of healthcare services offered by the PNFP, and at the same time reduce or eliminate user fees for certain priority care services. The implementation guideline outlined under the PNFP section indicates that partnership with PNFPs will significantly increase 'sustainability, access, efficiency, equity, and quality of healthcare services by allowing them to maintain their administrative autonomy' (Government of Uganda Ministry of Health, 2010).

The Three Common Health PPP Models

Three common Health PPP business models have been largely adopted across the world as demonstrated in Table 10.1.

Most of the infrastructure-based health PPPs combine these functions into three best models:

Infrastructure-Based Model: a contracting partner constructs, maintains or renovates public health facilities.
Discrete Clinical-Service Model: the private partner expands and improves the capacity of healthcare service delivery.
Integrated PPP Model: private sector takes on the role of providing a more comprehensive package of healthcare infrastructure and service delivery.

Characteristics of the Three Common Health PPP Models

Health PPPs generate several opportunities to influence private sector expertise and resources to enable sufficient capital in more large-scale projects that advance the local public and national health goals, such as improving the quality of healthcare service delivery (Chen *et al.,* 2020), and increasing access to care and affordability of healthcare services (Pagoni & Patroklos, 2019). During the past years, governments all over the world have engaged private actors or investors to deliver quality services through PPP healthcare (Abuzaineh *et al.,* 2018), to achieve some functions as follows:

Design: this entails the design of the project, including the design of the facility and healthcare delivery model.
Build: this feature requires the private sector to take on the role of construction or renovation of healthcare facilities covered in the project.
Finance: the private sector assumes the responsibility of financing or co-financing the project.
Maintain: this entails the maintenance of a health facility and equipment as well.

Table 10.1 The Three Common Health PPP Models Adopted by Governments

Health PPP Models	*INFRASTRUCTURE-BASED MODEL*	*DISCRETE CLINICAL-SERVICE MODEL*	*INTEGRATED PPP MODEL*
Components of PPP Models	**Financing + Infrastructure +** clinical support services and non-clinical services	Clinical services	**Financing + Infrastructure** + clinical support services and non-clinical services
Private-partners Responsibilities	A private partner is given a contract to design, build, finance, and maintain (DBFM) healthcare facilities. Provision of non-clinical services can be covered here, such as cafeteria and laundry. Some advanced PPP projects include the provision of clinical support services like lab, radiotherapy, radiology, and chemotherapy.	Under this model, a private actor is contracted to provide discrete clinical services, such as specialty healthcare services and clinical support services	A private sector actor is contracted to design, build, finance, and operate (DBFO) healthcare facilities and provide clinical and non-clinical support services.
Common PPP Model	Design-Build-Finance-Maintain (DBFM), Design-Build-Operate-Transfer (DBOT), Design-Build-Finance-Maintain-Operate (DBFMO), Private-Finance-Initiative (PFI), Infrastructure PPP, Accommodation Model	Operation and management (O&M) contracts	Design-Build-Operate-Deliver (DBOD), Public-private Integrated Partnership (PPIP) Alzira model, Clinical Services PPP, Integrated PPP.
Level of project/service delivery	Low	Average	High

Source: Developed by the Authors

Operate: the private sector takes on the role of supplying required equipment, including IT equipment, and delivery and management of non-clinical support services.

Deliver: conduct the management and delivery of required clinical services and non-clinical support services.

The decision by a government to pursue a certain PPP model is largely driven by local public needs and the environment, which includes but is not limited to social and political factors. The responsibility and level of risk that the government seeks to transfer, which the private actor is willing to take on, are also key determining factors (Pagoni & Patroklos, 2019).

The PPPs in Health Sector in Uganda

Many healthcare projects and services have been implemented under PPP arrangements in regional referral hospitals (RRHs) in Uganda. As such, PPPs have largely become vital arrangements for government hospitals because they improved the quality of care and healthcare service delivery in Uganda. The primary data shows that PPPs are central arrangement for the government. As noted by one respondent, this is because:

1) they improve healthcare service delivery and hospital infrastructure through funding; 2) improve on the health standards; 3) provide the necessary funding to run different activities and projects; 4) improve on human resources through recruitment, training, capacity building, compensation of health workers, and 5) improve on medical supplies and equipment.

This study is in harmony with some of the previous studies regarding the reason for implementing health PPPs. The National Academies of Sciences, Engineering, and Medicine show that PPP is known for its capacity to improve service delivery. For example, a 1993 World Health Assembly Resolution urged the WHO to mobilise and solicit outstanding support from private partners in the health sector, including government institutions and NGOs (Buse & Waxman, 2001; National Academies of Sciences, Engineering & Medicine, 2016). This is because PPPs are key components in strengthening the entire health system through pooling resources and technical skills to ensure quality care and healthcare service delivery to patients (Ferreira & Marques, 2021).

Another study by Tshombe, Nduhura, and Nuwagaba (2020) shows that most African countries have recognised the need to have PPPs as apparatus to finance infrastructural projects in the region. The authors identify some development partners including the African Development Bank, the

International Monetary Fund, and the World Bank Group as key funders of the infrastructural development for emerging economies (Tshombe, Nduhura, & Nuwagaba (2020, p. 152). This study found that Korea International Cooperation Agency (KOICA) *and Japan International Cooperation Agency (JICA) partnerships also provide grants* through the construction and equipping of hospital facilities with equipment and medical supplies in almost all government RRH. Consequently, PPPs have been embraced as a means for procuring public goods and services to improve the lives of people, and governments have put their hope in the private sector partners.

This study found several NGOs providing healthcare services to the patients and essential equipment to most of the RRH. For example, Infectious Disease Institute (IDI) has improved human resources for RRH in Uganda. IDI partners train health workers and send them to the community to educate the patients in their own homes about the dangers and preventive mechanisms of infectious diseases, such as Ebola, COVID-19, HIV, and TB. IDI partnership has improved on microbiology and infrastructural development through the construction of laboratory facilities in some RRH, study participants noted. In addition, the study discovered that RHITES, known as Regional Health Integration to Enhance Services in North—Lango-Acholi sub-region—offers capacity building, and provide funds to purchase medical supplies and reagents, and sample collection tools. The project also delivers TB and HIV care and counselling services to patients as was evident in Soroti RRH.

Different partners have greatly contributed to improving the quality of care and service delivery than before. For instance, this study found Baylor Uganda playing an instrumental role in delivering treatment and management of diseases. For example, Baylor offers free treatment and management of HIV and supports people living with HIV/AIDS. They provide services like safe male circumcision (SMC) and have greatly improved staffing through recruiting and compensation arrangements. BAYLOR has also constructed a blood collection service centre, and offers family planning services to the community in a bid to improve the quality of life, study participants revealed. All these health projects and services have been implemented to offer quality care and improved service delivery to the population.

PPPs Improve the Quality of Care and Service Delivery to the Patients

This study examined the motivations for implementing health PPPs in the health sector on the pretext that they play an important role in improving care and healthcare service delivery to patients through human resources, infrastructure, funding, and medical supplies and equipment. The study indicates that private sector involvement improves human resource capacity through recruitment, training, and capacity building of staff. They also provide health-care services and equipment on time and in an efficient manner in terms of service delivery, medical supplies like ARVs, and non-clinical support like counselling services. Primary data indicates that:

> *Private partners offer subsidized healthcare services, drugs and sometimes even free medicine, provide non-clinical support like training, capacity building, and cleaning services to the hospitals, which in the end leads to improved quality care and efficient services. PPPs bring in crucial skills, and expertise in the heath sector, and improve the professionalism of health workers. Private partners provide funds every quarter to Lira Regional Referral Hospital (LRRH) to support the eye department finance the eye camps, offer transport funds to the patients, free drugs, which the Ministry of Health cannot provide to the patients. They also provide eye patients with free meals during the surgical period, and this has reduced the congestion at the hospital unit,* during the study interview, the participants noted.

Some of the previous works of literature indicate that notwithstanding substantial support and success, the provision of primary healthcare services by the government has its challenges, including limited funding, shortage of human resources, and poor infrastructure (Joudyian *et al.*, 2021). To address this challenge, PPPs are key tools to help improve infrastructure projects and healthcare service delivery to the population (Baig *et al.*, 2014; Engel & van-Lente, 2014; Oluoha, Umeh, & Ahaneku, 2014). For instance, Brad Schwartz and Bhushan (2004, pp.661–667) show that PPPs have improved immunisation equity in Cambodia. This signifies the need to embrace PPPs in Uganda's health system. In addition, the primary data shows that the government of Uganda lacks intensive monitoring:

> *[T]he monitoring and supervision on the government side are little, whereas private sector has strict monitoring and a supervisory mechanism that have significantly improved reporting and accountability, which lead to improved healthcare service delivery, study participants noted.*

PPPs support the government with finances because the budget of the Ministry of Health is limited to meet the current needs of Uganda's population.

This study reaffirms the research by Ferreira and Marques that compared the quality and support of both the public and private sectors in providing health services to the population. Their study shows that PPPs are implemented to carry financial and human resource burdens and through this arrangement, the government transfers risks to private partners. For instance, the authors maintain that in Portugal, health PPPs are implemented to build hospitals and provide clinical services (Ferreira & Marques, 2021), and they guarantee quality care offered on time (Woodson, 2016). Their study adds that the PPP arrangements ensure efficient and sustainable use of healthcare services and that the patients receive high-quality care and timely services equitably.

PPPs Support Infrastructural Development

Private sector partners are involved in design-build-finance and maintaining a health facility (Abuzaineh *et al.,* 2018). As such, this study found that health PPPs have done a tremendous job in improving the status of government hospitals' infrastructure through the construction of clinics (ART clinics), theatres, OPD, and emergency departments. For instance, Japan International Cooperation Agency (JICA) offers grants through the construction and equipping of hospital facilities with equipment and medical supplies in almost all government RRHs. Through this partnership, some emergency facilities and theatres were constructed at Mubende RRH, OPD at Lira RRH, and equipped and provided compensations to the health workers they employ. The data shows that 'JICA partnership has improved the status of the hospital infrastructure and expanded space for operations such as the OPD facility in Mubende RRH, Lira RRH, Soroti RRH, and Mubende RRH, ART clinics in Fort Portal RRH, and offers supports in quality improvement of the health services offered to the patients'.

Through PPPs, several modern facilities are built to increase the capacity of operations; for example, medical laboratories, hospital wards, and ART clinics have been constructed in most of the government RRH to offer support to children with sickle cell condition, heart disease, and liver problems, through designing, financing, construction, providing medical supplies, and other necessary material and equipment like eye equipment, slit lamp, scan machine, and protective gear. Most of these projects have been through health PPP models adopted, such as build-operate-transfer (BOT), build-lease-transfer (BLT), and design-build-finance-operate-transfer (DBFOT) among others (Abuzaineh *et al.,* 2018).

Most of these PPP models operate through funding, ownership control and management, risk-sharing and transfer, technical collaboration, investment approach, tax arrangement, and management of cash flows (Mehta, Bhatia & Chatterjee, 2010; Mohanty & Sahu, 2023). These partnerships have been possible through a long-term contract and collaboration between a government entity and a private party. The World Bank Institute indicates that a PPP is a long-term agreement between the government and a private company, which identifies a means of delivering public projects and services and, or assets, in which the private actors have the mandate to bear all risks and management roles (World Bank Institute, 2012).

PPPs Bridge Finance Gaps

According to the United Nations Economic Commission for Africa, health sector funding is still a problem for most developing countries (Aliko-Dangote, GBC Health & United Nations Economic Commission for Africa, 2019). As such, this chapter notes that the government of Uganda cannot meet its financial obligations of providing equitable and efficient services to the population. The biggest percentage of the government expenditure goes to salaries, which in the end leads to poor health outcomes. This study is in agreement with the previous work by Sundewall and Brady, which found that the government of Nigeria spends more on salaries and tertiary healthcare, vertical expenditure on government directorates at different units of the health sector. Moreover, the available limited funds are not well-managed and thus lead to stock-out, inadequate medical supplies, and poor health outcomes (Sundewall & Brady, 2019).

Consequently, PPPs are crucial for health sector funding and development in Uganda. For example:

> *[P]rivate partners provide funds to government hospitals where the government is not in a position to finance some projects and services needed to deliver quality care to the patients and any assistance rendered to the government hospitals either directly or through the Ministry of Health are important to improve the services delivery and the quality of care offered to the patients. For example, MILDMAY has greatly helped in service delivery and medical supplies, which the government may not manage, such as Result-based Funding of medical equipment and staff motivation, the study participants revealed.*

As such, there is no doubt that the private sector plays a key role in lobbying for government hospitals, such as MILDMAY in Mubende RRH helps the government to mobilise and raise funds outside the country, which in turn supports the operation of the entire hospital. The government of Uganda lacks enough funding to meet its constitutional mandate of ensuring quality care, and that efficient, equitable, and timely healthcare services are delivered to its citizens. This by default welcomes private sector entities to bring in funds and bridge the financial gaps, where the government is incapacitated to provide. Health PPPs offer great benefits for funding and implementing infrastructural projects and services, and in the case of Uganda, the health sector has become too expensive and resource-intensive for the government to finance using its resources.

This chapter reaffirms the findings of the previous research projects (Wang, Switlick, Ortiz, Zurita & Connor, 2012) conducted on health sector funding programmes. The authors show that there are funding gaps in the health sector in Africa, estimated at $66 billion per year. Private sector financing holds great potential for growth and development. It is important to note that PPP synergies are important to the development of health systems across the African continent (Wang *et al.,* 2012). For example, the government of Ethiopia has largely depended on the U.S. President's Emergency Plan for AIDS Relief (PEPFAR) partnership to provide almost everything from medical supplies to strengthening human resources to curbing HIV, TB, and prevention of other infectious diseases among its population. Therefore, the PPP arrangement registered tremendous success and impact on the community (Aliko-Dangote, H., GBC Health & United Nations Economic Commission for Africa, 2019).

PPPs Strengthen the Capacity of Human Resources

As international development agencies and donors continue to increase global funding in response to the world's pressing health issues, such as HIV/AIDS, TB, Ebola, and in support of the United Nations' 17 Sustainable Development Goals (SDGs), the concern of organisation and human resource capacity has become an important element in the health sector (Wyss, 2004). The capacity of human resources is less visible and yet important in the operational productivity, efficiency, supply chain improvement, and sustainability of healthcare services. For instance, in Indonesia, PPPs have been established and offer unique services and support to the health sector to address system inefficiencies, health quality, and other related gaps in achieving primary health coverage (Health Policy Plus, 2020).

In Uganda, PPPs have been recognised as a mechanism to improve on organisation and human resource capacity of government hospitals. The primary data contends that PPPs are key drivers for improved healthcare service delivery to patients. The involvement of the private sector helps the government RRHs to improve human resource capacity through recruitment, training, retention, and capacity building of staff.

> *Private sector improves the capacity of human resource, strengthen capacity building, provide health services and equipment in time, and are efficient in terms of service delivery, medical supplies like ARV drugs, consumable medical products such as* bandages, cotton wool, catheters, syringes, gloves, cotton wool, sutures, tubes, *and non-clinical support like counselling services.*

This study is in agreement with some previous studies, which indicated that private sector entities also emphasise the training of medical workers to improve the human resource management system and build organisation networks (Nkabane-Nkholongo *et al.,* 2015; Vian *et al.,* 2007). Previous studies contend that continuous mechanisms to address new issues and increase access to quality care and service do not only necessitate medical supplies and financial support, but also a huge investment in human resource development, and management is needed to improve service delivery (Dwyer *et al.,* 2006; Sekhri, 2009). Since human resources plays a significant role in improving healthcare service delivery to the population, this implies that the absence of a strong and competent health worker team would result in poor healthcare services delivery and clinical outcomes (Wyss, 2004). According to Vian *et al.* (2007, p.1), the ability of health organisations to improve quality and access to healthcare services largely depends on the capacity of the human resource, which requires huge investment in hiring and training programmes.

Essential Areas Are Not Given Priority by the Government

In Uganda, it has been reported that many health needs and the most urgent priorities of both men and women are not identified and attended to by the health systems (Ministry of Health, 1999). The study also indicates that in many cases the government of Uganda does not give priority to some of the most essential areas in the hospital and lacks interest in some areas. Consequently, when the private partners come in, they bridge that gap, especially where the government lacks a keen interest. The primary data illustrates that:

> *PPPs play an important role where the government has completely no interest, but are vital to the patients and community; so, if there are any private donors, willing to bring in such services and resources, it can help the common person and save millions of lives. Private partners venture and explore areas where the government has never entered due to financial challenge, inadequate and inexperienced labor force, study participants noted.*

Therefore, the current study is in harmony with the Ministry of Health report published in 1999. The report shows that the government of Uganda does not give priority to essential healthcare areas and needs, and the development and implementation of health policies and programmes that do not address gender issues, and thus, it shows little effort to how inequality affects the well-being of the population (Ministry of Health, 1999). Moreover, Watkins, Jamison, Mills, Atun, Danforth, Glassman and Alwan in 2018 showed that priorities should be given to eliminating mortality and disease control, especially in times of a pandemic (Watkins, *et al.,* 2018).

However, some previous studies continue to assert that healthcare priorities should be based on ethical considerations, public values, and scientific evidence (Sundewall, & Brady, 2019). Universal Health Coverage (UHC) involves the solidarity principle and should be based on human rights perspectives. It helps to direct health budgeting with the prioritised packages.

National Development Plan II (NDP II) states that Uganda's health financial year 2015/16–2019/20 priorities included universal access to family planning services, malaria management, minimising maternal death, development and improving the status of health infrastructure, reducing neonatal and child mortality and morbidity rate, the establishment of the National Health Insurance Scheme, and scaling up the prevention of HIV/AIDS (Initiative for Social and Economic Rights, 2018).

PPPs Supplement Government Efforts in Delivering Healthcare Service

The primary data shows that Uganda's health sector is too wide for the government to effectively provide healthcare services that match its population. It was noted that:

> *The scope of healthcare service delivery is too wide, so the government alone can't address all health needs and issues, including limited and poor facilities, poor care, shortage of equipment and medical supplies, social support for the sick, including counseling services to the people living with HIV. Yes, the private sector indeed works hand in hand with government hospitals to support a lot of activities, for example, providing antenatal care services to pregnant mothers, clinical equipment and reagents for the equipment, carrying out community outreach where the government may not have the financial muscles and enough human resource to reach the local persons, study informants noted.*

PPPs are also important because government hospitals cannot offer services that everyone requires. As such, when private partners come in, they support these hospitals to provide healthcare services that match everyone's needs, efficiently and on time. The study found that 'PPPs support in delivering health education, through radio and television talk shows, which has helped in sensitizing and empowering the community about the primary health care'. Previous studies show that the private sector, such as NGOs, for-profit providers, and international donors, played an important role in the health financing and provision of care to the population (Whyle & Olivier, 2016).

The Best PPPs Model for the Health Sector in Uganda

This study assessed the best type of health PPP models for Uganda's health sector. Remarkably, the study found that Uganda's health sector has followed health PPP models while implementing projects and delivering healthcare services to the patients and community. However, there is no general conceptual framework used by the government of Uganda to implement PPP projects and services. This study found that, though not defined well in the PPP Act 2015 (Ministry of Finance, Planning & Economic Development, 2015), the Ministry of Health has embraced health models as: 1) an Infrastructure-based Model, 2) Discrete Clinical Services Model, and 3) Integrated Clinical Services Model in engaging with private partners to offer projects and healthcare services. Accordingly, the primary data identified Integrated Clinical Services as the best PPP model for Uganda's health sector. Consequently, this study concludes that Integrated Clinical Services Model is the best for Uganda's health system.

Figure 10.1 is a pictorial representation of an Integrated Clinical Service PPP model, showing how the health projects and services are procured; how the government and private sector engage with the community, stakeholders, and patients to identify the priority and health needs of the population. The model leverages private sector resources and expertise to deliver quality care services, medical supplies, consumable medical products, human resources, community health education, and infrastructural development. Therefore, adopting this health PPP model can help to align the effort and resources to improve the management of medical services, and to improve equity, quality, and access to care.

The goals of an Integrated Clinical Services PPP model are to improve healthcare services and balance the operating cost to both the government and patients who have limited access to healthcare and finances for better health services. Under this PPP model, the private sector takes the responsibility to design, build, finance, maintain, renovate, operate, and deliver health projects and services to the community. In doing so, the government procures private

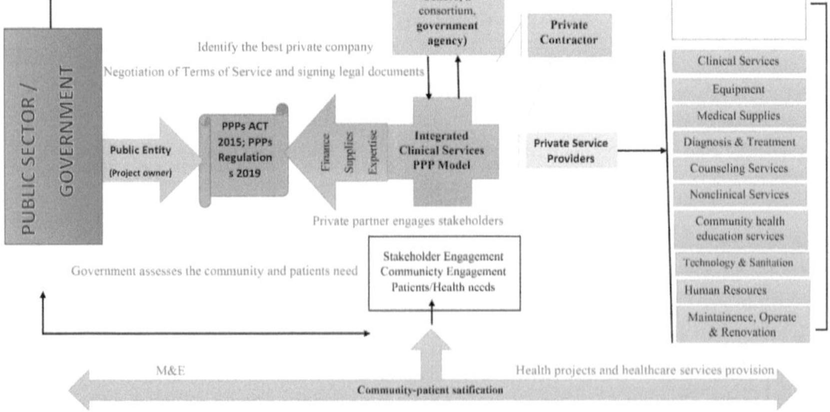

Figure 10.1 Integrated Clinical Services Health PPP Model. *Source*: Created by the author.

companies and transfers potential risks to the private companies (Abuzaineh *et al.,* 2018; Anderson *et al.,* 2006).

Moreover, the features and benefits of the Integrated Clinical Services Health PPP model include its roles and how it is implemented. The model allows private partners to offer multiple projects and healthcare services, including infrastructure, medical supplies, clinical equipment, and non-clinical services, such as human resources, capacity building, cleaning of the facility, and others (Abuzaineh *et al.,* 2018). However, this chapter calls for a strategic and an effective way of implementing these PPP models. As such, the Integrated Clinical Services PPP business model is the best, but there should be an effective approach to implement this model. For instance, the Integrated Clinical Services model should be based on the priority and urgent needs of the population.

In Valencia, Spain, for example, an Integrated Clinical Services PPP model was adopted to expand and include all referral clinics and primary care in the health district, and in most cases covered long-term healthcare goals. Though this arrangement requires more levels of community involvement and political support, it helps the private sector actors to gain control over the full spectrum of referrals and services for the selected population (Pagoni & Patroklos, 2019), and thus enables them to have further efficiencies and include more comprehensive healthcare promotion strategies that contribute to the overall improvement of services delivery (Abuzaineh *et al.,* 2018). In addition, the 2nd PwC/UCSF PPPs report in the series includes lessons learned from Latin America, which provides an overview of the three Integrated Clinical Services PPP contracts—awarded in Peru to construct the Hospital Guillermo Kaelin de la Fuente, Torre Trecca, and Hospital Alberto Leopoldo Barton Thompson. The report shows that Peru was among the first nations in Latin America to implement this type of PPP model and to incorporate non-accurate hospitals within the scope of the projects and services provided to the community (Abuzaineh *et al.,* 2018).

This chapter notes that an Integrated Clinical Services PPP model allows a private company to design a project, construct, finance, operate, and provide clinical support and non-clinical services to the facility. The qualitative data reveals that an Integrated Clinical Services PPP Model puts the private sector in the role of managing all ancillary support services, such as the delivery of non-clinical support services (radiology, laboratory, cafeteria, housekeeping, and clinical support services), consumable medical products such as bandages, cotton wool, catheters, syringes, gloves, sutures, and tubes, and identify and manage clinical equipment and patient systems, which are essential for delivering quality care to the patients. The transition of service delivery from public management is a key change agent, which requires key considerations and pre-planning management change (Raman, 2012). Generally, the private sector plays a key role in the design and management of all the human resources for healthcare services and support services.

CONCLUSION

The current study examined the reason for the implementation of health PPPs in Uganda's health sector. It identified the best health PPP model for Uganda's health sector. A mixed research method was used, where quantitative and qualitative data were collected. The body of literature indicates that PPPs have been recognised across the world as an important approach to infrastructure development and improved service delivery to the population. This study adds and maintains that PPPs are an important mechanism for government because they improve health facilities through design, financing, and construction, and human resource capacity through recruitment, training, and capacity building of staff. They also provide equipment on time and in an efficient manner, medical supplies like ARVs, medical beds, mosquito nets, and non-clinical support, like counselling services.

Health sector PPPs are crucial because they bridge the financial gaps through funding many health programmes and infrastructural development, medical supplies, and equipment. For example, the partnership of Japan International Cooperation Agency (JICA) *has provided* grants through the construction and provision of necessary equipment and medical supplies to the government RRHs. Through partnerships, the status of government health facilities such as OPD, clinics, theatres, emergency units, and ICU departments have been built and some revamped in RRHs. This chapter shows that the government of Uganda cannot offer products and services that meet everyone's needs, and the involvement of PPPs supplements the government's efforts. Consequently, when private sector entities collaborate with the government, they offer support to the government through funding, projects, clinical services, and non-clinical support services to the regional referral hospitals. Such support is not only limited to funds but also assistance in delivering health education, through radio and television talk shows, for example, IDI and Mildmay Uganda have helped in sensitising and empowering the community about primary healthcare. This is evident that the private sector partners, such as non-government organisations, for-profit providers, and international donors, play an important role in the health financing and provision of improved healthcare to the community.

Despite the lack of a precise PPP model for Uganda's health sector and the community's lack of knowledge about the nature of the health PPP models being implemented, the analysis of this study found that the government through the Ministry of Health has implemented health PPP models namely: 1) Infrastructure-based Model, 2) Discrete Clinical Services Model, and 3)

Integrated Clinical Services Model in engaging with the private sector to deliver projects and healthcare services for the features of these models. Accordingly, the study identified Integrated Clinical Services as the best health PPP model for Uganda's health sector.

In conclusion, for the government of Uganda to expand and improve its infrastructure and healthcare services delivery to the community, the PPPs should be fully implemented as an important alternative that lies between the public procurement framework and the private sector. This is important for the government because it brings private sector efficiencies, innovation, resources, such as competencies of human resources, and necessary funding to improve public infrastructure and services, especially when the government has limited funds to meet its budget requirement. Under PPP Act 2015, the government enters into a contract with the private sector, including for-profit making and not-for-profit making to transfer risks and management roles and expect improved public service delivery.

REFERENCES

Abuzaineh, N., Brashers, E., Foong, S., Feachem, R., & Da Rita, P. (2018). PPPs in healthcare: Models, lessons and trends for the future. Healthcare public-private partnership series, No. 4. San Francisco: The Global Health Group. *Institute for Global Health Sciences, University of California, San Francisco, and PwC. Produced in the United States of America*, 4, pp. 1–52.

Abuzaineh, N., Brashers, E., Foong, S., Feachem, R., Da Rita, P. (2018). PPPs in healthcare: Models, lessons and trends for the future. Healthcare public-private partnership series, No. 4. San Francisco: The Global Health Group, Institute for Global Health Sciences, University of California, San Francisco and PwC. Produced in the United States of America.

Aliko-Dangote, H., GBC Health, & United Nations Economic Commission for Africa. (2019). Healthcare and Economic Growth in Africa: Public-Private Partnerships. Addis Ababa, Ethiopia: ECA Printing and Publishing Unit. http://gbchealth.org/wp-content/uploads/2019/02/HealthReport_eng_fin_9Feb.pdf.

Aliko-Dangote, H., GBC Health, & United Nations Economic Commission for Africa. (2019). Healthcare and Economic Growth in Africa: Public-Private Partnerships. Addis Ababa, Ethiopia: ECA Printing and Publishing Unit. http://gbchealth.org/wp-content/uploads/2019/02/HealthReport_eng_fin_9Feb.pdf.

Alonazi, W. B. (2017). Exploring shared risks through public-private partnerships in public health programs: A mixed method. *BMC Public Health*, Vol.17 (1), pp.1–7.

Anderson, M. B., Petrie, M., Alier, M. M., Cangiano, M. M., & Hemming, M. R. (2006). *Public-Private Partnerships, Government Guarantees, and Fiscal Risk.* International Monetary Fund.

Anderson, S. (2012). Public, private, neither, both? Publicness theory and the analysis of healthcare organisations. *Social Science & Medicine*, Vol.74 (3), pp.313–322.

Asasira, J., & Ahimbisibwe, F. (2018). Public-Private Partnership in health care and its impact on health outcomes: Evidence from Ruharo Mission Hospital in Uganda. *International Journal of Social Science Studies,* Vol. 6(12), p.79.

Awor, P., Bisase, H., Lochoro, P., & Curtale, F. (2018). How is the partnership between the public and non-public sector evolving to strengthen universal health coverage in Sengooba, S. N., Kiwanuka, E., Rutebemberwa, E & Ekirapa-Kiracho, E (eds.), *Universal Health Coverage in Uganda: Looking Back and Forward to Speed up the Progress*. Makerere University, Kampala Uganda, pp.1–17. Available online: https://speed.musph.ac.ug/wp-content/uploads/2019/03/Chapter-7.pdf

Baig, M. B., Panda, B., Das, J. K., & Chauhan, A. S. (2014). Is public private partnership an effective alternative to government in the provision of primary health care? A case study in Odisha. *Journal of Health Management*, Vol. 16(1), 41–52.

Basabih, M., Prasojo, E., & Rahayu, A. Y. S. (2022). Hospital services under public-private partnerships, outcomes and, challenges: A literature review. *Journal of Public Health Research*, Vol.11 (3), 22799036221115781.

Bataringaya, J., & Lochoro, P. (2002). The framework for public private partnership in health. *Uganda Health Bulletin (Kampala, Uganda: 1995)*, *8*(3–4), 294–301.

Brad Schwartz, J., & Bhushan, I. (2004). Improving immunization equity through a public-private partnership in Cambodia. *Bulletin of the World health Organization*, *82*, 661–667.

Buse, K. and G. Walt. (2000). Global public-private partnerships: Part I: A new development for health? *Bulletin of the WHO*, Vol.78 (4), pp.549–61.

Buse, K., & Waxman, A. (2001). Public-private health partnerships: A strategy for WHO. *Bulletin of the World Health Organization*, Vol.79 (8), pp.748–754.

Cheng, Z., Wang, H., Xiong, W., Zhu, D., & Cheng, L. (2021). Public–private partnership as a driver of sustainable development: Toward a conceptual framework of sustainability-oriented PPP. *Environment, Development and Sustainability*, Vol. 23(1), pp. 1043–1063.

Dwyer, J., Paskavitz, M., Vriesendorp, S., & Johnson, S. (2006). *An Urgent Call to Professionalize Leadership and Management in Health Care Worldwide*. Boston, MA: Management Sciences for Health.

Engel, N., & van Lente, H. (2014). Organisational innovation and control practices: the case of public–private mix in tuberculosis control in India. *Sociology of Health & Illness*, *36*(6), 917–931.

Family Health International-360. (2012, August). The Role of Public–Private Partnerships in Strengthening Health Systems. Retrieved from www.fhi360.org/: https://www.fhi360.org/sites/default/files/media/documents/resource-public-private-partnerships-health-systems-strengthening.pdf [Accessed on 27 October 2022].

Ferreira, D. C., & Marques, R. C. (2021). Public-private partnerships in health care services: Do they outperform public hospitals regarding quality and access? Evidence from Portugal. *Socio-Economic Planning Sciences*, *73*, 100798.

Filip R, Gheorghita Puscaselu R, Anchidin-Norocel L, Dimian M, Savage WK. (2022). Global challenges to public health care systems during the COVID-19 pandemic: A review of pandemic measures and problems. *Journal of Personalized Medicine,* Vol.12 (8), pp.1295.

Government of Uganda. (2010). Health Sector Strategic and Investment Plan, p. 159; [Online] Retrieved from: http://www.health.go.ug/docs/HSSIP10.pdf; last accessed December 17, 2022.

Government of Uganda-Ministry of Health. (2010). Health Sector Strategic Plan III 2010/11-2014/15. [Online] Retrieved from: https://www.health.go.ug/docs/HSSP_III_2010.pdf [Accessed August 11, 2022].

Great Britain Treasury Taskforce, P. F. (1998). *Partnerships for Prosperity: The Private Finance Initiative*. Great Britain, Treasury, Taskforce Private Finance.

Hanson, K., Gilson, L., Goodman, C., Mills, A., Smith, R., Feachem, R. . . . & Kinlaw, H. (2008). Is private health care the answer to the health problems of the world's poor? *PLoS Medicine*, Vol. 5(11), pp.e233.

Health Policy Plus. (2020). *Improving and Supplementing the Public Healthcare Workforce with Public-Private Partnerships in Indonesia*. Washington, DC: U.S. Agency for International Development. http://www.healthpolicyplus.com/ns/pubs/18410-18736_IndonesiaPPPCaseStudy.pdf

Hellowell, M. (2012). The role of public-private partnerships in health systems is getting stronger. *Commonwealth Health Partnerships, 72.*

Hellowell, M. (2019). Are public–private partnerships the future of healthcare delivery in sub-Saharan Africa? Lessons from Lesotho. *BMJ Global Health*, Vol. 4(2), e001217.

Initiative for Social and Economic Rights. (2019). (ISER). *Achieving Equity in Health: Are Public Private Partnerships the Solution?* Kampala, Uganda: (ISER). Retrieved December 12, 2019, from www.iser-uganda.org /: https://www.iser-uganda.org/images/downloads/achieving_equity_in_health.pdf.

Jensen, J. (2016, June). A review of public–private partnership activities in health system strengthening. In *The Role of Public-Private Partnerships in Health Systems Strengthening: Workshop Summary*. National Academies Press (US).

Jomo, K. S., Chowdhury, A., Sharma, K., & Platz, D. (2016). Public-private partnerships and the 2030 Agenda for Sustainable Development: fit for purpose? DESA Working Paper No. 148 ST/ESA/2016/DWP/148.

Joudyian, N., Doshmangir, L., Mahdavi, M., Tabrizi, J. S., & Gordeev, V. S. (2021). Public-private partnerships in primary health care: a scoping review. *BMC Health Services Research,* Vol.21 (4), pp. 1–18.

Kwak, Y. H., Chih, Y., & Ibbs, C. W. (2009). Towards a comprehensive understanding of public private partnerships for infrastructure development, *California Management Review*, Vol. 51 (2), pp.51–78.

Mahoney, J. T., McGahan, A. M., & Pitelis, C. N. (2009). Perspective-The interdependence of private and public interests. *Organization Science*, Vol. 20 (6), pp. 1034–1052.

Mehta, A., Bhatia, A., & Chatterjee, A. (Eds.). (2010). *Improving Health and Education Service Delivery in India through Public–Private Partnerships* (Vol. 296). Asian Development Bank.

Ministry of Finance, Planning and Economic Development. (2015). Public Private Partnership Act, 2015. [Online] Retrieved from www.pppunit.go.ug/: https://www.pppunit.go.ug/sites/files/PPP%20Act%202015.pdf [Accessed August 10, 2022]

Ministry of Health. (1993). Report on Recommendations of the Health Policy Review Commission. [Online] Retrieved from library.health.go.ug/: http://library.health.go.ug/publications/policy-documents/report-recommendations-health-policy-review-commission [Accessed August 10, 2022].

Ministry of Health. (1999, September). National Health Policy. Retrieved from www.healthresearchweb.org: https://www.healthresearchweb.org/files/National_Health_Policy_1999.pdf

Ministry of Health. (2010, July). Health Sector Strategic & Investment Plan 2010/11—2014/15. Promoting People's Health to Enhance Socio-economic Development. Retrieved from www.health.go.ug/: https://www.health.go.ug/docs/HSSIP10.pdf [Accessed August 11, 2022]

Ministry of Health. (2012). National Policy on Public Private Partnerships in Health (NPPPPH). [Online] Retrieved from http://library.health.go.ug/publications/policy-documents/national-policy-public-private-partnership-health. [Accessed August 11, 2022].

Ministry of Health. (2015). Health Sector Development Plan 2015/16–2019/20. [Online] https://www.health.go.ug/cause/health-sector-development-plan-2015-16-2019-20/ [last accessed November 17, 2019]

Ministry of Health. (2016). MoH. Health Financing Strategy; at p. 8; http://health.go.ug/content/health-financing-strategy; last accessed November 17, 2019

Ministry of Health. (2017). Uganda's National Strategy for Public-Private Partnerships in Health 2016–2020. Kampala. https://pdf.usaid.gov/pdf_docs/PA00THFH.pdf: Ministry of Health.

Mohanty, U., & Sahu, A. (2023). Multi-sectoral approach in health sector: focusing on public-private partnership under the National Health Mission in India. *Population Medicine*, *5*(Supplement).

Nduhura, A., Nuwagaba, I., Settumba, J. P., Molokwane, T., & Lukamba, M. T. (2020). Public private partnerships: systematic review of available models for improving health care services. International Conference on Public Administration and Development Alternatives (IPADA).

Nkabane-Nkholongo, E. L., McIntosh, N., Grabowski, A., Vian, T., & Jack, B. W. (2015). Hospital public–private partnerships in low resource settings: Perceptions of how the Lesotho PPP transformed management systems and performance. *Health Systems & Reform*, *1*(2), 155–166.

Oluoha, C., Umeh, C., & Ahaneku, H. (2014). Assessing the contributions of private health facilities in a pioneer private-public partnership in childhood immunization in Nigeria. *Journal of public health in Africa*, *5*(1).

Ondategui-Parra, S. (2022). Public-Private Partnerships in Healthcare. Retrieved from healthmanagement.org/: https://healthmanagement.org/c/hospital/issuearticle/public-private-partnerships-in-healthcare [accessed on 27 October 2022].

Pagoni, E. G., & Patroklos, G. (2019). A system dynamics model for the assessment of national public–private partnership programmes' sustainable performance. *Simulation Modelling Practice and Theory*, Vol. 97, p. 101949.

Roehrich, J. K., Lewis, M. A., & George, G. (2014). Are public–private partnerships a healthy option? A systematic literature review. *Social Science & Medicine*, Vol. 113, pp. 110–119.

Sekhri, N. (2009). From funding to action: Strengthening healthcare systems in sub-Saharan Africa. World Economic Forum.

Sundewall, J., & Brady, E. (2019). Prioritizing essential packages of health services in six countries in sub-Saharan Africa. *Implications and Lesion for SRHR (unpublished report). PMNCH and Swedish International Development Agency.*

Sundewall, J., & Brady, E. (2019). Prioritizing essential packages of health services in six countries in sub-Saharan Africa. *Implications and lesion for SRHR (unpublished report). PMNCH and Swedish International Development Agency.*

Tashobya, C.K., Musoba, N. and Lochoro, P. (2007). Public private partnership for health in Uganda: will HSSP II deliver on the expectations*? Health Policy and Development*, Vol.5 (1), pp.50–58.

Tshombe, L. M., Molokwane, T., Nduhura, A & Nuwagaba, I. (2020). An analysis of public-private partnerships in the East Africa. *Research in World Economy*, Vol. 11(5), Special Issue, Sciedu Press, Canada, pp. 152–163.

United Nations Economic Commission for Europe (2016). UNECE PPP Standard for Healthcare Policy (Proposed Draft): Retrieved December 4, 2019, from. https://wiki.unece.org/display/pppp/Health+policy?preview=/23758291/31065240/UNECE%20healthcare%20PPP%20standard%20-%20Public%20Review%20-%20v2.1.pdf

United States Agency for International Development. (2016). USAID. Uganda Private Sector Assessment in Health: p. 22

Vian, T., Richards, S. C., McCoy, K., Connelly, P., & Feeley, F. (2007). Public-private partnerships to build human capacity in low-income countries: findings from the Pfizer program. *Human Resources for Health*, Vol. 5 (1), pp.1–11.

Wang, H., Switlick, K., Ortiz, C., Zurita, B., & Connor, C. (2012). *Health Insurance Handbook: How to Make It Work* (Vol. 219). World Bank Publications.

Watkins, D. A., Jamison, D. T., Mills, T., Atun, T., Danforth, K., Glassman, A. . . . & Alwan, A. (2018). Universal health coverage and essential packages of care.

Whyle, E. B., & Olivier, J. (2016). Models of public–private engagement for health services delivery and financing in Southern Africa: a systematic review. *Health Policy and Planning*, Vol. 31(10), pp. 1515–1529.

Woodson, T. S. (2016). Public private partnerships and emerging technologies: A look at nanomedicine for diseases of poverty. *Research Policy*, Vol. 45(7), pp. 1410–1418.

World Bank Group. (2016). Independent evaluation group. *Public-Private Partnerships in Health: World Bank Group Engagement in Health PPPs*. World Bank. Retrieved from https://ieg.worldbankgroup.org/sites/default/files/Data/reports/lp_Health_PPP_1116.pdf [Accessed on 27 October 2022].

World Bank Group. (2018). *Procuring Infrastructure Public-Private Partnerships Report 2018: Assessing Government Capability to Prepare, Procure, and Manage PPPs*. World Bank.

World Bank Institute. (2012). Public-private Partnerships e Reference Guide Version 1.0. International Bank for Reconstruction and Development/International Development Association, The World Bank, Washington, DC.

World Bank. (2015, July 9). *The Public-Private Partnership Act (Uganda).* [Online] Retrieved from worldbank.org/: https://ppp.worldbank.org/public-private-partnership/library/public-private-partnership-act-uganda [Accessed August 10, 2022]

World Health Organisation. (2022). Universal Health Coverage, Available from: https://www.who.int/news-room/fact-sheets/detail/universal-health-coverage-(uhc). Date o access: 22 March, 2023.

Wyss, K. (2004). An approach to classifying human resources constraints to attaining health-related Millennium Development Goals. *Human Resources for Health*, Vol. 2(1), pp. 1–8.

Chapter 11

Public-Private Partnerships and the Quality of Public Service Delivery in Zambia

Royd Malisase, Tambulani C. Nyirenda and Moses Chewe

For a long time, the delivery of public services had traditionally been the responsibility of the government alone. However, the twenty-first century has seen a major shift towards the inclusion of the private sector in public service delivery through, among others, Public-Private Partnerships (PPPs). Modern PPPs can be traced to the 1980s, when countries began to liberalise their economies (World Bank, 2022a). PPPs have steadily grown with several low- and middle-income countries in Asia, Africa, and Latin America pioneering varied and improved forms of these partnerships. Equally, industrialised countries such as the United States, Australia, and most European countries have a number of PPP projects in infrastructure development and service delivery (Oktavianus, Mahani & Meifrinaldi, 2018).

In high-income countries, China alone had 14,000 existing PPP projects, totalling US$2.7 trillion in aggregate value (Reuters, 2018). Over the last three decades, over 121 low- and middle-income countries have seen total PPP investments in excess of US$2 trillion in over 5,000 infrastructure projects (World Bank, 2016). Despite the COVID-19 pandemic, in 2021 alone, investment commitments stood at US$76.2 billion across 240 projects, with sub-Saharan Africa receiving US$5.2 billion worth of investments across 26 projects. This included US$336 million worth of investments in Zambia (World Bank, 2022a). Africa needs infrastructure financing of US$170 billion a year by 2025, with an estimated financing gap of US$68 to US$108 billion a year (African Development Bank, 2020). PPPs are seen as a key element in narrowing this gap by crowding in private sector investments.

Zambia's foray into PPPs was driven by its indebtedness. In 1999, the country was highly indebted, with debts of US$6.5 billion, translating to almost 160% of its gross domestic product (GDP) (Madimutsa & Pretorius, 2018). The debt made it difficult for the country to afford to develop infrastructure and deliver the needed public services (Zambia Development Agency, 2014). In response, the government turned to relying on the private sector to finance, develop, and manage these infrastructures and services. Consequently, the country began pursuing PPPs in the early 2000s. However, by 2021, Zambia's overall debt rose to US$33.8 billion (or 133% of GDP) (International Monetary Fund, 2022). This implies that the country needs more PPPs for its future development needs.

For PPPs to succeed in guaranteeing quality service delivery, there is a need for governments to put in place the correct regulatory framework, utilise appropriate PPP models, assess service quality, and identify constraints (Mouraviev & Kakabadse, 2017; Shukla, Sharma & Thumar, 2016; Gwary, Asindaya & Abba, 2016; World Bank, 2018; Asian Development Bank, 2008). Therefore, the purpose of this chapter is to discuss PPPs and the quality of public services delivered in Zambia. To achieve its purpose, the chapter will be arranged as follows: This introduction is followed by an explanation of the meaning of PPPs; literature review; analysis of the regulatory framework for PPP; types of PPPs adopted in Zambia; the quality of services delivered through PPPs; the constraints associated with delivering services through PPPs; future prospects, and finally, a conclusion.

THE MEANING OF PUBLIC-PRIVATE PARTNERSHIPS

There is no precise, clear or accepted definition of the term Public-Private Partnership. Generally, the term is used to describe a wide range of contractual arrangements between the public and the private sectors for the provision of public goods and services (Shukla *et al.,* 2016; Gwary *et al.,* 2016). Although widely varied, PPP contracts require the private entity to undertake infrastructure projects or provision of services by assuming substantial financial, technical, and operational risks and, in return, receive consideration in the form of a fee from the state's revenue/budget, fees collected from users, or a combination of the two (Mouraviev & Kakabadse, 2016). In other words, PPPs emphasise reliance on private sector resources to improve the delivery of public goods and services.

In reality, countries have specified definitions of PPPs based on their regulatory frameworks (World Bank, 2022a). In Zambia's case, the Public Private Procurement Act, 2009, defines PPP as an 'investment through private sector participation in an infrastructure project or infrastructure facility' (Republic of Zambia, 2009). The Act excludes projects undertaken jointly by any public entities and projects taken over by a private sector entity through privatisation or dis-investment (Republic of Zambia, 2009). The Act does not limit the PPP models that can be entered into. This allows the private sector flexibility with regard to design, construction, delivery, and management of PPP contracts by focusing on the services to be delivered, rather than salient details of the construction (Zambia Development Agency, 2014; Republic of Zambia, 2009).

These partnerships are not always easy to execute and require monitoring from all parties involved. In the absence of this, challenges emanating from adoption and implementation of projects may end up outweighing benefits in the long run (Ullah, 2019; Tshombe, Molokwane, Nduhura & Nuwagaba, 2020). Nevertheless, PPPs are superior to traditional procurement in that the involvement of the private sector improves efficiency and effectiveness (Fombad, 2013; Hall, 2015; Kisitu, 2018). In addition, PPPs allow better utilisation of scarce public funding, reduce risks, quicken the completion of projects, and help introduce advanced technology. Private entities are also better equipped to provide resources, especially funding, as well as managerial, technical, and innovative expertise, thus potentially improving the quality of public services (World Bank, 2022a).

LITERATURE REVIEW

To guard against bottlenecks in the implementation of PPPs, governments across the globe have put in place regulatory frameworks (Tshombe *et al.*, 2020; World Bank, 2022b; Vallée, 2018). Usually, these frameworks encompass a PPP Act, a PPP Policy and a PPP Unit. These are supplemented by an act and institution in charge of public procurement. In addition, various sector policies, acts, and the institutions tend to have provisions necessary for the integration of PPPs (World Bank, 2018; Muleya, Zulu & Nanchengwa, 2019). Most African countries have developed PPP regulatory frameworks, leaving less than 10 entirely without them (Vallée, 2018). African countries with robust PPP frameworks include South Africa, Mauritius, Uganda, Ghana, Gambia, Nigeria, Egypt, and Zambia. Outside Africa, PPP regulatory frameworks have been established in Europe, Asia, North America, Latin America, and Australia (World Bank, 2022b; World Bank, 2022c). For example, the European Union has PPP laws under the stewardship of the European PPP Expertise Centre. In China, PPPs are overseen by the Public-Private Partnerships Center. Federal states such as the United States, Australia, and Brazil have PPP laws and institutions at both the federal and state levels. In most countries, PPP units are established under the ministry responsible for finance and national development/planning. In some countries, such as Nigeria, Pakistan, and New Zealand, PPP functions are embedded in institutions responsible for infrastructure development (World Bank, 2022b & World Bank, 2022c).

Most regulatory frameworks are not adequate to deal with PPPs. Most projects, especially in Africa, that reach financial closure tend to do so only after circumventing these frameworks (Mouraviev & Kakabadse, 2017; Vallée, 2018). The laws are muddled and thus end up impeding rather than encouraging PPP projects. Even where laws are well structured, contracting authorities tend to lack expertise, knowledge, and intergovernmental cooperation. They also come under immense political pressure to conclude or cancel transactions (Axis Consulting, 2013; Abioye, 2016; Fombad, 2013). This creates a need for governments to improve their PPP frameworks by clearly delineating the roles and responsibilities of all participating stakeholders and empowering them to deliver projects (World Bank, 2018).

Once the proper regulatory framework is in place, the next step is to select the best PPP model; one in which the benefits outweigh the costs associated with implementation of projects. Literature reveals at least 25 different types of PPPs (Yuan, Zheng, You & Skibniewski, 2017; Mouraviev & Kakabadse, 2016; Shukla *et al.,* 2016; Gwary *et al.,* 2016; Kwak, Chih & Ibbs, 2009). Madimutsa and Pretorius (2018) place potential PPP models into four broad categories. The first category comprises PPPs that require public institutions to pay for goods or services delivered by private entities. They include Build-and-Transfer (BT), Service Contract, Supply-Operate-and-Transfer (SOT), and Build-Lease-and-Transfer (BLT). These models allow public entities to concentrate on their main functions while the services are contracted out to private entities. The public entity is also able to set quality standards that it would not have been able to meet itself (Fombad, 2013; Gwary et al., 2016). Examples of projects under these models include the 450MW Temane Gas-Fired Plant in Mozambique and the construction of Chiremba Road and ZB Water Augmentation Project in Zimbabwe (Zimbabwe Economic Policy Analysis and Research Unit, 2016; World Bank, 2022a). There is need to minimise the risks of awarding lucrative contracts to connected friends and relatives of politicians who offer high prices with poor expertise (Fombad, 2013).

The second category comprises PPPs that require private entities to finance, construct, and operate a project for a specific period of time before transferring it to the public sector. They include Build-Operate-and-Transfer (BOT), Build-Own-Operate-Transfer (BOOT), Build-Transfer-and-Operate (BTO), and Rehabilitate-Operate-and-Transfer (ROT) (Madimutsa & Pretorius, 2018). In these models, the private entity meets the cost of construction (or rehabilitation) and operation and recoups income by charging members of the public a fee for use of the infrastructure (Mouraviev & Kakabadse, 2016). If the fees are inadequate, the public partner may top up the difference. If the fees are high, the private entity may split earnings with the public entity (Shukla *et al.,* 2016).

It is important to determine the best contract period before ownership and control are handed back to the public entity. A short concession period disadvantages the private entity while the public entity loses out under a prolonged one. The common contract period tends to be 25 years (Gwary *et al.,* 2016; World Bank, 2018). These tend to be the preferred models for developing new infrastructure, accounting for over 30% of all projects (Madimutsa & Pretorius, 2018; Hammami, Ruhashyankiko & Yehoue, 2006; Loxley, 2013). These models were used in South Africa to construct two maximum prisons in Bloemfontein and Louis Trichardt with a combined capacity of 3,000 inmates, the 250 MW Bujagali Hydro Power Plant in Uganda and the Hamma Seawater Desalination Plant in Algeria (Ullah, 2019; Farlam, 2005; Harper, 2015). Others are the Vancouver Landfill Project in Canada, Costa Rica's San Jose-San Ramon Highway project and the Anglo-French Channel Tunnel in the United Kingdom and France (United Nations, 2008; Magro, 2015; Briggs & Mitchell, 2018).

The third category comprises PPPs that require private entities to finance, construct, own, and operate infrastructure without transferring it back to the public sector (Madimutsa & Pretorius, 2018). They include Build-Own-and-Operate (BOO), Rehabilitate-Own-and-Operate (ROO), and Contract-Add-and-Operate (CAO). These models, especially BOO, are the most popular accounting for close to 40% of all projects (Hammami *et al,* 2006, p.12; Loxley, 2013, p.487). This is because they allow the private entity to permanently own the infrastructure. Examples include Kutch and Pipavav Railways in India and Xiamen Airport Cargo Terminal in China. However, there is need for the government to maintain some control over the prices and quality of services provided under such models.

The fourth category comprises PPPs that transfer the responsibility of managing a public infrastructure from a public to a private entity. They include Concession, Lease, and Management Contracts (Madimutsa & Pretorius, 2018). The private entity usually earns money through service charges and, where necessary, a fee from the government (Mouraviev & Kakabadse, 2017). Ideally, the contract should give the private entity a high level of managerial autonomy while ensuring service quality, maintenance, and, where necessary, improvement in the infrastructure itself. Most initial contracts are short term, between five to 15 years, to enable performance assessment before deciding to renew, re-negotiate, or revoke the contract (Asian Development Bank, 2008; Kisitu, 2018).

These models, especially, concessions, are popular in the electricity and railway transport sectors. Notable examples of electricity concessions include Umeme Limited in Uganda, Compagnie Ivoirienne d'Electricité in Ivory

Coast, Veolia in Gabon, the National Grid Corporation of the Philippines, and several generation and distribution utilities in Brazil (Malisase, 2021). Rail concessions include Camrail in Cameroun, Tanganyika Rail in Kenya, Transrail in Senegal-Mali, Belgrano Norte in Argentina, and Armenian Railway in Armenia (Abioye, 2016; World Bank, 2022a). However, if poorly structured and monitored, these models may be detrimental to service quality on account of poor management by the concessionaire, failure to fund capital investments, corruption, and political interference (Kwak et al., 2009; Kisitu, 2018; Asian Development Bank, 2008).

Generally, the impact of PPPs on the quality of service provision remains mixed. Positive results have been recorded in electricity supply, transportation, education, and water and sanitation. In Morocco, a rural electrification programme under PPP resulted in increased access to electricity in rural areas from 16% to 98% (Ullah, 2019). Improvements in the reliability of electricity supply were also recorded in Uganda, Cameroon, Ivory Coast, Gabon, Australia, the Philippines, and Germany (Malisase, 2021). In the United States, the Milwaukee Parent Choice Program increased access to quality education for underprivileged children (LaRocque, 2008). Success was also recorded in the transport sector with the San Jose-San Ramon Highway, Chiremba Road and the Anglo-French Channel Tunnel, which led to reductions in accidents and travel time (World Bank, 2022a; Zimbabwe Economic Policy Analysis and Research Unit, 2016; Briggs & Mitchell, 2018). The Hamma Seawater Desalination Plant improved quality of clean drinking water in Algeria while the Vancouver Landfill improved solid waste management in Vancouver, Canada (Ullah, 2019; United Nations, 2008; Magro, 2015).

Negative results have led to dilapidated infrastructures, inadequate supply, and exclusion of the poor due to high tariffs (Hall, 2015; Mfunwa, Taylor & Kreiter, 2016; Ngoma, Mundia & Kaliba, 2014). In Africa, five countries account for more than 50% of all successful PPP activity: South Africa, Morocco, Nigeria, Egypt, and Ghana (African Development Bank, 2020). Most PPP contracts, especially railway concessions, have been cancelled. Concessionaires failed to invest in the railway networks leading to dilapidated infrastructure and failure to meet demand due to inadequate trains. Cancelled railway concessions include Sizarail in Congo Brazzaville, Transgabonais in Gabon, Transrail in Senegal-Mali, and Madarail in Madagascar (Abioye, 2016). Examples of PPPs leading to high tariffs can be found in Uganda, Nigeria, Gabon, and Ivory Coast where electricity became too expensive for poor customers after supply was taken over by private entities (Malisase, 2021). In France, water supplied by municipalities was found to be 16% cheaper than that provided under PPPs (Hall, 2015).

The negative effect on service provision has been the result of a number of constraints encountered by both the private and public entities. The main constraints include lack of or poor regulatory frameworks, corruption in contract allocation, lack of capital to fund improvements and maintenance of projects, poorly structured contracts, poor monitoring of implementation, and poor management by the concessionaires (Kwak et al., 2009; Kisitu, 2018; Asian Development Bank, 2008; World Bank, 2018). Other constraints are political interference, political instability, lack of political will, and lack of trust between public and private sector actors (Hall, 2015; Seeletse, 2016; World Bank, 2022a; World Bank 2022b).

THE REGULATORY FRAMEWORK FOR PUBLIC-PRIVATE PARTNERSHIPS IN ZAMBIA

The regulatory framework for PPPs consists of a series of laws, regulations, policies, guidelines, and government institutions (Vallée, 2018; Republic of Zambia, 2009; World Bank, 2022a). A quality regulatory framework is important to control the PPP process and ensure success by helping to identify successful projects, guide them effectively, and balance public and private interests (World Bank, 2022b). Before the establishment of the regulatory framework, only two of the five PPP projects entered into were successful, with the remaining three being cancelled. This failure was mainly the result of poorly structured PPP contracts that favoured private entities while lacking proper legal backing (Muleya *et al.,* 2019; Axis Consulting, 2013).

This prompted the government to develop the necessary regulatory framework, beginning with the PPP Policy in 2008, which laid the foundation (Zambia Development Agency, 2014). Guided by the policy, the country enacted the Public-Private Partnership Act, 2009, as amended by the Public-Private Partnership (Amendment) Act, 2018, and the Public-Private Partnership (Amendment) Act, 2021 (Republic of Zambia, 2011; Republic of Zambia, 2018; Republic of Zambia, 2021). The purpose of the PPP Act is two-fold: to promote and to manage PPPs. To promote PPPs, the Act provides guidelines aimed at encouraging private entities to partner with the government. For instance, section 7 requires the selection and awarding of contracts to be based on competitiveness, fairness, and transparency (Axis Consulting, 2013). Sections 3 and 4 remove unnecessary restrictions by allowing the use of any appropriate PPP model in infrastructural development and service delivery (Republic of Zambia, 2009). The 2018 and 2021 amendments strengthened the powers and functions of the Public-Private Partnership Department, Public-Private Partnership Council, and Public-Private Partnership Technical Committee (Republic of Zambia, 2018; Republic of Zambia, 2021).

The Act and its amendments also provide clear guidelines relating to procedures for evaluating, selecting, negotiating, and terminating contracts, concluding PPP projects, and resolving disputes between public and private entities (Republic of Zambia, 2009; Republic of Zambia, 2018). For example, the 2018 amendment identified project viability and compliance with environmental regulations as some of the selection criteria. The Public Procurement Act, 2020, sets provisions for bidding and bidder selection as well as procurement for projects (Republic of Zambia, 2020). The Zambia Development Agency Act, 2006, established the Zambia Development Agency, tasked with creating an economic environment conducive to a private sector-driven economy (Axis Consulting, 2013).

The major institutions are the Public-Private Partnership Department, Public-Private Partnership Council, Public-Private Partnership Technical Committee, Zambia Public Procurement Authority, the Zambia Development Agency, and Ministry of Finance and National Planning (especially the Investment and Debt Management Department). Sector ministries, agencies, and local authorities play the role of contracting authorities (Republic of Zambia, 2009; Republic of Zambia, 2018; Evdorides & Shoji, 2013). The PPP Department is tasked with implementing guidelines provided in the PPP Act and its amendments. It also advises the government on administrative procedures relating to PPPs and monitors the process of selecting private sector partners.

It also monitors the implementation of contracts to ensure that they are completed on time. The PPP Council, chaired by the minister in charge of finance, formulates PPP policies and ensures competition, transparency, and fairness in the process of selecting and approving projects. The Council also conducts project inspections at any given stage (Evdorides & Shoji, 2013). The PPP Technical Committee, chaired by the Secretary to the Treasury, comprises various ministerial permanent secretaries and representatives of various relevant institutions such as the Engineering Institution of Zambia, Zambia Environmental Management Agency, and Zambia Public Procurement Authority (Axis Consulting, 2013). Functions of the Committee include providing technical advice to the PPP Department and PPP Council, examining and shortlisting projects, and recommending projects for approval.

The Investment and Debt Management Department examines government financing of PPPs. The Zambia Public Procurement Authority manages the bidding process and approves major procurements for PPPs that involve the construction of infrastructure (Republic of Zambia, 2020). The Ministry of Infrastructure, Housing and Urban Development has overall technical and oversight responsibility for such projects. Contracting authorities, public institutions permitted by law to enter into PPP arrangements, are responsible for evaluating project proposals and forming ongoing relationships with the private partner (Evdorides & Shoji, 2013).

As can be seen, the regulatory framework is robust and capable of promoting and managing PPPs. Nevertheless, similar to observations in other countries, it has limitations. Firstly, some of the laws seem to conflict with each other. Despite amendments, the PPP Act tends to conflict with the Zambia Development Agency Act and the Public Procurement Act with regard to the powers and functions of various institutions. In addition, having too many participating institutions causes functional overlaps and coordination constraints. This results in prolonged negotiations and failure to reach financial closure (Mwanaumo, Nsefu, Mambwe & Lindunda, 2020). The regulatory framework also fails to clarify procedures to guide contracting authorities and private entities in the management of PPP projects. There is also a lack of sector-specific guidelines and vague and/or inadequate procurement procedures for PPP projects. This leads to poorly negotiated contracts that end up being cancelled after public outcry. The laws also relatively fail to protect private sector investments leading to reluctance from many established investors to commit resources (Muleya *et al.,* 2019; Axis Consulting, 2013).

TYPES OF PUBLIC-PRIVATE PARTNERSHIPS ADOPTED IN ZAMBIA

Before the enactment of the PPP Act in 2009, the Zambian government only entered into five PPP projects, rising to 16 by 2016 and more afterwards (Axis Consulting, 2013; Zambia Development Agency, 2014; Mwanaumo *et al.,* 2020). Since the PPP Act does not limit the PPP models, the government is free to utilise any model of its choice. Nevertheless, the only models implemented in Zambia so far are service contracts, BOT, BOOT, BOO, concession, and lease (Madimutsa & Pretorius, 2018; Zambia Development Agency, 2014; Muleya *et al.,* 2019; Ngoma *et al.,* 2014). Although the newly elected government cancelled contracts or abandoned negotiations for a number of PPPs on 20 August 2021, shortly after getting into power, the country still has quite a few PPPs running (International Monetary Fund, 2022).

Zambia only has small service contracts involving private companies providing catering, cleaning, and security services on premises of public organisations. For instance, cleaning and security service contracts are present at Chainama Hills College Hospital and the University of Zambia (Madimutsa & Pretorius, 2018). The Lusaka City Council has service contracts with various companies for solid waste management (Chulu, 2017). The government has signed service contracts with agricultural-based businesses to help in the supply of inputs to beneficiaries of the Farmer Input Support Programme

(Indaba Agricultural Policy Research Institute, 2015). These service contracts tend to be small and short term, between a month and two years, and are thus hardly considered relevant PPPs in the grand scheme.

Like in many other countries, BOTs in Zambia have been applied to the construction of physical infrastructure such as border crossings, road management, shopping malls, and television networks. Projects under the BOT model and its variants include the Kasumbalesa One Stop Border Post. In July 2009, the Zambian government entered into a 25-year contract with the Zambian Border Crossing Company to construct and operate the border post between Zambia and the Democratic Republic of Congo. The border post became operational in 2011 but the government overturned the contract in 2012, before renegotiating it in 2015 (Willie, 2020). The other is TopStar Telecommunications Corporation Limited, a joint venture between Zambia National Broadcasting Corporation (40%) and StarTimes of China (60%).

In 2016, the company was awarded a 25-year contract to build infrastructure and manage the US$373 million digital migration, and provide a digital television transmission network (African Media Barometer, 2021; Bwalya, Mutale & Kunda, 2022). Another one is the 65-year contract, signed in 2001, between the Lusaka City Council and China Henan, for the financing, construction, operation, and transfer of Luburma Market (commonly known as Kamwala Market), situated in Lusaka. Similarly, in 2010, the University of Zambia granted a 25-year land lease to Graduare Property Development Zambia Limited for the construction, operation, and transfer of East Park Mall (Zambia Development Agency, 2014; Mwanaumo, 2020).

Several contracts under BOT have been cancelled at various stages. One example is the Advanced Road Traffic Management System (ARTMS) project between the Road Transport and Safety Agency and Intelligent Mobility Solutions. The company was awarded a 17-year US$110 million contract in 2017 to provide intelligent transportation systems in traffic management, safety, and security through the use of speed cameras, road signs, vehicle inspection centres, and other road safety enforcement equipment. However, the contract was cancelled in 2020 on allegations of corruption and illegalities in the signing contract (Ncube, 2020). In addition, the government abandoned negotiations for the development of the 750MW Kafue Gorge Lower Power Station in 2015, preferring to fund and run it itself.

The BOOT model applies to the 120MW Itezhi-Tezhi Hydro Power Plant, owned and operated by Itezhi-Tezhi Power Corporation Limited on a 25-year contract from 2016. The company generates power and sells it to ZESCO Limited on a power purchase agreement (Energy Regulation Board, 2022). The BOO model is equally associated with power plants. Examples include the ongoing construction of the US$210 million 40MW Kabompo Hydro Power Project by Copperbelt Energy Corporation and the US$690 million

247MW Kalungwishi Hydro Power Project by Lunzua Power Authority (Copperbelt Energy Corporation, 2022).

The three major concessions, either cancelled or not renewed, are Zambia Railways Limited, Mulobezi Railway, and Mpulungu Harbor. In December 2003, Railway Systems of Zambia was awarded a 20-year concession to operate freight and passenger trains from the Copperbelt to Livingstone on railway infrastructure owned by Zambia Railways Limited. This was in return for a fixed concession fee of US$253.5 million and a 5% share of turnover (Railways Limited, 2013). The contract was cancelled in 2012 due to poor performance. Similarly, in 2003, Leasons General Contractors was awarded a 10-year concession to operate freight and passenger trains on the Mulobezi Railway, from Livingstone to Mulobezi, in return for a fixed concession fee and a percentage of turnover.

The concession was not renewed when it expired in 2013 (Malisase, 2021). In 2000, Agro Fuel Zambia was awarded a 25-year concession to maintain and operate Mpulungu Harbour. The concession was cancelled in 2010 after the concessionaire failed to make contractually agreed investments deemed necessary to improve service delivery (Zambia Development Agency, 2014). Equally, most leases have been cancelled with active ones consisting of small game camps and lodges (Malisase, 2021). Similar to observations in other countries (Gwary et al., 2016; Kwak *et al.,* 2009; World Bank, 2022a), the BOT model seems to be the most popular and successful, while concession and lease are the least successful, with most contracts cancelled due to poor performance.

THE QUALITY OF SERVICES DELIVERED THROUGH PUBLIC-PRIVATE PARTNERSHIPS

Similar to situations in other countries, the quality of services provided through PPP in Zambia is mixed. For instance, the border services provided by the Zambian Border Crossing Company at the Kasumbalesa One Stop Border Post significantly improved compared to when it was under government control (Muleya et al., 2019). The newly built border infrastructure had improved operational processes and computerised systems, leading to a smoother flow of traffic and efficient clearing and immigration processes. However, Willie (2020) discovered that the government-run Chirundu Border was more efficient at releasing imports and exports, taking an average of 24.1 hours compared to 39.4 hours at the Kasumbalesa Border.

Railway Systems of Zambia and Leasons General Contractors somewhat improved the operations of Zambia Railways and Mulobezi Railway, respectively. For instance, because of enhanced logistics arrangements and train speed, Railway Systems of Zambia improved transit time between Durban and the Copperbelt from an average of 45 days to about 15 (Sata, 2007). However, both concessionaires failed to invest in the maintenance and replacement of infrastructure. This led to the deterioration of trains and rail tracks, resulting in train derailments and loss of life and property (Zambia Railways Limited, 2013). Equally, the train fleet remained static. For instance, the *Leasons General Contractors* only operated a single train once a week, transporting both people and livestock on the *Mulobezi Railway* line.

The 163 kilometre journey between Livingstone and Mulobezi took two days because the train could only travel at 15 km/h due to the poor condition of the track (Malisase, 2021). This inconvenienced passengers, especially when rural roads became impassable in the rainy season. The two companies managed to transport only 12% of the market's total freight. Despite the poor performance, concessioners continued to demand their concession fees (Zambia Railways Limited, 2013). Zambia's experience mirrors that of Congo Brazzaville, Gabon, Senegal–Mali, and Madagascar which equally cancelled railway concession on account of mixed performance (Abioye, 2016).

Lusaka City Council's collaboration with various companies to manage solid waste has equally had mixed results. On one hand, the involvement of the private sector has improved the rate at which solid waste is collected in the district. On the other hand, only 15% of the solid waste produced is collected, causing waste to accumulate in open areas along the city's streets (Chulu, 2017). This is comparable to the impact of the Vancouver Landfill Project in Canada (United Nations, 2008, Magro, 2015; Briggs; Mitchell, 2018). A similar situation was observed in the agriculture sector where private agro-dealers have improved beneficiaries' access to the Farmer Input Support Programme. The agro-dealers have improved input procurement, storage, and transportation thus giving recipient farmers easier access to a wider variety of high-quality agricultural, livestock, and fisheries inputs (Indaba Agricultural, 2015). However, the cost of inputs has gone up, with beneficiaries paying more than those who pay cash. And some farmers have reported significant delays in receiving fertilizer, which reduce maize yields (Competition and Consumer Protection Commission, 2019).

Equally, the quality of services provided by TopStar was mixed. In general, the company was successful in assisting the country's transition from analogue to digital television transmission. This improved signal strength, quality, and reach. There was also a marked improvement in terms of picture and sound quality as well as diversity of programming (African Media Barometer, 2021). However, the company began offering media and television services as a content provider rather than its original mandate as a content distributor.

It began to stifle competition by blocking some non-state broadcasters from accessing its distribution network. Political leaders exploited this monopoly to suppress media freedom by ordering the company to remove critical private broadcasters from its distribution network (Bwalya *et al.,* 2022). It also increased the price of subscriptions, charging roughly US$1.60 per month for the least expensive bouquet, six times higher than the originally envisioned price. TopStar has also been accused of promoting Chinese culture by flooding its bouquet with Chinese language channels that funnel Chinese propaganda (African Media Barometer, 2021; Bwalya *et al.,* 2022).

With regard to the ARTMS project, only the speed camera component was partially implemented. And despite the contract being valued at over US$110 million, between July 2018 and March 2019, only three out of 116 districts, namely, Lusaka, Kafue, and Chisamba, had cameras on select roads. The speed cameras were of poor quality and required being physically placed on sides of the roads in the morning and removed in the early evening. However, the project somehow improved road safety, as evidenced by the high compliance to speed limits observed on Lusaka roads (Ncube, 2020). Nevertheless, it should be noted that this PPP was unnecessary since the Road Transport and Safety Agency had the financial and technical capacity to undertake the project on its own.

While China Henan was able to build the required infrastructure at Luburma Market, the shops were deemed to be of poor quality. Coupled with poor maintenance, most of the shops began to crack and fall into disrepair within 10 years. This negatively affected the safety of vendors and shoppers, making it difficult for businesses to operate effectively (Mwanaumo, 2020). The company's insistence on charging rentals in dollars priced out locals. Similarly, Mpulungu Harbour's concessionaire failed to make the required investment to improve the operations. Rather, it overcharged cargo operators in addition to favouring some at the expense of others (Zambia Development Agency, 2014). PPPs pricing out the poor is a common phenomenon that has been reported worldwide (Hall, 2015).

PPPs in the electricity sector have generally had a positive impact on services. For instance, Itezhi-Tezhi Hydro Power Plant added 120MW to installed capacity, helping the country reach surplus generation capacity (Energy Regulation Board, 2022). This improved electricity accessibility and reliability. This is similar to Uganda, Cameroon, Ivory Coast, Gabon, Australia, the Philippines, and Germany. Nevertheless, unlike these countries, PPPs in electricity generation in Zambia did not lead to a significant increase in electricity tariffs. The country's tariffs of US¢6.33/kWh are less than half of the US¢13/kWh average obtaining in sub-Saharan Africa (Malisase, 2021).

CONSTRAINTS ASSOCIATED WITH DELIVERING SERVICES THROUGH PUBLIC-PRIVATE PARTNERSHIPS

Even with the development of the legal and institutional framework, very few PPPs have succeeded in Zambia (Muleya *et al.,* 2019). Only five large-scale PPP projects can be considered successful namely, Luburma Market, Kasumbalesa One Stop Border Post, Itezhi-Tezhi Hydro Power Corporation, TopStar, and East Park Mall. And even from these, the quality of service provision remains mixed. Most of the earmarked projects under PPP failed to take off and the few that reach the operational stage do so after years of procrastination and major renegotiations. And even among these, a significant number still get cancelled due to several constraints, mostly connected to limitations in the regulatory framework (Mwanaumo *et al.,* 2020; Axis Consulting, 2013). These include lack of technical capacity; political interference; corruption; lack of clear sector-specific guidelines and regulations; bureaucratic hurdles; and financial constraints.

Neither the PPP Act nor other supporting legislation provides comprehensive instructions to contracting authorities and private entities on how to undertake activities throughout the PPP cycle. Additionally, there is no policy directive that states conditions under which projects should be undertaken through PPP rather than conventional public procurement (Republic of Zambia, 2018). For instance, there was no need to employ PPP for the ARTMS project when the Road Transport and Safety Agency was capable of undertaking the project alone (New Diggers, 2020). Similarly, negotiations for a number of projects, like the Kafue Gorge Lower Power Station, have been abandoned in favour of the government going at it alone. These ties in with the observations that some governments tend to use PPP as a panacea for development, and thus applying them to inappropriate projects (Hall, 2015; World Bank, 2022a).

Key institutions, like the PPP Department, PPP Council, and PPP Technical Committee, are filled with unqualified and incompetent personnel who lack the technical capacity to oversee PPP negotiations, implementation, and monitoring. These officials are appointed on political grounds rather than technical qualifications (Republic of Zambia, 2009; World Bank, 2022b; Evdorides & Shoji, 2013). For example, Mwanaumo *et al.* (2020) found that the 65-year contract for Luburma Market was poorly negotiated due to a lack of technical competence among officials from Lusaka City Council. Similarly, Intelligence Mobility Solutions ended up being awarded a US$110 million contract to install speed cameras when it actually cost only US$10 million to execute (Ncube, 2020).

In addition, the contract ended up being unknowingly illegally signed by the head of the contracting authority (the chief executive officer of the Road

Transport and Safety Agency) rather than the Minister of Finance. Another illegally signed contract was a BOT with Track Investments Limited to construct tollgates and collect toll fees; only to be abandoned after realisation that the law at the time did not permit private entities to collect toll fees (The Mast, 2015). It is suspected that other contracts might have similar illegalities. While this is consistent with other developing countries' experiences, it has been noted that the technical competence of public officials in developed countries contributes to the high success rate of PPPs in those countries (World Bank, 2018; World Bank, 2022a).

Political interference is the use of political pressure to cancel concessions, impose price controls, or enact unfavourable policies. For instance, low tariff rates is one of the impediments to PPPs in electricity generation. Currently, Zambia's tariff rate of US¢6.33/kWh, set in 2017, is not cost reflective (Malisase, 2021). Whenever the regulator, the Energy Regulation Board, accepts ZESCO Limited's request for tariff hikes, politicians force a reversal following complaints from members of the public. Consequently, many PPP projects in construction of power generation plants stall as investors fear making losses (Ntumbo, 2021; Malisase, 2021). Similarly, the PPP Council being composed of politicians leads to political meddling, rather than technical knowhow, characterising negotiations. This leads to poorly structured projects that are not based on extensive research (Ncube, 2020; World Bank, 2018; Ngoma, *et al.*, 2014). Negotiations and contracts are frequently cancelled on the whims of politicians as exemplified by the mass cancellations upon the change of government in August 2021 (International Monetary Fund, 2022). This situation is similar to other developing countries where intricate connections and interplay of politics and patronage stifle the growth of PPPs (Kisitu, 2018; Asian Development Bank, 2008; Hall, 2015; Seeletse, 2016).

Another constraint is corruption in the awarding of contracts. It leads to contracts being awarded to political cronies who lack the financial and technical capacity to implement the projects. For instance, TopStar was single sourced to undertake the digital migration project. This led to accusations that the contract was poorly phrased to the detriment of broadcasters. This is similar to the single sourced awarding of the ARTMS project to a company permitted to deposit speeding fines in an unapproved account. This allowed the siphoning of the money by various government officials. As a result, despite the company's failure to meet the terms of the contract, it was shielded from criticism (Ncube, 2020). Similar cases of corruption impeding the success of PPPs have been reported in other African countries like South Africa, Uganda, Kenya, and Nigeria (Kisitu, 2018; Tshombe *et al.*, 2020; Vallée, 2018).

Lack of decentralisation leads to bureaucratic hurdles because too many institutions are involved in decisions at each stage of the project cycle

(Ngoma et al., 2014; Muleya et al., 2019). Once a contracting authority identifies a potential partner, it seeks guidance from the PPP Department which in turn seeks technical advice from the PPP Technical Committee. If the project involves the construction of infrastructure, then the Technical Committee seeks input from the Ministry of Infrastructure, Housing and Urban Development. If the project is found to be technically sound, then approval is sought from the PPP Council (Axis Consulting, 2013). If the project involves financial commitment from the government, then the Investment and Debt Management Department in the Ministry of Finance and National Planning assesses the government's ability to fund the projects. The PPP Council, together with the Zambia Public Procurement Authority, then steps in and begins the tendering process and negotiation of the contract. Only then does the Minister of Finance sign the final contract.

In most cases, Cabinet Office or the Office of the President tends to also take an active role in the approval process (Republic of Zambia, 2009; Evdorides & Shoji, 2013; Axis Consulting, 2013). This makes the process long, leading to breakdowns in negotiations or projects taking years before reaching financial closure. Bureaucratic hurdles have also been cited as critical issues in many other countries, including Uganda, Tanzania, Lesotho, Malawi, Kenya, and Zimbabwe (Ngoma *et al.,* 2014; Kisitu, 2018).

Riddled with unsustainable debt, the government fails to participate in PPPs that require public financial commitments. Equally, difficulties in raising project finances, especially from local investors, lead to projects either being cancelled or taking years before getting off the ground. One reason for the cancellation of the Zambia Railways Limited concession was that the concessionaire failed to make the agreed-upon US$64 million investments in the rail infrastructure (Zambia Railways Limited, 2013). Although contracts for Kabompo and Kalungwishi Hydro Power projects were both awarded in 2008, they are yet to be completed (Copperbelt Energy Corporation, 2022). The public's inability to pay cost-reflective tariffs explains the aforementioned low investment in electricity generation as well as reluctance to invest in, or expand, service provision to rural areas.

FUTURE PROSPECTS

Zambia seems to have a bright future with regard to service delivery through PPPs. Even with the mass cancellations of contracts and negotiations in the past, the new political regime has shown an affinity for engaging the private sector in development. To that effect, a number of possible projects are at various stages of tendering, feasibility, contract negotiations, and infrastructure construction. They include the potential BOT for the construction of the 321km Lusaka-Ndola Dual Carriageway at a significantly lower amount than the US$1.26 billion the previous government tried to construct it at. As well as the rehabilitation of the railway infrastructure by Team Sweden Rail (Njenga, 2022). It is important to note that the future success of PPPs will depend on the country eliminating constraints, especially those related to the institutional framework and political interference. This will increase the confidence of private investors to partner the government in the delivery of public services. So far, this looks promising as the country is in the process of repealing and replacing the PPP Act to, among others, improve the institutional framework and eliminate political interference (Republic of Zambia, 2023). It is expected that the new Act and other measures will help create technical capacity and clear sector-specific guidelines as well as reduce political interference, corruption, bureaucratic hurdles, and financial constraints.

CONCLUSION

The importance of PPPs to Zambia's development, especially the delivery of public services, cannot be overemphasised. It is for this reason that the government has, over the years, established a regulatory framework to guide the process. Through this framework, policies, laws, guidelines, and institutions have been developed. These include the Public-Private Partnership Policy of 2008 and the Public-Private Partnership Act, 2009, and its 2018 and 2021 amendments. These are supplemented by the Public Procurement Act, 2020, and the Zambia Development Agency Act, 2006. These laws guide the promotion and management of PPPs in the country while protecting the interests of the government, private investors and the public.

These laws have in turn led to the establishment of robust institutions comprising the Public-Private Partnership Department, Public-Private Partnership Council, Public-Private Partnership Technical Committee, Zambia Public Procurement Authority, Zambia Development Agency, Ministry of Finance and National Planning, and various contracting authorities. These institutions identify potential PPP projects, undertake feasibility studies, and manage the tendering process, negotiations, implementation, monitoring, and evaluation. Guided by this regulatory framework, the country has undertaken a number of projects employing variations of service contracts, BOT, BOOT, BOO, concession, and lease.

These projects have been undertaken in transport, solid waste management, agriculture, border control, electricity generation, television services as well as market, and mall management. The quality of services provided from PPPs has been mixed. Some projects have improved quality of service delivery while others failed leading to cancellation of contracts. These mixed fortunes are the result of a number of constraints, most of which are related to the weaknesses in the regulatory framework. These include a lack of technical capacity, political interference, corruption, a lack of clear sector-specific guidelines and regulations, bureaucratic hurdles, and financial constraints. In addition to compromising quality, these constraints have led to a number of PPP projects failing to take off or decisions being reversed at the infrastructure construction or operation stage. Nevertheless, the country's future prospects look bright, provided the ongoing amendments to the regulatory framework manage to curtail most of the constraints.

REFERENCES

Abioye, O. (2016). Privatisation of the Nigerian Railway Corporation: An Evaluation of Critical Choice, PhD thesis, Cardiff Metropolitan University.

African Development Bank. (2020). *Supporting Public Private Partnerships in Africa: African Development Bank ready to scale up*. Available from: https://www.afdb.org/en/news-and-events/press-releases/supporting-public-private-partnerships-africa-african-development-bank-ready-scale-37804 Date of Access, 10/11/2022.

African Media Barometer. (2021). *A Home-Grown Analysis of the Media Landscape in Africa: Zambia 2021,* Friedrich-Ebert-Stiftung (FES), Windhoek, Namibia.

Asian Development Bank. (2008). *Public-Private Partnership Handbook*, Asian Development Bank, Mandaluyong, the Philippines, pp. 1–100.

Axis Consulting. (2013). *PPP Country Paper: Zambia*, Research Report Submitted to SADC-DFRC 3P NETWORK Public-Private-Partnership Working Group.

Briggs, T., & Mitchell, P. (2018). The Channel Tunnel and High Speed 1- a legal perspective. *Revue d'histoire des chemins de fer*, (48–49), pp. 143–155.

Bwalya, E.M.M., Mutale, M., & Kunda, E. (2022). Digital Television Migration In Zambia: Who Are The Real Beneficiaries? *International Journal of Scientific and Research Publications*, Vol. 12 (7), pp. 383–396.

Chen, Y., & Woo, R. (2017). China Overhauls $2.69 Trillion Public-Private Projects as Debt Fears Rise. *Reuters*. Available from: https://www.reuters.com/article/us-china-economy-ppp-idUSKBN1DH0DE Date of Access: 1/11/2022.

Chulu, I. (2017). Effectiveness of Garbage Collection by Private Companies: A Case Study of Lusaka, Master's thesis, University of Zambia, Lusaka, Zambia.

Competition and Consumer Protection Commission. (2019). *Agro-Input (Fertilizer) Value Chain Study in Zambia*, Study Carried Out under the Zambia Agribusiness and Trade Project (ZATP). Available from: https://www.ccpc.org.zm/media/research/Agro-Input-Value-Chain-Study.pdf Data of access: 26/12/2022

Copperbelt Energy Corporation. (2022). *Annual Report 2021*, Copperbelt Energy Corporation, Kitwe, Zambia.

Energy Regulation Board (ERB). (2022). *Energy Sector Report-2021*. Energy Regulation Board, Lusaka Zambia.

Evdorides, H., & Shoji, M. (2013). Public–Private Partnerships for Road Infrastructure Services in Zambia. *Management, Procurement and Law*, Vol. 166 (MP6), pp. 277–285.

Farlam, P. 2005. Working Together: Assessing Public-Private Partnerships in Africa, *NEPAD Policy Focus Series,* South African Institute of International Affairs, Johannesburg, South Africa

Fombad, M. C. (2013). Accountability Challenges in Public–Private Partnerships from a South African Perspective. *African Journal of Business Ethics*, 7 (1), pp. 11–25.

Gwary, M. M., Asindaya, Z., & Abba, M.A. (2016). Public-Private Partnership as Panacea for Effective Extension Service Delivery: Review of Experience and Potential in Nigeria. *Net Journal of Agricultural Science*, Vol. 4 (3), pp. 50–55.

Hall, D. (2015). Why Public-Private Partnerships Don't Work: The Many Advantages of the Public Alternative, Report, Public Services International (PSI), Greenwich, United Kingdom.

Hammami, M., Ruhashyankiko, J.F., & Yehoue, E.B. (2006). Determinants of Public-Private Partnerships in Infrastructure, IMF Working Paper WP/06/99, International Monetary Fund, Washington, DC, United Sates of America.

Harper, P. (2015). Public-private partnerships and the financial cost to governments: Case study on the power sector in Uganda, Report, Jubilee Debt Campaign, London, United Kingdom.

Indaba Agricultural Policy Research Institute. (2015). Opportunities and Challenges in Enhancing Agricultural Development in Zambia. Advisory Note submitted to The Ministry of Agriculture and Livestock. Available from: Retrieved January 20, 2023 from https://renapri.org/wp-content/uploads/2021/11/IAPRI_white_paper.pdf Date of access: 20/01/2023

International Monetary Fund. (2022). Zambia: Request for an Arrangement Under the Extended Credit Facility—Press Release; Staff Report; Staff Supplement; Staff Statement; and Statement by the Executive Director For Zambia, *IMF Country Report No. 22/292,* International Monetary Fund, Washington, DC, United Sates of America.

Kisitu, B. M. (2018). Public-Private Partnership (PPP) Challenges in National Agricultural Extension Systems in Uganda: Towards a New Model, PhD thesis, North-West University, North West, South Africa.

Kwak, Y.H., Chih, Y., & Ibbs, C.W. (2009). Towards a Comprehensive Understanding of Public Private Partnerships for Infrastructure Development. *California Management Review*, Vol. 51 (2), pp. 51–78.

LaRocque, N. (2008). *Public-Private Partnerships in Basic Education: An International Review*, CfBT Education Trust, Reading, United Kingdom.

Loxley, J. (2013). Are Public–Private Partnerships (PPPs) the Answer to Africa's Infrastructure Needs? *Review of African Political Economy*, Vol. 40 (137), pp. 485–495.

Madimutsa, C., & Pretorius, L.G. (2018). Public-Private Partnerships and Industrial Relations in the Public Sector in Zambia, *African Journal of Public Affairs*, Vol. 10 (4), pp. 310–325.

Magro, J.M.V. (2015). *Public-Private Partnership in Latin America: Learning from experience,* Development Bank of Latin America, Caracas, Venezuela.

Malisase, R. (2021). Privatisation of ZESCO Limited: In search of an appropriate method, PhD thesis, North-West University, North West, South Africa.

Mbewe, Z. (2022). Cabinet Agrees to Replace PPP Act. *News Diggers*. Available from: https://diggers.news/local/2022/03/11/cabinet-agrees-to-replace-ppp-act/ Date of Access: 11/11/2022.

Mfunwa, M., Taylor, A., & Kreiter, Z. (2016). Public-Private Partnerships for Social and Economic Transformation in Southern Africa: Progress and Emerging Issues. *Southern African Journal of Policy and Development*, Vol. 2 (2), pp. 6–17.

Mouraviev, N. & Kakabadse, N. (Eds.). (2017). *Public-Private Partnerships in Transitional Nations: Policy, Governance and Praxis*, Cambridge Scholars Publishing, Newcastle upon Tyne, United Kingdom, pp. 1–276.

Mouraviev, N., & Kakabadse, N.K. (2016). Conceptualising Public-Private Partnerships: A Critical Appraisal of Approaches to Meanings and Forms. *Society and Business Review*, Vol. 11 (2), pp. 155–173.

Muleya, F., Zulu, S., & Nanchengwa, P. (2019). Investigating the Role of the Public Private Partnership Act on Private Sector Participation in PPP Projects: A Case of Zambia. *The International Journal of Construction Management* Vol. 20 (6), pp. 598–612.

Mwanaumo, M.E., Nsefu, M.K., Mambwe, M., & Lindunda, M.M. (2020). *African International Conference on Industrial Engineering and Operations Management: Risk analysis and management in public private partnerships of urban markets in Lusaka, Zambia*, 2nd African International Conference on Industrial Engineering and Operations Management held in Harare, Zimbabwe, from 7th to 10th December, 2020, pp. 1384–1395.

Ncube, S. (2020). Speed Camera Contract Was Canceled because It Was Illegally Signed by RTSA CEO—Kafwaya. *News Diggers*. Available from: https://diggers.news/local/2020/10/06/speed-camera-contract-was-canceled-because-it-was-illegally-signed-by-rtsa-ceo-kafwaya/?fbclid=IwAR0LVWM_d18hv_EEm_VVih3t-8MIbTHdx-7z-L6lHaLN5si13lS6rJtxvZ_g Date of access: 1/1/2023.

Ngoma, S., Mundia, M., & Kaliba, C. (2014). Benefits, Constraints and Risks in Infrastructure Development via Public-Private Partnerships in Zambia. *Journal of Construction in Developing Countries*, Vol. 19 (1), pp. 15–33.

Njenga, M.F. (2022). PF govt paid China Jiangxi $30m for Lusaka-Ndola dual carriageway with no roadworks done. *News Diggers*. Available from: https://diggers.news/local/2022/06/06/pf-govt-paid-china-jiangxi-30m-for-lusaka-ndola-dual-carriageway-with-no-roadworks-done/ Date of Access: 11/1/2023.

Ntumbo, G. (2021). Zambia: Understanding Cost-Reflective Fuel, Electricity Tariffs. *Times of Zambia*. Available from: http://www.times.co.zm/?p=113412 Date of Access: January 11/01/2022.

Oktavianus, A., Mahani, I., & Meifrinaldi. (2018). A Global Review of Public Private Partnerships Trends and Challenges for Social Infrastructure. *MATEC Web of Conferences*, 147 (2018), pp. 1–9

Republic of Zambia. (2009). *Public-Private Partnership Act, 2009*, Government Printer, Lusaka, Zambia, pp.75–116.

Republic of Zambia. (2011). *Public-Private Partnership Policy and the Act 2009*, Ministry of Finance and National Planning, Lusaka, Zambia.

Republic of Zambia. (2018). *Public-Private Partnership (amendment) Act, 2018,* Government Printer, Lusaka, Zambia, pp. 223–234.

Republic of Zambia. (2020). *Public Procurement Act, 2020,* Government Printer, Lusaka, Zambia, pp. 121–200.

Republic of Zambia. (2021). *Public-Private Partnership (Amendment) Act, 2021,* Government Printer, Lusaka, Zambia, pp. 211–212.

Republic of Zambia. (2023). *The Public-Private Partnership Bill*, 2023. Government Printer, Lusaka, pp. 1–63

Sata, J. (2007). A Look at Zambia's Rail Transport. *Zambia Daily Mail.* Available from: http://nlpi.net/wp-content/uploads/2013/01/2007-01-30-ZAMBIA-DAILY-MAIL-A-Miror-on-Zambia-Rail.pdf Date of Access: 17/12/2022.

Seeletse, S.M. (2016). Performance of South African Private-Public Partnerships. *Problems and Perspectives in Management*, Vol. 14 (2), pp. 19–26.

Shukla, R., Sharma, S., & Thumar, V.M. (2016). Role and Importance of Public Private Partnerships in Agricultural Value Chain and Infrastructure, *International Journal of Commerce and Business Management*, Vol. 9 (1), pp. 113–118.

Tshombe, L.M., Molokwane, T., Nduhura, A., & Nuwagaba, I. (2020). An Analysis of Public-Private Partnerships in East Africa, *Research in World Economy*, Vol. 11 (5), pp. 152–163.

Ullah, A. (2019). Public Private Partnerships as Catalyst for Infrastructure Development in North Africa, *West Asia and North Africa: Changing Paradigms,* pp. 3–23 Available from: https://dx.doi.org/10.2139/ssrn.3336679 Date of Access: 10/11/2022.

United Nations. (2008). *Guidebook on Promoting Good Governance in Public-Private Partnerships*, United Nations Publications, Geneva, Switzerland.

Vallée, M. (2018). PPP Laws in Africa: Confusing or Clarifying? *World Bank Blogs*. Available from: http://blogs.worldbank.org/ppps Date of Access: 25/1/2023.

Willie, A. (2020). *Does the Current Concessioning Regime of Border Posts Infrastructure Yield Optimal Trade Efficiency for Africa? Lessons for COMESA*. Available from: https://www.comesa.int/wp-content/uploads/2020/10/Adam-Willie-Revised-Paper-15-09-20.pdf Date of access: 20/12/2022.

World Bank. (2022a). *Private Participation in Infrastructure (PPI) 2021 Annual Report*, The World Bank, Washington D.C., United Sates of America.

World Bank. (2022b). *PPP Units around the World*. The World Bank, Washington, DC. Available From: https://ppp.worldbank.org/public-private-partnership/overview/international-ppp-units Date of Access: 1/11/2022.

World Bank. (2018). *Procuring Infrastructure Public-Private Partnerships Report: Assessing Government Capability to Prepare, Procure, and Manage PPPs,* The World Bank, Washington, DC.

World Bank. (2016). *The State of PPPs: Infrastructure Public-Private Partnerships in Emerging Markets & Developing Economies 1991–2015*, The World Bank, Washington, DC.

The World Bank. (2022c). *Public-Private Partnerships Laws / Concession Laws,* The World Bank, Washington, DC. Available from: https://ppp.worldbank.org/public-private-partnership/legislation-regulation/laws/ppp-and-concession-laws Date of Access: 2/11/2023

Yuan, J., Zheng, X., You, J., & Skibniewski, M.J. (2017). Identifying Critical Factors Influencing the Rents of Public Rental Housing Delivery by PPPs: The Case of Nanjing. *Sustainability*, Vol. 9 (3), pp. 1–22.
Zambia Development Agency (2014). *Public–Private–Partnerships in Infrastructure Development in Zambia*, Zambia Development Agency, Lusaka, Zambia.
Zambia Railways Limited. (2013). *Five Year Strategic Plan for the Period 2014-2018*, Zambia Railways Limited, Lusaka, Zambia.
Zimbabwe Economic Policy Analysis and Research Unit. (2016). *Status and Performance of Public-Private Partnerships in Select Eastern and Southern African Countries*, Macroeconomic and Financial Management Institute for Eastern and Southern Africa (MEFMI), Harare, Zimbabwe.

Chapter 12

The Governance Framework Question in Public-Private Partnerships (PPPs)

The Case of Independent Power Producers (IPPs) in Zimbabwe

Edson Basera, Gideon Zhou, and Alouis Chilunjika

In the wake of capital-constrained public power utilities characterised by demand outstripping supply, the Independent Power Producers (IPPs) are emerging as potential models of financing infrastructural development in the electricity sector across the globe. The IPPs are non-utility generators that sell electricity to state power companies, end consumers, or wholesale electricity traders (Eberhard, Gratwick, Morella & Antmann, 2016). The African Development Bank (2019, p. 103) notes that the Zimbabwe Electricity Supply Authority, 'the integrated power utility, faces an unsustainable financial situation that leaves no room for new investments'.

The chapter argues that given Zimbabwe's constrained fiscal capacity, engaging the IPPs as models of the PPPs is critically important to increase electricity supply in the country. The African Development Bank (2011) asserts that the African continent's energy sector requires USD29 billion annually, but most African governments, Zimbabwe included, are confronted with fiscal constraints that affect their infrastructural development plans. Power Africa (2021) argues that this limited fiscal space has been exacerbated by the Covid-19 pandemic and the resulting response and recovery efforts. On the same note, Alloisio (2021) highlighted that for the PPPs to be attracted in sub-Saharan Africa, a specific institutional ecosystem that embraces a greater level of human capital endowment and the ability to adopt contemporary and innovative technologies is a critical factor.

Drawing from the above literature tone, Zimbabwe in particular and Africa in general are looking for private sector capital to spur infrastructure development in the electricity sector. In this light, the chapter argues that effective

PPP governance which, inter alia, entails developing and supporting the PPP policy, legal and regulatory frameworks to attract private capital and negotiate complex public-private partnership arrangements is critical. Against this backdrop, this study empirically examined the governance success factors needed to enhance the effectiveness of the IPPs as well as constraining factors in Zimbabwe. The chapter winds up by proposing measures to strengthen the effective governance of the IPPs as frameworks of financing electricity infrastructural development in Zimbabwe.

THEORETICAL AND CONCEPTUAL ANALYSIS

The discourse of the PPPs is informed by eclectic theoretical underpinnings. In this regard, the PPPs broadly fall within the rubric of the New Public Management (NPM) and New Public Governance (NPG) frameworks. Resultantly, public management as an area in ferment draws from economics using theories such as Transactional Cost as well as the Principal-Agency which inform the discourse of the PPPs in financing public service, despite the argument by academic scholars that the NPM is not a tangible action of programme but a tendency. The Principal-Agency theory formalises assumptions about the distribution of property rights and information in writing the constitution of the organisation. The population as the principal, monitors politicians and the bureau as agents to ensure they abide by the contractual agreements. To guarantee effective performance, the agents (employees, contractors or third parties) should be the best candidates selected on a competitive basis, a factor which is core to the PPP success (Ayee, 2005).

The transaction theory emphasises on the role of the state in defining the basics of contractual arrangements between the state and investors on existing technologies and natural endowments (Ayee, 2005). Weimer and Vinning (1993 cited in Ayee, 2005) assert that transactions are vulnerable to compliance threats. Thus, investors will resist entering into contracts unless there is credible commitment that other parties will not opportunistically exploit their vulnerability. To that end, the central question of the political economy is how governments can make credible commitments that assure investors that their investments will not be appropriated and the capital supplied will not be debased (Blackburn & Christensen 1989 cited in Ayee, 2005). In this vein, the central theory argument resonates with the study's concerns as contract monitoring and credible government commitment to protection of property rights are central to the successful implementation of the PPPs.

Related to the foregoing governance issues, the NPG framework advocates cooperation and stakeholder networks to promote innovation and improve public service delivery (Osborne & Nasi 2013). Trist (1981) and Huxham (2000) cited in Nkomo and Nhema (2015) argue that networks build trust and resolve social problems and are therefore integral to the functionality of the PPPs. Similarly, Public Administration scholars argue that collaborative governance helps to solve problems that exist under partnership arrangements (Robinson 2015; Nkomo & Nhema 2015). Huxham and Vangen (2000) cited in Nkomo and Nhema (2015) assert that under collaborative arrangements diversity, complexity and dynamism cause collaborative inertia. Thus, governance in partnerships requires time and effort, in which partners must support the development of mutual aims, trust and understanding—necessary for the continuity of the partnerships.

A critical analysis of the above public administration eclectic theoretical framework shows that issues such as contract management, effective regulation (for environment protection, quality of life and economic well-being), economic measurements (output, efficiency and value for money), competitive selection, government support, investment guarantees, political commitment, effective management, incentives, network and governance systems are covered. These built-up public administration theories by and large cast light into the study as the above traits are essential for the effective governance of the IPPs in Zimbabwe.

LITERATURE REVIEW

Definition of the PPPs and IPPs

There is no universally accepted definition of the PPP. However, World Bank (2012) defines PPP as a long-term agreement between a private party and a public sector agency with the aim to provide a government asset or service in which substantial risk and management obligation is borne by the private investor. Equally important, the Netherlands Ministry of Foreign Affairs (2013) defines the PPP as a form of cooperation between government, businesses, NGOs, trade unions and knowledge institutions in which they agree to work together to attain a common goal or carry out a specific task, jointly assuming the risk and responsibility as well as sharing their resources and competencies. Thus, the government or its agency can partner with either domestic or foreign private investors with a view to narrow the funding and efficiency gaps towards financing infrastructural development.

With the setting of the study being the electricity sector, scholars have emphasised on the existence of hybrid PPPs in the electricity market. For example, Christensen and Laegreid (2011) defined it as a combination of private sector, government and state-owned enterprises (SOEs) working together. In the same vein, Heldeweg, Saunders and Hamsen (2015) averred that whether it is private model or public-private collaboration, good governance in the energy sector does matter and as such the collaboration should be labelled hybrid energy governance partnerships. In the energy sector, the concept of IPPs is gaining traction across the globe.

In an IPP framework, the private sector enterprise, a state-owned utility and the Department of Energy (DoE) collaborate with a view to deliver sustainable energy to the national grid (Nel, 2018). The United Nations Economic Commission for Africa (2011) emphasised that the partnership between IPPs and state-power utility is reinforced and defined by the power purchase agreement (PPA) which is its bomb-proof aspect. Most of the IPPs exist as variant models in the form of Design-Build-Finance-Operate-Maintain (DBFOM), Design-Build-Finance-Operate (DBFO), Design-Construct-Manage-Finance (DCMF), Build-Operate-Transfer (BOT), Build-Transfer-Operate (BTO), Build-Own-Operate-and-Transfer (BOOT) or Build-Own-Operate (BOO) depending on the nature of the contract between the government and the private electricity producer (World Bank, n.d, online; Chilean Concession Law, n.d, online; Delmon, 2010, p. 12).

THE PPP GOVERNANCE'S COUNTRY EXPERIENCES IN THE ELECTRICITY SECTOR: SAMPLED COUNTRIES

Empirical evidence in this section is strengthened by an elaboration of detailed account of cross-country experiences with regard to governance of the IPP projects in the electricity sector. These empirical PPP success cases have been corroborated by an Eclectic Public Administration Theoretical Framework.

Uganda

In 2006, the Ugandan government implemented the public-private partnerships in the energy sector to remedy electricity shortage in the country (Nsasira, Basheka & Oluka, 2013). Despite the Bugali project being rated the African Power Deal of the year in 2007, Nsasira *et al.* (2013) and United Nations Economic Commission for Africa (2011) argued that the project developers paid lip service to environmental and social concerns as it failed to compensate displaced people. Further to the above Bugali case, Nsasira *et al.* (2013) argued that the other Buganda small-scale independent power producers were marred by corruption across the entire procurement chain, thereby undermining institutional sustainability. The sustainability gaps in the above cases underscored the fact that policymakers in nascent, emerging, developed and the mature PPP markets must give serious consideration to the sustainability of the PPPs as models for enabling the provision of public goods and services.

The Latin American and Asian Experiences

Faced with transmission constraints and high prices of electricity, both the Latin American and Asian countries have engaged private players to invest in the electricity sector under public-private sector arrangements (Mckenzie, 2018). Latin American countries such as Brazil, Mexico and Peru as well as other Asian countries such as China improved the sustainability of the IPP projects through embracing openness and transparency in the planning of power expansion; transparency and predictability in the competitive procurement of generation capacity; robust oversight by the ministry and the energy regulatory body as well as efforts towards improving the operational and financial sustainability of the electricity distributors (Vagliasindi, 2013; United Nations Economic Commission for Africa, 2011; Eberhard *et al.*, 2016). Hall (2015) notes that across Latin America, the IPPs are concentrated in a few countries, as Brazil and Mexico account for 65% of all the IPPs, while Colombia, Chile and Peru account for a further 15% .

Vagliasindi (2013) pointed out that in China the sharp increase in renewables posed challenges to the stability of the transmission systems. Vagliasindi (2013) further pointed out that Mexico used an open-season approach with new transmission divided between Federal Electricity Commission (FEC) and private investors, and it facilitated better regulatory and technical certainty. Similarly, Sly and Copley (2017) argued and emphasised that aging transmission and distribution grid networks deter investors from investing in power generation.

This therefore implies that to ensure sustainability of the IPPs in electricity generation, there is need to consider the co-existence of the private investors and SOEs towards investment in strong and reliable transmission grid networks to minimise power losses and improve efficiency. Emphasising on the need for a strong transmission and distribution infrastructure, International Monetary Fund (2013, p.30) notes, 'Also, any country relying on hydropower will have to invest in transmission to allow heavy seasonal power loads to be efficiently routed through the system'.

According to Hall (2015, p.20), government guarantees have been presented as important in the sustainability of the PPPs as models of financing infrastructural development in the electricity sector. In this case, the International Financial Corporation (IFC) presents the Central Java 2,000MW coal-fired IPP as a success story. Hall (2015) noted that the IFC advised Java on the IPP system structuring and also advised the Indonesian government to provide guarantees through the newly created Indonesia Infrastructure Guarantee Fund (IIGF).

The Sub-Saharan IPP Experiences

Faced with inadequate electricity and extreme poverty in the midst of limited fiscal space, IPPs had spread across sub-Saharan Africa between 1990 and 2014 and are now present in 17 countries including South Africa, Tanzania, Kenya, Nigeria and Uganda (Eberhard *et al.,* 2016). Using an empirical study of five sub-Saharan African countries of South Africa, Tanzania, Nigeria, Kenya and Uganda, the IPP success is attributed to the development of a centralised task team with the experienced PPP advisers in the National Treasury, an IPP unit for renewable energy, local and international transaction advisers, inflexible PPAs, competitive bidding, project financing, sound economics (solar cheaper than coal), appropriate risk-sharing and political support (Nel, 2018; South African Department of Energy, 2015; Eberhard *et al.,* 2016). Using the Ugandan case study, Nsasira *et al.* (2013) and United Nations Economic Commission for Africa (2011) argue and emphasise the need for: effective monitoring and regulation of the IPPs to ensure compliance with performance targets, corruption reduction through independent transaction advisers, the involvement of independent agencies such as Transparency International to oversee the bidding processes, training at national and sub-national levels as well as enabling legal and regulatory frameworks.

Lessons Drawn for the Effective Governance of the IPPs

A critical evaluation of the sampled IPP country experiences in the electricity sector shows that those countries that offer enviable performance on the IPPs such as Indonesia, China and Tajikistan in Asia; Jordan in the Middle East; Brazil, Mexico and Peru in Latin America; South Africa, Tanzania, Kenya, Uganda and Cote d'Ivoire in the sub-Saharan Africa have managed to embrace a mix of the following five IPP governance factors:

1. *Robust Oversight by the Ministry of Energy and Power Development and the Energy Regulatory Body.*
   The Ministry assists in policy formulation and the planning of dynamic power programmes. In the same vein, the regulatory body will assist in coming up with cost-reflective tariff frameworks to ensure the sustainability of power projects (Eberhard *et al.,* 2016). Latin American electricity projects such as Brazil, Mexico and China offer enviable examples in which robust oversight and regulatory frameworks guaranteed the sustainability of the electricity PPP projects.
2. *Enabling Legal and regulatory Frameworks (cost-reflective tariffs)*
   There is need for a legal and regulatory framework that protects investors, lenders and government in the PPP contract (World Bank, 2009).

However, Turley and Semple (2013) argue for flexible legal frameworks that cope up with changes in the environment. The cases of the South African Renewable Energy Programme and that of Uganda offer enviable example in this respect. These two countries have sound, fair, accountable and independent electricity regulators that guarantee sustainable cost-reflective tariff frameworks for the provision of electricity (Eberhard *et al.,* 2016).

3. *Transparency and Predictability in the Competitive Procurement/Bidding of Generation Capacity.*

The World Bank (2011) emphasised that there is need for competition and transparency in tender processes as procurement processes which reduce costs across the entire project spectrum. However, Eberhard *et al.* (2016) argued that competition does not matter as some markets do not find more investors to warrant competition. Vagliasindi (2013) emphasised that Latin American countries such as Brazil, Mexico, Peru as well as China strengthened the sustainability of the electric PPP projects through embracing openness and transparency in power planning and procurement.

4. *Improved Operational and Financial Sustainability of Electricity Distributors.*

   Aging transmission and distribution grid networks deter investors from investing in power generation. This therefore implies that to ensure the sustainability of the PPPs in electricity generation, there is need to consider the co-existence of private investors and SOEs towards investment in strong and reliable transmission grid networks to minimise power losses and improve efficiency (Sly & Copley, 2017, Vagliasindi, 2013, International Monetary Fund, 2013, Eberhard *et al.,* 2016). Vagliasindi (2013) emphasised that in both China and Mexico, private investors invested heavily in the transmission and distribution infrastructure networks of electricity so as to minimise technical losses.

5. *Dedicated and Competent Staff Cemented by Training and Capacity Building at Both National and Sub-National Levels.*

   The World Bank (2011) emphasised that capacity building and appropriate staffing for project selection and structuring is crucial since it ensures that the PPP projects meet standards such as value for money, financial viability, affordability and sustainability. The World Bank (2011) further argued that this stage demands sophisticated and experienced advisors which can gobble up 3 to 10% of initial project capital outlay in developing countries. According to Sulser (2018), the 430MW Azito IPP project in Cote d'Ivoire was sustainable because of a dedicated and competent staff.

The IPPs Sector in Zimbabwe

Citing the Minister of Finance and Economic Development Mthuli Ncube, journalist Farirai Machivenyika writing in the *Herald* of 6 December 2022 (Herald, 2022a) indicated that the Zimbabwe Energy Regulatory Authority (ZERA) had licensed over 50 IPPs and while 30 of them were operational, just over half of them are small operations designed to meet the in-house needs of the company building the station rather than to generate power for the grid. Further, Journalist Zvaimaida Murwira highlighted that against electricity demand requirement of 1850MW against constrained supply, Zimbabwe was importing the power deficit from Zambia, South Africa and Mozambique which implied that it was supporting the IPPs in those exporting countries.

In view of the foregoing, Murwira also citing Minister Mthuli Ncube suggested that the government was supposed to support the IPPs since the authorities knew that IPPs were in need of a government guarantee, a viable tariff of US 10.30 cents per KWHr and currency convertibility for their proceeds. Substantiating the foregoing, Murwira quoted the Permanent Secretary Gloria Magombo in the *Herald* of 7 December 2022 (Herald, 2022) who noted that the government had secured funding to increase the capacity of the IPPs as well as increase the uptake of the net metering programme so that IPPs contribute immensely to the national grid.

According to Journalist Kennedy Nyavaya writing in the Energy Transition (2022), in September 2022, the ZERA had registered over 60 clean energy IPPs yet only about 3% had managed to start operations and supplying to the national grid. The Energy Transition (2022) further stressed that those IPPs operating account for 5% of the expected output of 7000MW. Further, Kennedy Nyavaya, in the Energy Transition (2022), attributed the low contribution of the IPPs to inadequate funding, further emphasising that the ZESA should collaborate with the struggling IPPs and should also channel more of its funds towards clean energy to maximise their potential.

The chapter is motivated to narrow the above gaps in the governance of the IPPs as variant models of the PPPs in the electricity sector in Zimbabwe. Inspired by the reviewed IPP country experiences, the chapter examines the governance of the IPPs in Zimbabwe with a view to suggesting best practices to strengthen the effective governance of the IPPs across the country.

METHODOLOGY

This study used documentary review through the use of desk-top research whereby global experiences on the IPP governance frameworks, the PPP definitions and the PPP scenario on the Zimbabwean environment were done. Additionally, key informant interviews were also conducted targeting key respondents drawn from private players and Zimbabwe Electricity Supply Authority and the Ministry of Energy and Power Development who consented to the research undertaking. In the IPP sector, the key respondents comprise experts and senior managers drawn from private players. The study whose principal aim was to examine the fundamental IPP governance framework in Zimbabwe targeted 26 respondents in each of the identified sectors drawn through purposive sampling for the 5 key informants and random sampling for the 21 questionnaire participants.

The study used a key informant interview guide to answer the following questions: How many IPPs are in operation and in what form do they exist? To what extent do conditions in the electricity sector comply with the IPP governance indicators? How are contracts and licences issued and are due processes being followed? What are the major challenges impinging the effective governance of the IPPs in Zimbabwe? What measures should be implemented to strengthen the effective governance of the IPPs in the electricity sector in Zimbabwe?

The study used qualitative approach in analysing and discussing its findings. Literature analysis and content analysis were utilised to analyse the data. On the basis of quantitative data analyses, the 5-point questionnaire set was computed into the spread sheet with a view to assessing the extent to which the ZESA has successfully embraced the IPP governance factors to attract investors towards financing electricity infrastructure. The analyses were used to propose an IPP governance and policy framework to enhance the effectiveness of the IPPs as electricity infrastructural development financing models for Zimbabwe.

RESEARCH FINDINGS AND ANALYSIS

Response Rate

This section presents and displays the number of respondents against the targeted respondents. Table 12.1 displays the response rate.

Noteworthy is that the study distributed questionnaire to 21 respondents who were selected at random to examine the governance of the IPPs in the electricity sector in Zimbabwe and there was 100% response rate. Furthermore, the study also purposely sampled five key informants and interviewed them to verify some key questions with regard to governance of the IPPs in Zimbabwe.

Presentation and Discussion of Research Findings

The presentation and discussion of results are research-question focused.

Table 12.1 Response Rate

Category of employment	*Target Respondents*	*Number of respondents*	*Response Rate (%)*
Government Organisations	18	18	100
Private players	5	5	100
Development Finance Institutions	2	2	100
Others	1	1	100
Total	**26**	**26**	**100**

Source: Developed by the authors

How many IPPs are in operation and in what form do they exist?

This question investigated the number and forms of the PPPs manifesting in the electricity sector. The study noted that the Electricity Act of 2002 makes provision for the Independent Power Producers (IPPs) to participate in electricity generation (Government of Zimbabwe, 2002). Forms of the IPPs in the electricity sector in Zimbabwe include: (a) less than nine mini-hydro power stations that are primarily BOO with an estimated MW capacity of 35MW, (b) four co-generation (bagasse and timber) stations which are also BOO with an estimated MW capacity of 97MW; (c) five coal/thermal, gas and diesel stations that are primarily BOOT with an estimated MW capacity of 6000MW and lastly 70 solar stations which are BOO with an estimated MW capacity 1200MW, 10 of which are operational with an estimated MW capacity of 20MW (Magombo, 2021). The abovementioned include four major typologies of IPP projects in the electricity sector in Zimbabwe.

In the review period 1998–2021, the country has been experiencing erratic electricity supplies as demand has been outstripping supply which results to load shedding. According to Magombo (2021), as on 6 December 2021 the ZPC was producing 1400MW from its power stations across the country against a peak demand of 1700MW which gives a deficit of at least 300MW which is sometimes closed through importing and load shedding. Moreover, the study results indicate an increasing urban expansion and industrialisation resulted in the ZPC failing to cope with the increase in demand due to financial constraints. In this regard, the four categories of the PPPs of the IPP projects in nature and scope were established to complement the ZESA to cover the electricity supply gap with a motive to exporting the surplus power into the SADC regional markets.

First, under the mini-hydro projects category which are mainly located in the Manicaland Province, there is the 1.1MW Nyamingura plant located in Honde Valley and was established in October 2008; the 2.75MW Pungwe A power plant in Honde Valley which was established in March 2014; the 15.25MW

Pungwe B station in Honde Valley which was established in March 2014; the 3.8MW Duru power plant in Honde Valley which was established in February 2012; the 1.6MW Kupinga station in Rusitu Valley in Chipinge which was established in December 2014; the 3.72MW Pungwe C station along Pungwe River which was established in December 2015; the 2.3MW Hauna station in the Ngarura River in Honde Valley which was established in July 2016; and the 0.3MW Claremont and the 2.06MW Tsanga B power stations both in Nyanga which were established in April 2017 and May 2018, respectively. Second, under the co-generation category there is the 35MW Triangle power station in the Lowveld of Masvingo Province which was established in December 2006; the 39MW Hippo Valley power plant in the Lowveld which was established in August 2007; and the 18.3MW Bagasse Green Fuel plant in Chisumbanje of Manicaland Province which was established in September 2011.

Third, under the coal/thermal, gas and diesel categories, the PPP projects are at various levels of construction while some are partly functioning. In this case, there is the upgrade of Hwange 7 and 8 projects which started on the 1 August 2018 and are expected to add 600MW into the national grid in 2023. There is also the 2100MW coal-fired Lusulu project in Binga in the Matabeleland North Province which has been on the cards since 2011 and is failing to take-off due to funding challenges. Another one is the 2400MW coal-fired Gokwe-Sengwa project in the Midlands Province which has been on the cards since 1998. The Gokwe-Sengwa project is failing to take-off due to various challenges such as the perceived poor quality of coal as well as financial challenges. The Gokwe-Sengwa project is being coordinated by the Rio-Zim, (Private Limited) a diamond mining company.

Fourth, under the solar energy category there are various projects notably the 2.5MW Centragrid Power Station in Nyabira (Harare) which was established in June 2016; the 2.5MW Riverside Power Station in Mutoko district of Mashonaland East Province which was established in December 2018; the 2.25MW Nottingham Estates which was established in June 2017 in Beitbridge in Matabeleland South Province; and the 5MW SolGas Power Plant which was established in August 2020 in Hwange district of Matabeleland North Province. The existing PPPs of the IPP projects in nature are significant for the study because they provide the empirical basis for examining the fundamental governance frameworks on the operations of IPPs in Zimbabwe. The IPP cases also provide lively experiences on the constraining factors as well as assisting the study in proposing measures for strengthening the governance of the IPP projects.

To what extent do conditions in the electricity sector environment in Zimbabwe comply with IPP governance indicators?

This question analyses the extent to which conditions in the electricity sector environment comply with five IPP governance indicators. Through the responses from the structured fill-in questionnaires and interviews, respondents were asked to assess the extent to which conditions in Zimbabwe's electricity sector environment comply with the IPP critical success factors on a Likert scale rating with scores like: [very good (4), good (3), moderate (2), fair (1) and poor (0)] as shown in ensuing sections. This entailed questioning the governance systems in place to ensure the sustainability of the IPP projects.

Variable 1: Robust oversight by the Ministry of Energy and Power Development with Sound and Effective Zimbabwe Energy Regulatory Authority.

Twenty-five per cent of the participants rated the variable from very good to good as they indicated that the Ministry is effective in its oversight responsibility and that the regulator is fair and impartial in the exercise of its role. The majority of respondents (i.e., 75% of the respondents) rated the variable from moderate to poor as they indicated that the Ministry is not proactive but reacts to situations as they arise, further emphasising that it is very difficult for the ZERA to come up with a cost-reflective tariff framework since the decision will have negative political and economic effects. For example, subsidies are removed and retained again. Further, respondents cited gaps in the competitive procurement framework.

Variable 2: Transparent and predictable licensing framework.

Forty-six per cent of the participants rated the variable from very good to good as they in each case indicated that the Second Republic is making significant strides in the ease of doing business indicators. Respondents in this respect emphasised that there are transparency and accountability systems that are emerging in the Second Republic. In light of this, 54% of the respondents rated the variable from moderate to poor as respondents established that the licensing framework is marred by corruption and bureaucracy as it takes five years to get a power generating license because there are too many requirements that are needed to operate an IPP project. They cited the Chivayo–American company dispute on the IPP licenses where a U.S. company had won the tender to construct the Gwanda Solar Project but the tender was allegedly given to Wicknell Chivayo who did not perform the contract.

Variable 3: Coordinated PPP unit with experienced adviser.

Forty-six per cent of the respondents rated the variable from very good to good as they highlighted that the PPP unit is at its emerging phase (skills development is taking place). They further indicated that most policymakers in Zimbabwe are still on the learning curve on area of the PPPs and PPP workshops are being rolled out. However, 54% of participants rated the theme from moderate to poor as they indicated that the outfit is not visible on the ground and its performance has not yet been seen.

Variable 4: Capacity building, appropriate staffing and retention of developed staff throughout the project cycle.

Fifteen per cent of the respondents rated the variable from very good to good as they indicated that capacity is being developed through training and development workshops. However, the majority of respondents which accounted for 85% of the total respondents rated the variable from moderate to poor as they argued that while capacity is being developed, retention is difficult due to the volatile macro-economic-environment-induced poor remuneration. Further, respondents established that the ZESA used to send officers to the United Kingdom, India and Malaysia for six-month exchange programmes in the areas of generation, transmission and distribution but the programme stopped in the late 1999. They also indicated that skills transfer between the ZETDC staff to IPP project implementers is difficult due to mobility gaps and overstretched financial resources.

Variable 5: Cost-reflective tariffs.

In light of the cost-reflective tariffs, 19% of the respondents rated the variable from very good to good as they indicated that tariffs are being adjusted on regular basis and there is pay-per-use plan (prepaid metering and billing). However, 71% of the total respondents rated the variable from moderate to poor as they indicated that in line with the New Public Governance Framework, robust engagement of various stakeholders and wider consultations are done to come up with a tariff framework and there is bureaucracy in the approval of the framework by the government. Respondents further argued that the tariff is not cost reflective because the government is the one that approves it and it considers social and political implications in setting a tariff framework (hence there is no autonomy on the part of the IPPs in coming up with the tariffs). Thus, economic viability and sustainability of the power generation are somehow ignored. Compared to the SADC region the average tariff for Zimbabwe is US$0.08 per kilowatt versus US$0.14 for the SADC region. As such, it can thus be argued that, 'the tariff framework does not allow investors to recoup their return on investment within 25–30 years of the PPP project operation'.

Drawing from the above governance indicators, the study argues that quality of institutions and governance framework is of fundamental importance to strengthen the sustainability of the IPP projects.

With regard to empirical experiences, the cases of Kenya, South Africa, Uganda and Nigeria embraced sound and quality institutional framework to ensure the success of the PPP projects. In the same vein, Latin American electricity projects such as Brazil, Mexico and China offer enviable examples in which robust oversight and regulatory frameworks guaranteed the sustainability of the electricity PPP projects. Overall, in the context of Zimbabwe, like questionnaire respondents, interviewees rated the institutional, legal and regulatory frameworks to be moderate (2). Although interviewees noted that both the Ministry of Energy and Power Development and the ZERA are supporting the IPP projects, it was also argued that there is too much government interference in projects and there is fragmented coordination within government institutions. Interviewees noted that most investors who get licenses have no technical and financial capacity to ensure the take-off of the projects.

Although Eberhard *et al.* (2016) argued that competitive bidding is suitable in emerging market and advanced economies, the cases of Kenya, Nigeria, South Africa, Tanzania and Uganda have sustainable PPP projects due to embracing of the competitive bidding in the tender process. As opposed to the unsolicited bidding framework, competitive bidding creates value for money as more efficient and cost-effective measures will be adopted. However, in the Zimbabwean case interviewees argued that there is more of unsolicited bidding as opposed to competitive bidding in the licensing framework. In Uganda, the 250MW projects were marred by corruption across the procurement chain as the Uganda Energy Regulatory Authority (ERA) failed to provide guidelines for a fair, open and competitive bidding process.

Competitive and cost reflective tariff framework is critical to ensure the sustainability of the PPP projects. The empirical cases of South African Renewable Energy Programme and that of Uganda offer enviable examples in this respect. These two countries have sound, fair, accountable and independent electricity regulators that guarantee sustainable cost-reflective tariff frameworks for the provision of electricity (Eberhard *et al.*, 2016). In the Zimbabwean context, interviewee 2 emphasised that the tariff framework is just cost recovery but not economic. However, interviewee 4 who is from the academic field argued that the tariff framework is good but there is a lot of inefficiencies, high salaries to management, among others. There is power theft, underrating of charges due to poor corporate governance. Additionally, there are technical losses due to antiquated machinery and commercial losses due to gap in collection.

How IPP contracts and licenses are issued and are due processes followed?

Study respondents stressed that licenses took at least six months and due-diligence exercises are not performed with regard to whether the investors have sound balance sheets to embark on the projects as the contractors would have no technical and financial capacity to ensure take-off of the projects. The study respondents emphasised that in the case of Zimbabwe due to political connection, the IPP investors get licenses which they use to scout for financiers while others are being used for speculative purposes. This results in a situation whereby investors who are issued with licenses sit on them for speculative tendencies.

What are the major challenges impinging the effective governance of the IPPs in Zimbabwe?

A synthesis of the views expressed by the respondents revealed the following as major challenges impinging the governance of the IPPs in Zimbabwe.

Gaps in cost reflective tariff framework

Study respondents argued that lack of a cost-reflective and competitive tariff framework has been affecting the sustainability of the IPPs in the electricity sector with potential huge private players skirting investment in the Zimbabwe power sector. In view of the above, there is need for the ZERA to come up with a competitive and cost-reflective tariff framework in line with macro-economic trends prevailing in Zimbabwe as well as the SADC regional trends. Empirical literature is also awash with evidence of the ZESA losing private players due to non-cost-reflective tariff framework for the period running 1998 and 2021. Whereas in the SADC region the average tariff framework is US$0.12 to US$0.14 per k/h, in Zimbabwe the average has been ranging between US$0.07 and US$0.09 per k/h for the period 1998 to 2021, a scenario which needs improvement.

Unserviced and unmaintained grid network

Cumulatively, 29% of respondents gave out that unserviced or unmaintained grid network results in bushes encroaching the grid transmission line and disrupting the transmission of electricity during the rainy seasons.

Bureaucracy and red tape to reduce time for accessing investor licenses

Nineteen per cent of respondents emphasised that bureaucracy and red tape in accessing investor license and land use certificates from local authorities derail the implementation of the power projects and can lead to investor fatigue which hampers the sustainability of partnership projects.

Unavailability of capital and material resources

A cumulative 68% of the respondents highlighted that the volatile and dynamic macro-economic environment with the IPP constraining factors such as inflation, shortage of foreign currency, shortage of raw materials, external shocks are affecting the long-term business strategy and creditworthiness of the offtaker and that of the IPP projects. The shortage of resources such as transformers, poles and vehicles affect the operating efficiency of the ZESA and therefore the sustainability of the IPP projects as models of financing infrastructural development in the electricity sector.

Limited grid transmission capacity to accommodate the IPP demands

Study respondents hinted that the grid impact assessment gap also affects the long-term sustainability of the IPP projects. Some IPP projects are required to scale down their capacity as they are told by the offtaker that their production capacity/potential cannot be accommodated into the grid network due to grid capacity constraints. As one respondent on questionnaire noted:

> Some projects like thermal solar that an IPP might want to be connected to the grid will require a grid impact assessment which might affect uptake of some solar projects as such projects are intermittent.

Brain drain and gaps in capacity building and staff retention

Study respondents noted that brain drain in the power sector impinges the sustainability of the partnership projects as more than 50% of engineers are leaving the country to scout for greener pastures due to non-competitive salary structures.

Lack of a competitive bidding framework

Cumulatively, 8% of the respondents argued that unsolicited/non-competitive bidding characterises the awarding of tenders for the PPP power projects. These respondents argued that, unlike the competitive bidding, this unsolicited bidding framework compromises value for money as investors would inflate the costs of the project and compromise on issues to do with feed-in tariff.

CONCLUSION AND POLICY RECOMMENDATIONS

Drawing from the discussion of research findings above, the chapter proposed some measures to strengthen the effective governance of the PPPs in the electricity sector in Zimbabwe as follows:

- There is a need for the ZERA to come up with a competitive and cost-reflective tariff framework in line with the macro-economic developments prevailing in Zimbabwe as well as the SADC regional trends.

- The need for routine maintenance or servicing of power lines is crucial to ensure uninterrupted supply of electricity to domestic and industrial consumers as well as to the export market.
- There is a need for the government to create a one-stop centre for the power investors to provide real-time services to investors in the electricity sector.
- The government should attract and incentivise investors who will provide intermediate products and services in the electricity sector, such as manufacturing of transformers, copper cables and poles, among other required materials to strengthen the sustainability of the IPPs as infrastructural development financing frameworks in the electricity sector.
- The ZETDC may need to invest in increasing or upgrading transmission grid capacity to accommodate the demands of private partners.
- There is a need to attract and retain skilled labour by paying USD-pegged competitive salaries that are in tandem with the SADC regional trends. Deliberate policies towards building the capacity of work force and project managers will also enhance the sustainability of the IPP projects.
- There is a need for Zimbabwe to adopt a competitive bidding framework in awarding tenders to power projects with a view to enhancing value for money in these IPP projects.

REFERENCES

African Development Bank. (2019). *Zimbabwe Infrastructure Report 2019.* Tunis Belvedere: African Development Bank.

African Development Bank. (2011). *Infrastructure and Growth in Zimbabwe: An Action Plan for Sustained Strong Economic Growth.* Tunis Belvedere: African Development Bank.

Ayee, J. R. A. (2005). *Public Sector Management in Africa,* Economic Research Working Paper Number 82 (November 2005). Tunis Belvedere: African Development Bank (ADB).

Alloisio, I. (2021). *The role of Public Private Partnerships in the energy transition infrastructure financing in Sub-Saharan Africa.* Energy and Climate. 10th Florence School of Regulation-European University Institute's Annual Conference (10th–11th June 2021). Available on: https://fsr.eui.eu/the-role-of-public-private-partnerships-in-the-energy-transition-infrastructure-financing-in-sub-saharan-africa. [Accessed 1 January 2023].

Chilean Concession Law. (not dated). PPP Reference Guide (n.4) 7*/PPP Knowledge lab, "PPP Reference Guide, Version 3. Available on: https://pppknowledgelab.org/guide/sections/83-what-is-the-ppp-reference-guide/ [Accessed 20 October 2022].

Christensen, T. and Laegreid, P. (2011). Complexity and Hybrid Administration: Theoretical and Empirical Challenges. *Public Organization Review,* Vol. 11, pp.407–423.

Delmon, J. (2010). Understanding Options for Public-Private Partnerships in Infrastructure. Sorting out the forest from the trees: BOT, DBFO, DCMF, Concession, Lease. . . . *Policy Research Working Paper 5173.* The World Bank (Finance Economics and Urban Development).

Eberhard, A. A., Gratwick, K.N., Morella, E, and Antmann, P. (2016). *Independent Power Projects in Sub-Saharan Africa. Lessons from five key countries,* 2016 International Bank for Reconstruction and Development. Washington DC: World Bank.

Energy Transition. (2022). As Energy Poverty Persists and Prices Soar, Zimbabwe Urgently Needs Sustainable Answers. (The Energy Transition: The Global Energiewende) of 20 September). Available on: https://energytransition.org/2022/09/as-energy-poverty-persists-and-prices-soar-Zimbabwe-urgently-needs-sustainable-answers/. [Accessed 20 December 2022].

Government of Zimbabwe. (2002). *Electricity Act, Number 4 of 2002* (Chapter 13:19). Harare, Zimbabwe: Government of Zimbabwe Printers.

Hall, D. (2015). Why Public-Private Partnerships Don't Work? The many advantages of the public alternative. *Public Service International Research Unit* (PSIRU), University of Greenwich, UK. Available on: https://www.world-psi.org/. [Accessed 20 December 2022].

Heldeweg, M. A, Saunders, M and Hamsen, M. (2015). Public-Private or Private-Private Energy Partnerships? Towards Good Energy Governance in Regional and Local Green Gas Projects. *Energy Sustainability and Society,* 5(9), pp. 1–12. Available on: https://doi.org/10.1186/s13705-015-0038-8/. [Accessed 20 January 2022].

Herald. (2022a). *We Are Working on IPPs Tariff Concerns.* (The Herald of 6 December). Available on: https://www.herald.co.zw/were-working-on-ipps-tariff-concerns/. [Accessed 20 December 2022].

Herald. (2022b). *Measures Taken to Ease Power Shortage.* (The Herald of 7 December). Available on: https://www.herald.co.zw/measures-taken-to-ease-power-shortage/. [Accessed 26 December 2022].

International Monetary Fund. (2013). *Energy Subsidy Reform in Sub-Saharan Africa: Experiences and Lessons.* Washington, DC: IMF. Available on: https://www.imf.org>pub>afri132. [Accessed 4 August 2022].

Magombo, G. (2022). Measures Taken to Ease Power Shortage, The Herald of 7 December. Available at: at: https://www.herald.co.zw/measures-taken-to-ease-power-shortage/. (Accessed 26 December 2022).

Magombo, G. (2021). Presentation to the Ministry of Foreign Affairs and International Trade for Diplomats, 6 December 2021. Harare: Zimbabwe

Mckenzie, B. 2018. *The Rise of Corporate PPAs 2.0.* (An Update—July). Available on: www.bakermckenzie.com. [Accessed 1 January 2023].

Nel, D. (2018). An Assessment of Emerging Hybrid Public-Private Partnerships in the Energy Sector in South Africa, *International Journal of Economics and Finance Studies,* Vol. 4, (1), pp. 33—48.

Netherlands Ministry of Foreign Affairs. April 2013. *Public-Private Partnerships in developing countries: A Systematic literature review.* The Netherlands, Amsterdam: The Policy and Operations Evaluation Department. Available on: https://www.government.nl/.../2013/.../iob-study-public-private-in-developing-countries/. [Accessed 18 December 2022].

Nkomo, K and Nhema, A.G. (2015). Implementing Public-Private Partnerships (PPPs) in the transport sector in Zimbabwe: Challenges and prospects: *Global Business and Economics Research Journal*, Vol. 4 (7), pp. 40—70.

Nsasira, R, Basheka, B. C and Oluka, P.N. (2013). Public-Private Partnerships and Enhanced Service Delivery in Uganda: Implications from the Energy Sector, *International Journal of Business Administration,* Vol. 4(3), pp. 48—60.

Osborne, S.P, Radnor, Z and Nasi, G. (2013). A New Theory for Public Service Management? Towards a (Public) Service Dominant Approach, *The American Review of Public Administration*, Vol. 43(2), pp. 135—158.

Power Africa. (2021). *Advancing Public-Private Partnerships to Accelerate Energy-Sector Development.* (The Power Africa of 29 November). Available on: https://powerafrica..medium.com/advancing-public-private-partnerships-to-accelerate-energy-sector-development-25b9bbaa81. [Accessed 1 January 2023].

Sly, A and Copley, A. (2017). *Policy Brief: Closing the financing gap for African Energy Infrastructure: Trends, challenges, and opportunities* (April 2017). Washington DC: Brookings Institution.

South African Department of Energy Press Release. (15 June, 2015). Public-Private Partnerships Success Story, South Africa announces more utility renewables, Pretoria, Available on: https://www.bluehorizon.energy/public-privatepartnership-success-story-south-africa. [Accessed 15 November 2022].

Sulser, P.O. (2018). *Infrastructure PPPs in the Most Challenging Developing Countries: Closing the Gap.* Great Britain, London: Euro-money Trading Ltd (International Financial Law Review).

Turley, L and Semple, A. February (2013). *Financing Sustainable Public-Private Partnerships*. International Institute for Sustainable Development. Available on: https://www.iisd.org>ppp-financing. [Accessed 20 December 2022].

United Nations Economic Commission for Africa. (2011). *Public-Private Partnerships in Africa's Energy Sector: Challenges, Best Practices and Emerging Trends.* Addis Ababa, Ethiopia: United Nations Conference Centre, 30 June to I July 2011.

Vagliasindi, M. (2013). *Revisiting Public-Private Partnerships in the Power Sector.* Washington, DC: The World Bank.

World Bank. (not dated). *Concessions, Build-Operate-Transfer (BOT) and Design Build Operate (DBO) Projects, Public-Private Partnership in Infrastructure Resource Centre.* Available on: https://www.ppp.worldbank.org/public-private-partnership/agreements/concessions-bots-dbos/. [Accessed 20 November 2022].

World Bank. (2012). *Public-Private Partnerships- Reference Guide Version 1.0.* Washington, DC: World Bank.

World Bank. (2009). *Tool-Kit for Public-Private Partnerships in Roads and Highways: Overview and Diagnosis,* Washington, DC: World Bank.

World Bank. 2011. *Principles for Public-Private Partnerships (PPPs) Effectiveness in Developing Countries.* Washington, DC: World Bank Group.

Zunguze, T. (2016). *Defying the Odds: Understanding the Critical-Success Factors for Financing Independent Power Producers in Zimbabwe.* South Africa: University of Cape Town—Graduate School of Business. Available on: https://open.uct.ac.za>bistream>handle. [Accessed 3 December 2022].

Conclusion and Recommendations

Alex Nduhura and Innocent Nuwagaba

This book has provided theoretical and empirical evidence on the application and experience of Public-Private Partnerships (PPPs) in Africa. Reading through the chapters of the book, a number of conclusions come to the fore. These are detailed in this final chapter. The chapter subsequently suggests some recommendations. In drawing the conclusions, what has come out clear is that there is a mixed bag of successes and challenges in terms of the implementation of PPPs throughout African countries. Further to this, it is also evident that there is still a lot to be done in terms of popularising PPPs and realising full benefits of implementing the same. In most African countries, PPPs have been adopted for different purposes. Whilst there are commonalities in relation to the drivers for PPPs, these, nonetheless, tend to differ from country to country.

Some of the key drivers identified for adopting PPPs (in Botswana and Kenya) include: risk allocation; access to private capital; value for money (VFM) (see chapter 6); need for effectiveness; the need for service delivery; public interest as well as potential benefits (see chapter 7). The recognition of PPPs for improving specific sectors in African economies cannot be overemphasised. To illustrate, PPPs are recognised to reside with the evidence and have further potential to improve the reliability of infrastructure such as (reliable) power supply. Good road network; airport and seaport transportation; telecommunication; good water supply and proper sanitation; and educational institutions and health services are essential prerequisites for rapid socio-economic development and national security enhancement (see for instance Chapters 6, 8 and 10). PPPs are confirmed to have resulted in providing VFM—for money increased road network and reduced traffic—a key measure for economic prowess of countries.

In South Africa, the use of appropriate models is recognised as apt for the success of PPPs. For the country's road sector, the design-finance-build-operate-transfer (DFBOT) model has been popular; however, due to the fact that most roads installed by government are not in good state amidst declining resources, the adoption of the improve-finance-maintain-operate-transfer (IFMOT) model is proposed (see chapter 9). This is justified because the roads exist yet funds to improve and maintain them are largely unavailable. Notwithstanding, it is important to note that PPPs tend to deliver services at a price much higher than those for services delivered directly by government.

Reasons advanced for such trends identified include the fact that private actors borrow finances at higher rates and that they receive collections in local currency despite borrowing in foreign currency. Further challenges linked to the implementation of PPPs in Africa include corruption which is seen as a major ingredient for higher user fees for PPP services since costs borne to corruption are silently absorbed and recovered. Other challenges include the engagement of private sector partners without adequate technical, managerial, financial and marketing resources in PPP operations. It is also necessary for governments at national and state levels to secure sufficient political will in terms of continuity of PPP projects embarked on by previous administrations (see chapter 8).

This book concludes that PPPs in Africa have a place in development. PPPs are now mainstreamed in official government documents such as national vision statements and national development plans. Therefore, the understanding and recognition of the PPPs as a service delivery mechanism in Africa is no longer essential but a must for scholars, private actors, administrators and policymakers. PPPs support service delivery by providing and improving infrastructure quality and quantity. While the choice to adopt PPPs has been due to the need to attract and access private capital, we recognise that the need to diversify the objectives of PPPs should extend from capital and include innovation but most importantly pursuit of efficiency and effectiveness gains.

It is also concluded that PPPs have a place in developing and emerging countries in Africa. No matter the stage in economic development, countries that integrate PPPs in their service delivery paths are likely to benefit from the adoption of PPPs. We note, however, that while PPPs resonate with benefits, they can also provide negative externalities in development. This calls for the need to anchor the practice of PPPs on theories that have been discussed, secure political support, establish strong legal, regulatory frameworks and improve the way PPPs are governed.

THEORETICAL FOUNDATIONS UNDERPINNING STUDIES ON PPPs

The book provides for the understanding of PPPs from a diverse theoretical lens. Theories provide the impetus for research (Silverman, 2000). As argued by Suppes (1974), the significance of theories to research include i) analogy; ii) being used as a device for reorganising experiences; iii) reorganising complexity; iv) being used to solve a problem; and v) being used to avert the triviality of empiricism. Typically, as scholars, we use theory as a lens that can inform the understanding of the subject matter under investigation. This book reviewed a number of theories (see chapter 1) in order to set the tone for subsequent chapters. The chapter demonstrates that PPP transactions can be understood using the governance theory. The theory facilitates us to appreciate how PPPs are governed. This is done through various means such as stakeholder interactions, their use of power, and legal, regulatory and institutional frameworks.

Other theories analysed include agency theory that presupposes several important issues, namely: government will always be held responsible for the action of private actors, information asymmetry exists and governments must always invest in capacities necessary to sustain their regulatory function in PPP arrangements. Additionally, the agency theory presupposes that while governments delegate their role to private actors under PPP arrangements, it is important that governments continuously monitor the actions of private actors and ensure that PPPs continue to deliver in the interest of the public. Further theories discussed include the network, transaction and cost-based theories. The network theory acknowledges that PPPs operate as a network of actors. This brings complexities but at the same time provides opportunities that need to be exploited. Therefore, the need to adopt the principles of network governance becomes important if PPPs are to deliver the dream of government.

The transaction cost theory implies that when transacting within PPPs, it is important to note that private actors will always seek to minimise costs in order to increase profit for themselves. Applied to PPPs private actors may lapse on operation and maintenance schedules, and seek to increase user fees unjustifiably. This implies that there is a need to watch all actions of PPPs. This can be done through instituting and implementing robust performance measures rewarded by both incentives and disincentives. The chapter concludes with the resource-based view theory. Applied to PPPs, PPPs are justified because they help to provide access to resources that may not be available or deficient in government.

Therefore, by adopting PPPs in service delivery, PPPs provide opportunity for governments to access resources, such as capital, innovation, among other resources, that may not be available in the right quantity and quality as may be required. The Integrated PPP Model discussed in chapter 1 asserts that the private sector takes on the role of providing a more comprehensive package of healthcare infrastructure and service delivery.

THE TELEOLOGY OF PUBLIC-PRIVATE PARTNERSHIPS

The Teleology of Public-Private Partnerships

Conclusions on the purpose of PPPs are discernible through the book. Indeed factors that gave rise to the initiation and introduction of PPPs to African countries have been debated and analysed. Of equal and critical significance is the purpose for which PPPs exist to serve. As Eagleton observed, one cannot interpret (much less formulate) politics without addressing the question of purpose, the ends deciphered and the means by which those ends might be achieved (Griffiths, 2018, pp. 905, 906). In this book, as the authors grappled with questions of service delivery, efficiency, provision of public infrastructure and source of finance and technical expertise, the question of ends has never felt more important. PPPs, in this regard, exist to serve various purposes.

Acquisition of private capital: Governments throughout the world have been faced with a dire need to change ways through which they procure public assets and services (see chapter 3). Pressure to change the standard model of public procurement arose because of public debt, which grew rapidly during the 1970s and 1980s (Tharun, 2014, p. 56; Molokwane, 2019, p. 159). The need to access private capital has been confirmed as the most popular reason for the adoption of PPPs. One of the primary reasons for adopting PPPs has been efficiency and effectiveness in affairs of government; however, attaining such has proved to be costly, hence the resolve by some governments to acquire private capital by engaging private partners. The adoption of PPPs on grounds for private capital has delivered below the expectations of the greater public as the adoption has overshadowed the benefits that PPPs deliver. This has resulted in mismatch of perceptions and expectations, painting dark image of PPPs; yet PPPs are key catalyst for development. A focus on diverse benefits is recommended for PPPs to improve their publicness (see chapters 3, 4 and 5).

Private provision of public infrastructure: As has been evident throughout out the post-independent Africa, majority of African governments have not been able to provide public infrastructure due to both indigenous and exogenous factors. Topical in the provisions of public infrastructure are for example: quality of infrastructure; quality of service delivery; management and governance of PPPs; technology and skills transfer; financing of projects, among others. The diversity of the infrastructure and service needs by governments relates to the multiplicity of factors that come into play in the implementation of PPPs. Among others, these include: a lack of technical capacity; political interference; corruption; a lack of clear sector-specific guidelines and regulations; bureaucratic hurdles; and financial constraints (see chapter 12).

Some governments have been seen to be compromising quality in the provisions of public infrastructure. This is adds to existing constraints that often led to a number of PPP projects failing to take off or decisions being reversed at the infrastructure construction or operation stage. Nevertheless, the country's future prospects look bright, provided the ongoing amendments to the regulatory framework manage to curtail most of the constraints. In Zambia for instance (see chapter 11), the quality of services coming forth as an outcome of projects in various sectors implemented through PPPs reflects mixed results. It has been found that some projects have improved quality of service delivery while others failed leading to cancellation of contracts. These mixed fortunes are the result of a number of constraints, most of which are related to the weaknesses in the regulatory framework. In a different vein, there is anecdotal evidence of successful PPP infrastructure and services in the African continent. These include electricity provision in: Kenya (see chapter 3); Uganda (see chapter 3); South Africa, Tanzania, Kenya and Nigeria (see chapters 5, 7, 8 and 9). PPPs have similarly been implemented in the road transport, water and health sectors (see for example chapters 8, 10, 11, 12).

Axiomatic and Inexorable factors: Contemporary global events authoritatively gave rise to the adoption of PPPs. The most convincing justification for the introduction of PPPs comes from the post-2007 fiscal strictures. Anecdotal cases constituting these shocks include: (i) the Global Financial Crisis (2007–2009); (ii) the 2014–2015 global commodity crash; (iii) COVID-19 pandemic; and (iv) the invasion of Ukraine [the Russo–Ukrainian War, which began in 2014, intensified on 24 February 2022 when Russia invaded Ukraine] (UNCTAD, 2022) (see chapter 3). Beyond the aforementioned inexorable factors there are nonetheless axiomatic factors. These include: ease of doing business; relief to government fiscus; conducive legal framework; and availability of domestic and capital and debt funding (see chapter 6) (Molokwane, 2019, pp. 162–165).

INSTITUTIONAL, LEGAL AND REGULATORY FRAMEWORKS REQUIRE STRENGTHENING

An effective PPP legal framework provides a starting point for effective implementation of PPPs in Africa (see chapter 4). Countries implementing PPPs in the African continent have made efforts to put in place, the Institutional, Legal and Regulatory Frameworks. Whilst some have PPP legislation, others have PPP policies and implementation framework. Those with the latter have found themselves having to develop PPP guidelines and/or regulations to augment their public procurement (see chapters 2 and 6). Others have various pieces of legislation that they use for implementing

PPPs; for example, Nigeria uses its Infrastructure Concession Regulatory Commission Act whilst the Public Tenders Law in Egypt is used in specific instances although the country has a specific PPP Law. Countries with no specific PPP legislation apply alternative legal instruments as their basic legal instrument for the implementation of PPPs. UNECE (2008) views building an effective legal framework as an integral element for the success of PPPs (see chapter 5).

Conclusively, there is an agreement that a legal framework is a prerequisite for any type of PPP activity. The legal framework does not only have to be in place, it must be well-designed, detailed, and clear. When PPP laws and regulations exist investment in PPPs will increase as their success becomes highly likely. PPP laws are recommended because they cushion against various types of PPP-related risks (e.g., political risk, etc.), creating increased investor confidence in the PPP markets. This is because legal and regulatory frameworks provide certainty, which is key for PPP concessions as their tenure is quite long. A PPP legal framework is very fundamental in determining successful implementation of any PPP project.

Governments must respect and put in place robust sound laws and regulations in order to create the confidence that drives investor interest in PPP markets. In order for a PPP law to deliver on the promises of PPPs, five core indicators were identified and derived from various pieces of literature. These include: legal definition and recognition of PPPs in a legal system; institutional mechanisms; clarity of PPP implementation process, dispute resolution schemes; and lastly, transparency and accountability. Whereas these indicators play a significant role in building a strong PPP legal framework, they must not be seen as ends but rather, as means to ends (see chapter 5).

RECOMMENDATIONS

PPPs remain a viable alternative of financing and providing public infrastructure and service through the engagement of private partners. The success of PPPs in the African continent however is reliant on satisfying a number of demands. Recommendations for possible success in the private provision of public infrastructure and services include some of those stated below. Due to the stakeholders that manifest in PPP arrangement, politics emerges as a critical factor. It must be conceded that PPPs require political will of leaders in order for the same to be adopted and implemented. To a significant degree, the success of PPPs is also reliant on the will of leaders as politics can equally distort the success and potential for PPPs. Effective management of stakeholders in this regard is good politics for PPPs. To illustrate, there is need to identify and manage stakeholder interests, power and expectations, and put in place sound PPP policies and laws. Second, it has been recognised that in order to escalate PPP adoption and success rate, a number of proposals should be out in motion. These include (a) correctly identifying and selecting projects where PPPs would be viable; (b) structuring contracts to ensure an appropriate pricing and transfer of risks to private partners; (c) setting up an encyclopaedic and transparent fiscal accounting and reporting standard for PPPs; and (d) introducing legal, regulatory and monitoring frameworks that ensure appropriate pricing and quality of service. Third, building a strong institutional framework is also a key ingredient of sustainable PPPs. Finally, PPP provides synergy and contributes a combination of skills, abilities, and power for producing the best results. Neither the public nor the private sector is capable by itself of solving the numerous problems in the sectors in which strategic partnerships have been invited. Government must therefore strive for critical policy reflection, value for money and developing capacities to regulate the adoption and implementation of PPPs.

REFERENCES

Griffiths, D. (2018). Teleology, *Victorian Literature and Culture*, Vol. 46 (3/4), pp. 905, 906.

International Monitory Fund. (2004). *Public Investment and fiscal Policy,* The Fiscal Affairs Department and the Policy Development and Review Department, (In consultation with the other departments and in cooperation with the World Bank, and the Inter-American Development Bank).

Molokwane, T. 2019. Short Term Public-Private Partnerships—A starting point for Botswana in Sebola, M. P & Molokwane, T. (Eds.). *4th Annual Conference of International Conference on Public Administration and Development Alternatives (IPADA),* Southern Sun, OR Tambo International Airport, South Africa from 3rd to 5th July, 2019, pp. 159–167.

Silverman, D. (2000). Doing Qualitative Research: A practical Handbook, Thousand Oaks CA: SAGE.

Suppes, P. (1974). The place of Theory in Educational Research. *Educational Researcher*, Vol. 3(6), pp.3–10.

Tharun, S. L. (2014). A study on Public Private Partnerships with Reference to Indian Infrastructural Projects, *International Journal of Business and Management Invention*, Vol. 3(10), pp. 56–63.

UNCTAD. (2022). *Rethinking the Foundations of Export Diversification in Africa*: *The Catalytic Role of Business and Financial Services*. United Nations Conference on Trade and Development, New York, NY.

UNECE. (2008). *Guidebook on Promoting Good Governance in Public-Private Partnerships*, United Nations Economic Commission for Europe, United Nations Publications, New York & Geneva, pp. 1–91

Index

Page numbers in *italics* refer to figures/tables

About the Editors and Contributors

EDITORS

Muhiya Tshombe Lukamba (PhD) is a professor in Public Management and Administration at the Vaal Triangle Campus of the North-West University in South Africa. He is the deputy director of the School of Government Studies, Vaal Triangle Campus. Tshombe holds a BA Honours in Public Administration, and MPhil (Energy Policy) from the University of Cape Town, and a Doctoral degree in Public Management from the Cape Peninsula University of Technology. He has supervised 8 PhD graduates, and more than 10 MA students. He has presented papers at various international conferences on topics such as Public Management, Human Resources, Comparative Public Administration, Public Sector Reform, Public Private Partnership, and Energy Security. He has authored more than 42 articles and two books: *New Public Management in Africa: Emerging Issues and Lessons* and *Public Administration in Africa: Performance and Challenges*, both published by Taylor and Francis Company.

Thekiso Molokwane (PhD) holds a PhD in Public Administration. He is senior lecturer of Public Administration in the Department of Political and Administrative Studies, University of Botswana and an extraordinary professor of Public Administration at the North-West University in South Africa. His work experience includes working as a senior administration officer in the Office of the President and as a principal administration officer in the Ministry of Defence, Justice and Security both for the Government of Botswana. He has also worked as a principal lecturer at the Limkokwing University of Creative Technology in the Faculty of Business and Globalization in Gaborone, Botswana. His area of specialty is Public Private Partnerships and has broadly published on the same area as well as in other areas of Public Sector Reforms, Comparative Public Administration and Public Policy. Dr. Molokwane has multiple publications in the PPP area. He has also edited there (3) Books of Conference Proceedings published by the 'International Conference on Public Administration and Development Alternatives (IPADA)' as a guest editor (2019,2020,2021 and 2022). He has further co-edited four books namely: *Governance, Reforms and Public Affairs: Cases from Southern Africa,* pp. 1–310; *Public Administration in Sub-Saharan Africa: Development and Policy Nexus*, pp. i–312; *Public Management and Administration in Africa: The Quest for Resilience in Uncertain Times*, pp. 1–181 and; and *The Context of Public Administration in Southern Africa: Contemporary Issues and Future Perspectives.*

Dr. Molokwane teaches various Public Administration courses at both undergraduate and graduate levels. In addition, he supervises students' research projects at undergraduate, Masters and Doctoral degree levels. He serves as an external examiner for theses and dissertations for both Masters and Doctoral degrees.

Alex Nduhura (PhD) is a senior consultant and provides leadership as Head of the Department of Procurement, Logistics and Marketing at the School of Business and Management, Uganda Management Institute. He holds a PhD in Public Management and Governance from North-West University, South Africa, MBA (Makerere) and Graduate Chartered Diplomas from CIPS UK and CILT UK. He has worked at Stanbic Bank Uganda as a procurement manager; committee member at Standard Bank Group; aviation industry, agro processing and lecturer in universities in Uganda, South Africa, the UK and Rwanda. His practice, training, and consulting research interest include public private partnerships; supply chain management; cities and city marketing; comparative public administration; new public management; and public sector reforms with focus on public-private partnerships. He has edited conference proceedings and a book. He has also published in various journals as well as conference proceedings.

Innocent Nuwagaba (Ph.D) is currently a consultant (Procurement and Supply Chain Management) at the East and Southern African Management Institute (ESAMI), in Arusha, Tanzania. His qualifications include: PhD in Public Management and Governance from North-West University (NWU),South Africa, Master's in Business Administration (MBA) and Master's in Management Studies (MMS) (Procurement and Supply Chain Management); Postgraduate Diploma in Procurement and Supply Chain Management (PGD. PSCM) in addition to another Postgraduate qualification in Monitoring and Evaluation (M&E) and a Bachelor of Arts Degree in Education (BA.ED from

Makerere University, Kampala, Uganda). He is the chief editor of *African Journal of Public Administration and Environmental Studies*. He has done a lot of consultancy work for Public Procurement, Public-Private Partnerships, Monitoring and Evaluation and Project Management, World Bank Project of Social Impact Assessment, World Bank (WB) 2016 Procurement Frame Work and African Development Bank (ADB). He has examined a PhD in Public Management and Governance entitled A model for privatisation of state-owned enterprise: The case of South African Airways. He has published some research on PPP projects in Uganda: a case of Uganda National Roads Authority, qualitative analysis of PPP project contracts in the roads sector in Uganda, the principal agency relationship in PPP projects and the quality of election projects in Uganda, Implications of Land Reforms Projects for Nation building in Uganda: A focus on the War-torn Local Governments in Northern Uganda, Procurement Planning and Procurement Performance for Operations and Projects in Public Sector Entities—A Case of Uganda Management Institute, Extrapolating the Quality of Election Projects in Africa: A Contextual Analysis of Electoral Project Governance in Mukono Municipality, the impact of the oil and gas exploitation projects on the environment in western Uganda, An assessment of Public Private Partnerships (PPP) in the roads sector in Uganda. A case of Uganda National Roads Sector, Public Private Partnership (PPP) Projects in Uganda, A case of Uganda National Roads Authority (UNRA), a qualitative analysis of Public Private Partnership (PPP) Project contracts in the roads sector in Uganda. A Contextual Elucidation of Uganda National Roads Authority (UNRA), Truncating through the Crevasses of Customer Experience in Ugandan Retail Pharmaceutical Companies: Synthesizing the intermeshing of Service Quality & Customer Satisfaction, the Doldrums of Development Projects in Uganda: Gauging the role of PRDP Health Project on Antenatal Care Attendance in Lira District, Uganda, an assessment of Participants' Perception of Public Private Partnerships in Uganda: A Conceptual Analysis of PPPs and Value for Money for Uganda National Roads Authority published, Elucidation of principal agency relationship in adopting concession, leasing and contracting PPP models in the road sector, a synthesis of the public management of mobile data and Project performance: Lessons learnt from Ministry of Health (MOH), Kampala, Uganda, Public Private Partnership Projects and Regional Cooperation in The Horn of Africa and the East African Region in the era of COVID-19 pandemic, Accountability Paradox for the Success of Public Private Partnership (PPP) Projects in developing Countries and do Stakeholders Matter? Nexus of Public Private Partnership Projects for City Street Parking in Uganda.

CONTRIBUTORS

Edson Basera is a principal research officer in the Office of the President and Cabinet, Zimbabwe. He is currently studying a Doctor of Philosophy degree in the Department of Political and Administrative Studies, University of Zimbabwe. His research focuses on publicprivate partnerships. Edson holds a Master of Public Management from the Korea Development Institute, South Korea; a Bachelor of Science (Honours) in Administration degree from the University of Zimbabwe; and a Higher Diploma in Business Administration from the Zimbabwe Institute of Management where he is also an associate member. Edson is also a fellow of the Seoul G20 Global Leaders Forum, South Korea. Edson's research interests include Public Sector Reforms and Management, Public Sector Finance, Development Management, Investment Policy Analysis and Local Governance. In 2018, Edson co-authored an article: *South Korea's Expanding Development Tentacles in Sub-Saharan Africa: Zimbabwe's Experiences of Korean Benevolence* which received an international award and is published in *K-Developedia*, a South Korean international journal.

Thabo Daniel Borole holds a PhD in public management and governance from North-West University. He acquired a master's of education in education management a master's of development and management from North-West University. He obtained his BEd (honours) degree at the University of Johannesburg and a national diploma in technical education (mechanical) at Tshwane University of Technology. He has worked for both the Gauteng and North-West departments of education. Before joining the education sector, Dr. Borole worked for SA Bolt Manufacturers as a sales executive and is currently serving as a visiting research associate at North-West University. He is also consulting in the space of public-private partnerships focusing on the road subsector.

Emmanuel Botlhale (PhD) is a professor in Public Administration in the Department of Political and Administrative Studies and Acting Dean of the School of Graduate Studies at the University of Botswana (UB). His primary teaching interest area is Public Finance. His secondary teaching and research areas are public budgeting, fiscal administration, project management, public governance, and research methodology. Some of his recent publications include 'PPPs as instruments of public procurement in Botswana post-2007', *Int. J. Procurement Management*, *15*(4): 488–505. doi.10.1504/IJPM.2022.123191 [2022] and 'Public revenue diversification in Botswana during crisis times', *Forum for Development Studies*, *48*(2): 271–288. Doi: org/10.1080/08039410.2021.1898464 [2021].

Moses Chewe is a lecturer of Public Administration in the Department of Government and Management Studies at the University of Zambia. He holds a BA in Public Administration and Master of Public Administration from the University of Zambia. He is currently a PhD candidate in Public Management and Governance from North-West University, South Africa. His research interests include public sector management, civil society organisations, and occupational safety and health management. His most recent publications have appeared in *Review of Radical Political Economics*.

Alouis Chilunjika (PhD) is a holder of a PhD in Public Management and Governance from the University of Johannesburg, as well as a Master of Public Administration and a Bachelor of Science Honours degree in Administration both from the University of Zimbabwe. He is currently a senior lecturer in the Department of Political and Administrative Studies at the National University of Lesotho. His research interests include Public Finance, Public Policy, Public Administration, Corporate Governance, Local Governance, Political Science and Electoral Processes. He has published several journal articles and book chapters in these areas.

Richard Obinna Iroanya (PhD) is a professor in Security and Strategic Studies, University of Namibia. He received training in Political Science and International Relations. He holds the following qualifications from the University of Pretoria in South Africa: Doctor of Philosophy (DPhil) (International Relations); Master of Security Studies (MSS) and Postgraduate Honours degree (BA Hons) in International Relations. He obtained his Bachelor of Science (BSc) degree in Political Science from Nnamdi Azikiwe University, Awka, Nigeria. In addition, Dr. Iroanya has also received advanced training in Dynamics of Health and Society from Linköping University, Sweden; and, Ecole des Hautes Etudes en Sciences Sociales (EHESS), Paris, France, facilitated with European Union Erasmus Mundus Scholarship. As a result, he was awarded double master's degrees: Master of Social Sciences (MSocSci, EHESS, Paris); and, Master of Arts and Science (MASci, Linköping University, Sweden). Dr. Iroanya served as Postdoctoral Research Fellow at the Thabo Mbeki African Leadership Institute (TMALI), University of South Africa between 2015 and 2017. Before joining the Department of Security and Strategic Studies, School of Military Science, University of Namibia, he was a research fellow in the Department of Political Studies and International Relations, North-West University, Vaal Campus, South Africa between January and September 2018. He is a versatile scholar with extensive experience in research, curriculum development, and teaching, as well as monitoring and evaluation. He serves as external examiner to a number of universities in his areas of expertise, and has several peer-reviewed publications to his credit. He has participated in different national and international conferences, seminars, and training workshops where he presented papers. Dr. Iroanya has quantitative and qualitative research/data analytical skills common to the social sciences. He reads, writes, and speaks French fluently. He is a team player with a high capacity for tolerance and appreciation of diversity. His excellent social and communication skills are essential for harmonious relations and success in multi-ethnic and inter-cultural working environments.

Gosego Rockfall Lekgowe teaches law at the University of Botswana. He has taught both public law and commercial law. Some of the courses that he has taught include Tax Law, Banking and Negotiable Instruments Law and Constitutional and Administrative Law. Mr. Lekgowe has served as an assistant deputy editor of the *University of Botswana Law Journal* and served on various committees of the Department of Law. In 2015 and 2016, he served as assistant academic advisor during the World Trade Organization (WTO) Regional Trade Policy Course held at the University of Botswana. In 2020, Mr. Lekgowe participated in the study on Interventions to Improve the Food Security of Communities in Wildlife-Dominated Landscapes in Northern Botswana funded by the Food Agricultural Organization (FAO). He specialises in regional integration law. He has published on various legal areas including constitutional law, regional integration, and World Trade Organization law. Some of his publications include: 'Mmusi & Ors v Ramantele & Another: An opportunity missed to begin the burial of Attorney General v Unity Dow?' *University of Botswana Law Journal,* 15, 2012 ; 'The Right to Peaceful Assembly in Botswana: The Constitutionality of the Public Order Act', *University of Botswana Law Journal,* 18–19, 2014; 'Damages for Wrongful dismissal in Botswana: High Court and Court of Appeal at Loggerheads', *University of Botswana Law Journal,* 20–21, 2015; 'The trajectory of citizen economic empowerment in Botswana after fifty years: An endless road of hapless policies', *University of Botswana Law Journal,* 22–23, 2016; 'The Botswana—South Africa Deadlock—Escaping Botswana's Gallows', *University of Botswana Law Journal,* 25, 2017; and 'Removing a High Court judge for misbehavior under the Constitution of Botswana', *University of Botswana Law Journal,* 24, 2017. He is currently pursuing his doctoral studies at the University of Birmingham.

Royd Malisase (PhD) is a lecturer of Public Administration in the Department of Government and Management Studies at the University of Zambia. He holds a BA and an MA in Public Administration from the University of Zambia and PhD in Public Management and Governance from North-West University, South Africa. His research interests are public sector reform, public policy and local government administration. His most recent publications have appeared in *Review of Radical Political Economics* and *Zango: Zambian Journal of Contemporary Issues.* Dr. Malisase teaches various Public Administration and Human Resource Management courses at both undergraduate and graduate levels. In addition, he also supervises students' research projects at Undergraduate, Masters and Doctoral degree levels. He has served as an examiner for theses and dissertations for Masters Degrees.

Salomo Ndapulamo is a PhD student in Public Administration at the University of South Africa. He obtained his MA in Public Administration from the University of Namibia. His research focus areas are socio-economic development and strategic management in the Namibia context. Salomo teaches politics and strategic management at the School of Military Science of the University of Namibia.

Gabriella Nguluwe is a PhD student in Public Policy and Management at the University of South Africa. Her primary research interest is the intersection between policymaking and implementation. Gabriella teaches Public Management in the Department of Security and Strategic Studies at the School of Military Science, University of Namibia. She earned her MA in Public Management from the University of Namibia.

Tambulani C. Nyirenda is a lecturer and researcher in the Department of Government and Management Studies at the University of Zambia. He holds a BA in Public Administration and a Masters of Public Administration from the University of Zambia. His research interests are Governance, Health Policy, and Public Procurement. His most recent publications have appeared in the *Sexual & Reproductive Healthcare Journal, Clinics in Mother and Child Health,* and *BMJ Open.*

Joseph O. Obosi (PhD) holds a PhD in Political Science and Public Administration from the University of Nairobi. He is a senior lecturer at the Department of Political Science and Public Administration, University of Nairobi, where he teaches Public Policy and Administration, Comparative Politics and Research Methods. He has about 20 publications in books and refereed journals in the areas of water sector reforms, privatisation of water delivery, private–public partnerships, and health governance. He also coordinates Public Policy and Research Programmes at the Department of Political Science and Public Administration, University of Nairobi. He is a member of several international professional organisations such as International Public Policy Association (IPPA) and International Society for Urban Health. His recent publication is a chapter on *Public Private Partnerships and Public Policy in Africa* in Routledge *Handbook of Public Policy in Africa.* Dr. Obosi has consulted for Water Service Trust Fund and Catering Levy and Trustee Development, Insurance Regulatory Authority, Teachers Service Commission, Norwegian Refugee Council, Partnership for African Social Governance and Research (PASGR) and World Bank, among others.

John Paul Settumba (PhD) is a consultant in the Department of Procurement, Logistics and Marketing at the School of Business and Management, Uganda Management Institute. He holds a PhD in Public Management and Governance from North West University, South Africa, Masters in Procurement and Supply Chain Management (Makerere) and Graduate Chartered Diplomas from CIPS UK. He has worked in various capacities in the Public Procurement Management. His practice, training, and consulting research interest includes public private partnerships, health supply chain management, and public administration. He has also published in various journals as well as conference proceedings. He has published research on PPP projects in the health sector in Uganda.

Ivan Kiiza Twinomuhwezi (PhD) is a consultant/lecturer of Economics, Public finance and Public Policy Studies. He has a PhD in Education Policy Studies [Public Private Partnerships in Education] from the University of Pretoria (South Africa), and an MA in Economic Policy and Planning from Makerere University, Kampala-Uganda. He is the Head of the Department of Public Policy and Governance at Uganda Management Institute, which he joined in the year 2005. Ivan has widely participated in postgraduate research supervision, training and consultancy in areas of public-private partnerships (PPPs), public policy and governance, managerial and healthcare economics, public finance [fiscal and monetary policy issues], quantitative methods, sustainable development strategies, economic policy analysis, cost–benefit analysis, social impact assessment (SIA), social risk management (SRM) and education policy studies as part of his career. His research specialties are in the fields of public-private partnerships (PPPs), education policy studies, economic policy analysis, public policy analysis and governance, public sector management and evaluation, and public finance [taxation policy] among other contemporary socio-economic global policy issues in which he has conducted and published some research work. Besides, he has not only participated in reviewing PhD theses and masters' dissertations in policy-related studies as an academic research examiner but also peer reviewed some research journal papers for publication. His current research interests are on public-private partnerships and education policy studies for inclusive socio-economic transformation and sustainable development.

Gideon Zhou (PhD) is an associate professor of Public Administration in the Department of Governance and Public Management at the University of Zimbabwe. He has over 20 years of university teaching and consultancy experience in the areas of public policy analysis, management of public sector reforms, and budgeting and public finance governance. He holds a PhD (with specialisation in the areas of Public Administration), a Master of Public Administration, and a Bachelor of Science Honours Degree in Politics and Administration, all from the University of Zimbabwe. He is also a holder of a Certificate in Education (Secondary) from the then Gweru Teachers' College, then an affiliate of the University of Zimbabwe. He has published books, chapters, and journal articles in the areas of public policy, public sector reforms, public budgeting and fiscal resources governance, revenue resourcing in local authorities, corporate governance in public enterprises and public debt and parliamentary oversight, among others. His current research focus is on the feasibility of mainstreaming and utilising sustainable, transformative, innovative, and network governance models to enhance institutional service delivery in public sectors.

www.ingramcontent.com/pod-product-compliance
Ingram Content Group UK Ltd.
Pitfield, Milton Keynes, MK11 3LW, UK
UKHW041450071026
15587UKWH00010B/746

9 781666 931280